DESPERATION

DESPERATION

Surviving Hitler's Intention

Lydia Rychner-Reich

iUniverse, Inc.
New York Bloomington Shanghai

DESPERATION
Surviving Hitler's Intention

Copyright © 2008 by Lydia Reich

All rights reserved. No part of this book may be used or reproduced by any means, graphic, electronic, or mechanical, including photocopying, recording, taping or by any information storage retrieval system without the written permission of the publisher except in the case of brief quotations embodied in critical articles and reviews.

iUniverse books may be ordered through booksellers or by contacting:

iUniverse
1663 Liberty Drive
Bloomington, IN 47403
www.iuniverse.com
1-800-Authors (1-800-288-4677)

Because of the dynamic nature of the Internet, any Web addresses or links contained in this book may have changed since publication and may no longer be valid.

The views expressed in this work are solely those of the author and do not necessarily reflect the views of the publisher, and the publisher hereby disclaims any responsibility for them.

ISBN: 978-0-595-44553-0 (pbk)
ISBN: 978-0-595-69295-8 (cloth)
ISBN: 978-0-595-88880-1 (ebk)

Printed in the United States of America

Desperation—born of despair, created in a child's mind as she wishes, hopes for survival in a lost and hateful world filled with sorrow and tears.

Desperation—the lullaby of Naziboots, and the symphony of death with all its great masters of horror playing the instruments of torture.

And so, I wish to dedicate this book in memory of my beloved parents and sisters, who have fallen through those brutal Nazihands.

To my beloved mother, who taught me to always find the goodness in people; my beloved father, who taught me honesty; to my beloved sisters, who taught me happiness and laughter. Yes, this book I shall dedicate to you, beloved ones, who in my heart shall always be unforgotten. And you shall always be the great symbol of humanity!

Contents

ACKNOWLEDGMENTS ix
INTRODUCTION xi
MY CHILDHOOD 1
MY YOUTH 28
MY LIFE IN WAR-TORN POLAND 49
MY SORROWFUL TEENAGE YEARS 76
MY LIFE IN BONDAGE 103
SEARCHING FOR A LIGHT IN THE DARKNESS 128
DEPARTURE FROM GREABEN 173
BERGEN-BELSEN 180
FREEDOM 195
EPILOGUE 205

ACKNOWLEDGMENTS

I would like to thank my beloved Jack (Yankele) for his never-ending support of me and my huge endeavor to write this book. He has always supported me and given me encouragement. He drove me to night classes every night and watched the children while I learned how to type and to speak and write English better so that I could complete this book. He has worked so hard over these past sixty years to support me and our family and to make sure that we wanted for nothing. He truly is a blessing in my life. How lucky I was to be found by him after the war and to marry him.

I would also like to thank my children for their support and encouragement in getting this book published. I would be remiss in not singling out one of my children, Ron Kolman, my dear son-in-law, who took it upon himself to spearhead the publishing of this book. He has spent innumerable hours on the phone and on the Internet with the publisher, getting information in the beginning, setting up reviews of the book, sending the book out to the publisher, and many other myriad activities that have been necessary to get the publishing rolling. I cannot thank him enough for helping me realize my dream of publishing this book. My gratitude is without words for your kindness and the generosity of your time in listening to me and talking to me at any time of the day or night. You are truly a blessing to me and my family.

I would also like to thank everyone at iUniverse—for their patience and assistance in getting this book published. There were some delays over the past couple of years and I'm so glad iUniverse—stuck with us.

Last, but certainly not least, I would like to thank my beloved mother and father for giving me the few years that they were able to give to me. I enjoyed every single minute that I was allowed to have with them. I miss you both terribly and have never forgotten you, nor have I forgotten my beloved sisters, Ella and Cilly. You will all always be with me. To you this book is dedicated with all of my love.

INTRODUCTION

From the time I was liberated, I swore I would tell my story to honor my parents and my sisters. I wrote this story you are about to read almost forty-five years ago when the horrors of what had happened to my family were still very fresh in my mind. Writing everything down on paper helped me somehow deal with all of the tragedy I had already faced in my short life.

After I had completed my memoirs, my fourth child was born. I was so busy raising a family with four children between the ages of thirteen and newborn that I had no time for much else. I also began helping my husband Jack in establishing our new real estate endeavors. My life was consumed with my children and the business for years and years. And time just went forward. The catharsis of writing down in words what had happened during the Holocaust helped me try to live a normal life in the United States.

Then, almost thirty years ago, in 1978, my beloved Jack was diagnosed with Parkinson's disease. From that time on, I made it my mission to find a cure, or at least obtain the best medicines possible for Jack. As Jack's illness became worse, my life became consumed with caring for him and searching the world for new medicines.

It was not until a few years ago that I realized that time was running short. I was in my late seventies and I knew that I had better seriously try to get my story published and out there for the world to see. With so many naysayers denying the reality of the Holocaust, especially, in recent times, people in positions of power, I felt it was imperative to set the record straight. I witnessed the atrocities of this Holocaust that "never happened." I was there. I have firsthand knowledge. I am one of the last surviving witnesses. My story had to be published. The horrid history of what happened to the Jewish people (and many others as well) during World War II cannot be denied. It happened, and we who witnessed the events of that most tragic time in the history of the world must not let it ever be forgotten. Those who deny it must be silenced. I was there. I lived it. I am the history of the worst Holocaust that the world has ever experienced. What I saw with my own eyes no one can deny.

And so I set about to finally try to get my book published. Unfortunately, I lost approximately two precious years due to a family member's many promises to me that he would get my book published. I spent two long years with him, going over each chapter, recounting to him each of the many stories in the book, only to realize that I had been strung along for his own selfish benefit. When his promises turned out to be false ones, my disappointment was beyond devastating. I thought my dream of publishing my story for my parents and my sisters would never come true.

Then my children and I decided that we would search for the best publisher out there. We looked high and low and found our shining light, iUniverse. This publisher's dedication to getting out my story in my own words, written when I was only a young immigrant in this country, has touched me so. They have spent innumerable hours with me and my children in an attempt to finally publish this book. My son-in-law, Ron Kolman, has been passionate about ensuring that my story gets into print. Without iUniverse and Ron's commitment and enthusiasm for my story, you would not have the opportunity to share my story of desperation and of hope. Thank you all. Thank you for letting me into your homes and hearts.

Lydia Reich, 2008

MY CHILDHOOD

I was born in Gleiwitz, a nice little city in Germany's upper Silesia, the youngest of five children. When I was born, there were already two girls and two boys in our family. I don't recall too much from childhood, but this much I know: we were the luckiest children, with the best parents any child could wish for. At the time of my birth, we lived at Kronprinzenstrasse 1 in the back of a huge apartment building. Anti-Semitism was already powerful at that time, and we felt it, but children get used to anything, and so we were happy when a few gentile children would play with us. When I was still little, I often thought that one day they would see: *I shall get acquainted with Shirley Temple, and those that hate me so much will be sorry; then they will be happy if I even speak to them.* Well, I had my share of sorrow and my share of happiness as a child.

To introduce my family: my father had a painting business and he was a very good painter. He and my mother were good and honest people; this I always heard people saying. My father adored us, especially the younger ones. My mother was very strict with us, but still she was a mother like no other mother could be.

My oldest sister, Ella, was around thirteen years old when I was born. Then came brother Max. He was a little tough to bring up; my mother had many arguments with him. I loved him so dearly, my big wonderful brother. I was his pet and Mother's little darling. If anyone had dared to do anything to me, or if I were sick, Max would have gone through fire for me. How many times he fought for me with those little Nazibeasts! He was always my big hero.

After Max came brother Sigfried. I think he was a little jealous when my other sister and I were born. Until then, he had been the youngest and he could not understand how he could be replaced. My father loved him so very dearly. On more than one occasion I would hear my father bragging, "This will be my boy!" My mother also was very proud of him. He was so pretty, but Sigfried was wild and so was I. How proud and happy I was, when I was about eight years old, when people would look at me and say, "That is Sigfried number two."

Next came Cilly; she was about a year older than I. She called herself Dad's darling, as I called myself Mother's darling. A darling she must have been; at the age of five she was allowed to visit with my dad's relatives in France.

By the age of five, I started school. Not quite half a year thereafter, I became seriously ill. I had an absess under a tooth, and at that time people frequently died of such. My temperature soared to a high of about 107°F. They all feared for my life. My operation was very serious but it was successful. Today I still have a mark from it under my chin.

Well, after a lot of persuading, the landlord, who did not sympathize with Jews but liked their money, rented us a flat. There we had much space and comfort, but life got tougher each day. The newspaper *Stuermer,* edited by Julius Streicher, did nothing to ease the tension; with all those awful caricatures of Jews, it injected such hatred into the Hitler youth, and incited the jealousy of many of hostile neighbors. But as children, this, we thought, was our fate—to suffer and be beaten by the gentile. Sometimes I thought: *How lucky they are to be free; why aren't I that lucky?* Though times were hard, I remember joyous times when Mother took us to Jasehtchemp for summer vacation. This was a resort in Poland, and we went there because Jews were not permitted to visit summer resorts in Germany anymore. Soon it was to be forbidden in Jaschtchemp, too. But those times that we went were so wonderful. Mother was not so strict then; she always looked to make us happy, her only goal in life.

My mother's folks lived in Poland, so we went there quite often for visits. When my grandmother was still alive, what wonderful times we spent in her little room. Those joyous moments I shall always cherish in my memory. Her wrinkled, sweet face always created happiness. She died, I think, around 1936, and her grave was later destroyed by the Nazis. Her soul they were unable to destroy, and I shall always be comforted by the thought of it. In the same city in Poland, Bendzin, my mother's youngest brother Uncle Jacob lived together with Grandma.

In the same city also was Uncle Samuel, Mother's oldest brother. Uncle Samuel had five daughters, two of whom survived the war. Sally now lives in Denver, and Hanny resides in Australia. We went often to visit Mother's relatives in Bendzin. I loved it so much because they always welcomed us so warmly. When I was still very little, Uncle Jacob got married. Their lovely wedding took place at the home of the bride's aunt and uncle. They resided in Pogon by Sosnowitz, Poland. I am writing this because, as you will see, it is very significant later on; this aunt and uncle later were my in-laws, but they never lived to see this happy day—me marrying one of their three sons. You can say I have known Jack, my husband, almost all my life. The children of my in-laws, I am happy to say, survived this awful war, including one of the girls and all of the sons. A year after Uncle Jacob had married, a son was born to them. Pinjush was one of the most beautiful babies I've ever seen, and I loved him so much I don't think I could love my own children more dearly.

Near us in Gleiwitz there was also Mother's third brother, Uncle Heinz. He worked for the *Volkstimme* before Hitler came to power and Jews still could have such jobs. The *Volkstimme* was one of the biggest, if not the biggest, newspaper in Gleiwitz. Uncle Heinz came often to visit us, and we liked him very much.

I think my childhood was, even with all its little sorrows, one of the happiest episodes in my life. I shall always look back on it with great admiration for my beloved parents, who made it in any way possible, always keeping sorrow and pain away from us children.

In the apartment building where we lived we had a few nice neighbors, too, who sympathized with us even though we were Jews.

Mrs. Piela had a son and two daughters. She and my mother were good friends. She was a war widow who had a second husband—not a good one—so Mother helped her a little. Her son, who was much older than me, liked me very much. I can say he was like my third brother. It hurt very much when he became one of *them*, sought after by Hitler; how quickly he seemed to forget we knew each other. His half sister Mia was a good friend of mine, though older than me.

We had a beautiful allotment garden a little outside the city. There, my mother took Mrs. Piela's father to help out and Mother paid him nicely. The garden was Mother's pride, the most beautiful garden I have ever seen. Later our so-called best friend Mr. Piela took it away from us. It was the Nazi way of saying thanks to friends. Just like that, he wanted it, and they gave it to him, no questions asked.

Across the street from where we lived, there was another Jewish family who had a cigar and cigarette shop. They had two daughters and my sister Cilly and I were were good friends with those girls. Cilly and I shared nearly all the same friends throughout my childhood. We were very close to each other; we fought often but we were completely inseparable. Together we were the family darlings. Max could punish us, but minutes later he would be sorry and give us sweets.

All the friends I made when I started school had a nice club where we often met. There was a breathtaking beautiful park in Gleiwitz called the promenade. There was a swimming pool near our city, as well as a lovely place for sunbathing and playing Both Laband and Sandwiesen were very lovely places a little outside of the city. We went to a big forest outside of the city to hike. There you could find mushrooms, blueberries, boysenberries, etc. I was able to enjoy this pleasant life for such a short time.

When Cilly and I weren't quite nine years old, we were given our first watches. At that time it was quite a big occasion for a child to own a real watch. I will never forget this moment, how utterly happy we were, how proud.

But soon life stopped being rosy for Jews. Soon after life started to get miserable for us in Germany, Uncle Heinz got married and left for Israel. He later had twins who are, as I write this, studying at the University of Illinois.

One day, all of a sudden, we came face to face with death. As we returned home from our visit in Poland, brother Sigfried became gravely ill. The day the doctor pronounced it was typhoid, right away the Nazis came to take him from us. He was still a child at that time. The anti-Semitic forces were already working overtime, and they took him in such a mean way, as if he was no human being at all. I shall never forget the look of my parents. It was so awful, we thought Mother would commit suicide. Father's gentle face was a mask of stone from unshed tears. Never before had I seen my sweet father this way. At the hospital, Sigfried was not given much hope. Then came the crisis. My mother spent all day and night at the hospital. In temples in every city where our relatives lived, prayers were held for my brother. Then the unbelievable happened. He lived through his crisis; the doctors gave us hope.

We littlest ones did not know of his progress, for Mother did not want to give us too much hope, for then the disappointment would be more bitter. One day when Mother and Father came home from the hospital as usual, I asked, "Mama, how is Sigfried and when is he coming home?" And behind her, he waddled in, so skinny, but who can imagine this day of joy? And then, as if sorrow was not enough, he decided to leave Germany, for it had started already to become unbearable for us there.

The day came when he left for *Hachsharah* to prepare for the kibbutz in Israel. Mother cried bitter tears. Later, he came back for a few months, but finally came the day when we had to say good-bye, and forever. Awful was his good-bye—and so it started, the Swastika tearing our happy family apart. After all those happy holidays together, never again would we see him up there in choir in the temple. What heartache! Next, all of a sudden, Max left for Argentina. And one man, pouring salt on our wounds, said at the station to my brother, "One brother to Israel, one of you to Argentina; I think you people will never see each other again." Well, that was not the reason my brothers never saw their parents again, for when you live there is always hope. Only when one is murdered will you never see each other again. Max and Sigfried would see each other again, all right, for they were wise to escape the inferno in time. They gave themselves the best chance for survival by leaving this rotten Naziland in time.

Their new lives were by no means easy for them in the beginning, but Sigfried chose the life he wanted, and it made him happy. Israel was for him the fulfillment of his dreams. For Max, it was tough in the beginning. But later, when he had adjusted himself to the way of living in Argentina, he started to work for himself and things brightened. Back home, we had to to adjust to life without our brothers.

A short time before my brothers left, Ella, my oldest sister, went to Berlin to study at the Academy of Art. She was very talented in any way you can imagine. For instance, she could paint just from looking once at an object. She knitted most of her clothing, and what she didn't knit, she mostly sewed for herself. She even designed clothes. I don't think there was an object that she would not have been able to make. On top of it all, she was a very efficient secretary. At the academy, she studied painting and decorating.

With each day, then, Nazi Germany started to become worse and worse for us Jews. On almost all of the gentile store windows one could see those ugly signs: *"Juden Eintritt verboten!"* Jewish businesses were demolished and boycotted, including my father's. The Hitler Youth became the means to enforce the Nazis' hatred against us helpless people. They threw stones after us, spit at us, beat us—they were allowed to do anything, and we had to smile at it all. They called us names—one of their favorites was "stinking Jew"—any disgraceful name they could think of. It was much in line with Nazi culture when a little bandit scum flower of fascism tripped an old lady on the street only because he was a little brown Naziswine and she a Jew. I think those who saw all that, all those who went through what I shall report in the next chapters, will always feel a deep disdain for those who committed such acts. No restitution could clean such filth from our minds and hearts. After I survived, I said, "I shall always hate them with all my soul!" Today I can't even hate them; I feel just a deep disdain for them, and pleasure that they will have to live with fear for the rest of their guilty lives.

They will never have a peaceful moment, and always the horror they brought upon this earth will be in front of them.

Julius Streicher, nightmare of my childhood, wherever your soul is—it couldn't be in heaven—it will not be able to find any peace, for all the shame you helped bring upon my innocent people. Perhaps there are some of your people who will say that I am right. Do you remember the diabolical scheme, the picture that you put in the *Stuermer* about a Jew and an Arab in a bed? The Jew wanted to push out the Arab of the bed. This miserable picture was born in an evil mind, and underneath it was written, "The Jew takes my whole bed—help, Allah." Yes, the stoned Jew took his share of the bed, all right. Not in the dirty way you showed it, but the part that belongs to him. Streicher, shall I mention all of your beastly friends? So many of them, like a disease. But all the horror you brought upon us I shall tell, as well as I can, as I promised that I would, if I should be fortunate enough to live through this disaster.

Somehow once my brothers left home, life did not have the zest it used to have. With my brothers around, there was always some mischief to do, and the best part of it was that I could get away with it because I was was the youngest. For instance, when Max went away to a party and came home dead tired, sister Cilly and I had his box spring hooked up on strings. All of a sudden in the middle of the night we heard a big bump, and in the morning Max was sound asleep on the floor. The Purim plays taught us to not spoil our fun. I remember all those happy times our brothers used to take us on hikes, and all those nice birthday parties they would help Mother with to surprise us. It all used to be so much fun, but now with my brothers gone, there was only so much emptiness.

There was no one left anymore to protect us from those awful Hitler gangs. Now Cilly and I were on our own, and it was real tough. Sometimes it would take us hours to get home from school, although it should only take ten to fifteen minutes. For there they were, those little brown gangsters; they lurked in every corner to beat us up. And then, when we finally got home, we could hardly go out to play, for who would play with a Jew? Even going to the store, which used to be so much fun, was no fun anymore, for people who used to be friendly now looked the other direction; they didn't want to have anything to do with a Jew anymore.

So Mother made a decision, and one day she said that we were going to leave our house and move to another place near the school. This house that Mother had in mind belonged to a Jewish landlord. It was a lovely flat. The landlord was very nice, and many of our neighbors were Jewish. The atmosphere improved for us tremendously, and it was wonderful.

The landlord's granddaughter, Marianne, became a very close friend of ours. We got along greatly; she was very lonesome, for she was the only child. Soon thereafter, Cilly, Marianne, and I became a swell triangle. We went together to the movies, for at that time there was still one movie house left where the sign *"Juden Eintritt verboten"* wasn't hung out. Or we played in her grandfather's lovely garden, which lay at the back of the large yard. Or we went together to Sunday school.

Marianne lived with her mother in the apartment above us. We installed a silent telephone. From two cigarette boxes hooked together with a big string, closed on the end with a knot, we made our marvelous connection with each other, and till late at night we would send messages to one another. At times we sent goodies, and sometimes, when I couldn't resist it, I played little tricks on her, sending her a herring dressed in a coat and hat, or bitter almond, or onion peels—and sometimes the answer would be a frog or some other mischievous thing.

Now that I look back, those are my most precious memories. The Nazis forbade us everything, they destroyed everything, but as long as there was still breath in us, they could not destroy our good spirit. We always tried to be happy and make the best of everything. They forbade us to go here, they forbade us to go there, not the park anymore, not the swimming places, or the forest, or the hills for sleigh riding in a winter wonderland. But we never got discouraged. When they crammed us into classrooms just for Jews, we didn't despair; we somehow got along.

The Jewish Committee made a little park for the Jewish population, and it felt somehow much better there than to look into the faces of hatred on the other children that were now so hostile, trying to beat us up whenever they could find an occasion. And with all this, we still didn't get discouraged. Of course it was no fun to be segregated like that, but we got along. But when summer came, I was sometimes lonesome, I cannot deny it. I had always been the water rat; swimming was my life. When we were not permitted to swim in the public places anymore, this was the thing that hurt me the most. Whenever I felt a yearning for the nice cool water outside, I went into the bathroom, filled the tub full with water, and sat in it. I even tried to swim in it, always pretending that I was outside in Laband where the sun was shining and people were all around with gaity and laughter, back when everything was like it used to be and there was no segregation at all.

Living now at Bahnhofstrasse 6, I realized how much we had missed living on Kronprinzenstrasse between all those hostile neighbors. Even those that we once thought were our friends later would show who they really were. At night when I went to sleep, there was such wonderful peace now. It was not like in the old neighborhood, where the whole house was always in motion, day and night. Not far away from Kronprizenstrasse was Hutt Enterprises. This was a very big factory on the edge of Gleiwitz, not far from the railroad, and when we went to bed, we always felt as if the whole house was on a big swing.

When my parents first came to Gleiwitz near the end of World War I, Father had worked at this factory. As I understand, life was real tough for my parents in those times, but with a lot of patience and hard labor, sweat, and again hard work, my parents started to get ahead. When the brown Satan came to power, my father was already wonderfully well established. But all of those years of hard and honest work, the Nazis destroyed in a jiffy. How many times would I be stiff from fear, going around the block and seeing the huge *gas tanks* right there in back crowning the city of Gliewitz? I would think to myself, *If something happened to the factory, the whole city would be blown up into the air.* Later, when I remembered my childish fears, I thought about all the evil the Nazis had brought upon this earth, and I considered how wise it would have been if the Lord had let all the cities in Germany blow up into the air—how much disaster we would have been spared.

And then, well, again I thought differently. Living in our wonderful new surroundings on Bahnhofstrasse gave me time to think about a great many things—for instance, how wonderful life really could be if the Nazis would only leave us alone. Of course that was only a dream, for with each day the Nazis' hatred towards us grew stronger and stronger. The small room I shared with Cilly was so cute and cozy that, when in it, I forgot all of the outside world. I tried to stay inside my little heaven, as I called it, as much as possible, for outside there was hardly a place left that a Jew was allowed to go. Already by the end of 1937, we couldn't visit Jaschtchemp anymore.

At that time anti-Semitism in Poland also was at its peak. They tore the beards from the Jews and even inflicted pogroms on those poor, helpless people. They prohibited Jews from their summer or winter resorts, too. If there was a place that wasn't openly prohibited, one could feel one wasn't wanted there. Life in Poland was very tough, too, and although they saw how hard the Jews had it, the Nazis and their supporters still were jealous of what little the Jews had.

It wasn't fun to miss going to Poland, and with melancholy I looked back at those nice times we had spent in Jaschtchemp. The last time we were there, our former landlady wouldn't let us have rooms any more, so we rented one from a farmer on the edge of the forest. It turned out to be much nicer, and there I made friends with a big fat sow. It was a beautiful swine, much, much nicer than the ones most of our neighbors had back in Gleiwitz. At times when it got lonesome, it came upstairs looking for me. My parents, of course, had no idea about this great romance. One day my father was visiting us when the farmer brought a big wagon of hay. I don't know if it was the smell of the hay, or love for me, but piggy escaped from her pen, and guess who she chased all over the farm? I will never forget the picture of Dad running to my rescue. I don't remember who got tired first, Dad, or my secret admirer, because it didn't take long before all the hands were alert and it went on like a hog chase at the fair.

Today when I complain to my sister-in-law about how wild the children are, she always comforts me with this phrase: "One thing you haven't to worry about, they will never be half as wild as you were!" I think every child has a right to be wild, for childhood is so very short, and it ends all to soon. Childhood memories are always the most precious ones.

Even school had changed. The Nazis took almost all of our classrooms, leaving only two or three, so we had to go to school at all times of day to school. I remember that sometimes it was already dark outside when we had class. But somehow we got along fine. The washrooms, of course, were segregated at school. What German girl would be permitted to mix with a Jew?

There was in our classroom a girl by the name of Herta, I think—a miserable, ugly creature. I still have her in my classroom picture. Her father, as I understood, was Jewish and her mother, so she said, gentile. She always told us how much fun she had at holdiay time, for she would spend the Jewish holidays at her father's parents, and with her gentile grandparents, she would spend the other holidays. She always made such a big issue of it, and we kids at times felt a bit jealous. One day, all of a sudden, she said, "If I should become an Aryan, I would never forget you, all my wonderful friends. I would never call you names." One day she came to school no more, and later we saw her walking among the gentile children. When one of us kids called out her name, she asked the girls she was walking with, "What does this stinking Jew want from me?" Later our teacher told us that Herta was an Aryan, and that we were never to call to her again. I will never forget her face of hatred when she saw one of us, her former friends, and never had I heard worse words than the ones coming from her mouth. Never have I seen more maliciousness in anyone's face than hers when she saw how the other kids hated us. I think that this ugly face will also always be in my memory.

With all our oppression, kids will be kids.

There were not enough teachers to go around because of our segregation, but even with all of the hatred against us, we kids still had to have our fun and play jokes on our poor teachers. Those poor teachers, what they had to go through! I remember the day we stuck needles in the seat of a very unpopular teacher. Well, I don't think that a rocket could make a nicer jump. Not all of the kids knew about it, so it made the class roar with laugher.

One winter day, we had very late classes. It was snowing, and somehow my girlfriend and I got the brilliant idea of taking a snowball into class and putting it—where else?—on the teacher's chair. We didn't realize that the snow would eventually melt, but thought that when the teacher sat down, he would make a very cold discovery. The discovery came, all right, but too late. When classes were out, we did not have the fun we expected, but we were richly rewarded, for all of a sudden one kid shouted, "Tsk, tsk, teacher, what did you do?" From teacher's chair and up to our seats, a big water puddle was running. Poor teacher, his eyes looked with disbelief, his face astounded. I remember, too, those times when some of the boys poured sneezing powder on a teacher's desk. After we saw one of the Shirley Temple movies where she puts an apple on the floor so that the teacher trips, that trick became very popular at school. However tough life was, us kids still were searching for our fun. We never got discouraged.

One day our sister Ella mailed us a huge cardboard Shirley Temple doll from Berlin, and we were suddenly the most popular kids. Together with the doll, Ella sent us the most gorgeous dresses for it, like those Shirley wore in her movie roles, and from that day on, the doll became our most cherished possession. We were as proud of it as if it were Shirley in person.

Among our kids, like everywhere, were a few stuck-up ones. I never bothered with them, but when I had that doll, how funny it was to see those stuck-ups begging me to let them see it! Those show-offs came from very rich homes, but I never did like them—not out of envy, heaven forbid; from my early childhood on, I would always like people for what they were, not for what they had. All my life I lived that pattern. I always treated my friends friendly, and expected to be treated the same. It reminded me of a poem that sister Ella once had written into my diary. "For your friends, always choose good people and you won't lose, and do not ask if rich or poor; for God, all the people stay the same, be assured! Always talk as if your mother was near, and it's for sure you'll be, with luck on your way, don't fear!" Somehow, those few words were, throughout my life, an inspiration, and they shall always be. Money is good to own, that is one thing no one can deny—and if one does deny it, I doubt he really means it. But a real, true friend you will not be able to buy for all the riches on earth. And a person who thinks that he will be able to buy friends with money is, to me, the unhappiest person on earth.

There was another great hobby I had. From early childhood on, I just adored to perform. My greatest desire was to become a movie star. On holidays we always had plays at school. This was my life—there, I could stand in front of the audience and capture their hearts. Cilly and I used to be pretty good at dancing. When we were very, very little we would even perform solo. How much did I love tap and ballet! I remember people congratulating my parents after our performances. The last play I participated in was *Der Fledermaus*, by Johann Strauss. I was a cloud, and Cilly was a star. I wore a breathtaking white tulle gown with silver embroidery and blue chiffon. I still have the picture from this performance in my possession after all these years. How wonderful those memories are! What nice compliments I received, and how proud my parents looked! Liking the stage so much, it was natural for me to collect all the pictures I could get of all the movie stars. I knew almost all the stars at that time by heart. Some cigarette firms enclosed their pictures in each package of cigarette coupons, and my father, smoking quite a bit, I had the most beautiful collection. Pictures of Shirley Temple? I had countless, of course. To exchange those coupons, I had to go back to our old neighborhood, and there I visited my two friends from the cigar shop. I met quite often some of our old neighbors, too. I greeted them as I had always been taught, but they somehow didn't recognize me anymore. Mia looked at me like I was a stranger, and her brother Teddy—dear old Teddy, who used to play with me, who sung lullabies to me, fed me, comforted me when I was crying, and who would have done anything in the world for me when I was a baby!

Yes, Teddy, this is how I address you: you, too, became a Nazi, and, Teddy, you looked at me with such loathing, as if I were a crawling insect. It nearly broke my heart. When I came home later, crying in Mother's arms and telling her of my great sorrow about Teddy, him of all people (even today it is hard for me to understand it), my mother made me promise never to go into that evil house again. And so again, one of my nice childhood memories broke into fragments. If I had only known then how much sorrow lay ahead of me, I would have seen that that should have been the least bit of it. With all of this nastiness from the adults as well as from their children, one poem portrayed that picture. Although I know it in German, I shall try to translate it here. It describes so well how life really was in Nazi Germany.

THE LITTLE HERO

Down from my window, children are playing,
with no question asked if they are poor or rich,
for mostly to children it makes no difference which is which.
Just one stands in the corner forlorn and cries his sins.
He is a Jew, whom they despise. Already the smallest children,
brought up with hate in their minds, won't play together
with him anymore, the work of their parents brains.
Be strong, little man—you're a hero, my friend.
Lucky the Jew who can survive the struggle in this cold world!

I am always touched to tears when I remember this poem so full of wisdom, so much like the bitter reality it was harbored in. Our life being constant harrassment like that, I started to search for an answer, for the purpose that lay behind all that evil. I was still a child, but one grows up so fast in such a predicament. Almost all of the books which could have shed a light on it were gone; all those wonderful books by Jewish writers were the first to be destroyed by the Nazis. If some of those books were left, who would dare sell them or keep them out in the open? So I read the Bible. I wanted to find out what it was that made us so different from the others. For when everyone made such a big issue about a person, there must be something extra special about him—these were my thoughts as a child. I got very interested in the Bible, and I wanted to learn more about my faith.

I became a regular at Sunday school, and when I heard our rabbi speak and saw him up there on the altar, peace would come into my soul. I knew and felt that there was somebody up there who would protect us from all of that evil, who wouldn't let those diabolic forces destroy us. I read all of those wonderful psalms, and they brought a great deal of comfort to me. No matter how dark it was at that time, I knew that there was always the good Lord beside us. He would always find someone to save us. One of my favorites was the book of Moses, and the stories of how he had saved those poor unlucky Jews when they were slaves, and how miraculous it had been, the way he himself was saved by the man that was sent to destroy him.

I think that at that time my biggest comfort really was the Bible. Although my parents were no more as religious as they used to be back in Poland, my mother still tried with all of her heart to keep up her old traditions, for she came from a very religious home. My father's parents had been religious, too, but Father tried more or less to go with modern times in this regard. Mother had always taught us to respect the Sabbath. She explained to us kids how holy it was. She kept all of our other holidays, and our house was a strictly kosher home. We kids tried, when Mother wasn't paying attention, to modernize it a little, but when the fascists started their outrageous propaganda, they were not able to take our traditions and beliefs away from us, not even with all of their filthy lies. Our faith, it was deep grown into us. On Yom Kippur, the most holy of all holidays, how full the temple was with all the people staying there deep in prayer, clad in white for our innocence. I always nagged Mother to please let me fast all day, for I, too, wanted to feel important, and I, too, wanted to give my share.

Among our good friends was a girl by the name of Margit Reichman. She was such a devil that at times I even feared her for all those practical jokes she played on us. I don't think there was a thing that she was afraid of. She survived and is today in Israel.

My sister Cilly and I looked so alike that everybody always thought we were twins, and us being so close together, we made plans for our future. Always our plans were together. It was quite natural for us that we would marry, of course, on the same day, that our first children would be girls, and, of course, we would dress them alike, just as Cilly and I did. How much fun it would be when everybody thought they were twins. Later on, perhaps, we would both have boys, and those we would dress like twins, too. Such were our dreams as children, but like most of our dreams, they were never to come true.

My very first birthday without our brothers was one of the most lonesome ones I had ever known. There was no one to tease us like they used to, saying, for instance, "No gifts for you today; you have been a bad girl," or "Today for your birthday gift we will cut your braids. At least one." That one made me afraid to go to sleep, for I thought I might really find my pride cut off when I got up in the morning. Or one might be left, and what good would one braid do? Now on this lonesome birthday, there was no one here to take us to the Neue Welt, a wonderful place so full of fun; there one could see those cute midgets, and everything was colorful, so gay—but no brother was here to make this all come true. It wouldn't have done any good anyway, for as the brothers left just in the nick of time, all our fun went, too—Jews weren't allowed to go there anymore.

All sorts of memories entered my mind on this lonesome first birthday without my brothers. Once I got lost at Neue Welt, and I screamed until a policeman found me, sobbing, and brought me home. All those memories are so dear to me. That year the fair came to our city, and left without us visiting it. My memories of the fair are so full of gaiety and laughter. For what child wouldn't it be so? All those funny clowns; the lucky wheel, how very exciting; all those sweets one could only enjoy at the fair; all those wonderful goodies to win or to buy—but no more for us Jewish children to enjoy. How my heart cried in agony as I walked down the streets and saw all those happy children with all of their goodies and prizes. When they saw us, they stuck their tongues wide out to us. I cried myself to sleep in my mother's arms. "Why, Mother, why? What was my sin?" and my mother, with tears in her sweet and helpless eyes, gave me her only comfort: "Don't worry, my darling Hertzele, my heart's love, don't fear, Lydilein, the sun will shine again and your life will once again be sunshine and roses!" My so-dearly beloved mother. Why not for you? Why not for you to enjoy sunshine and roses again? My roses are the symbol of my freedom; all over the house I have them today. Mama, your sweet face will always be the most precious shrine in all of my memories. How much you tried to make it all up to us, as if you felt guilty for having us brought into this evil world so full of hatred. My sweetest of all mothers, any child would have been fortunate to have you. How you tried to buy for us more than you were able to afford that time—all of our so very lovely dresses! We didn't have to say a word, you just saw the sparkle in our eyes as we passed the windows on the street, and the next day we would have them.

I remember my last bathing suit; I have tried to copy it since, but was never successful. This was a highly expensive piece of clothing. Jews couldn't enter the store anymore by that time, but you just had to get it for me. You paid a gentile woman twice the amount it was worth so you could see me happy. And how proud I was of it! It's funny that I should remember it so vividly, this, of all things. It wasn't how much you paid for it—that was only a symbol—it was you, the way you always looked to make us happy. You wanted so very badly to protect us from all of that evil around us, but how impossible it was, for life got worse and worse with each new day to come. Those Naziboots haunted my dreams. Day and night one could hear their filthy growling and marching on the streets or in their Bierstube, singing those horrible songs of their idol, Horst Wessel, that were grafted into the youth. With fire in their eyes, they went into the streets in groups, ready to attack their helpless victims. And why not? They had those wonderful songs to live by, those songs of murder and conquest. "And if the blood of the Jew will squirt from the knife, we will feel doubly good." Or, "Heads are rolling, Jews are crying and in the streets is running blood." So it went, on and on, never to find an end. Or those murderes, clad in black—who wouldn't remember the SA, the *Sturmabteilung,* the storm troopers, and the marching that went on and on, murder gleaming in their eyes as they sang, "SA is marching, in same step and trot."

Those songs always haunt me, always singing about killing the Jews. All those pictures, like a madhouse, go by in my memories of my childhood. All of their propaganda about the filthy Jew was carried over the radio, too. They would not let a chance escape; their whole glory was to make the Jews suffer. Who could forget the Fuehrer's speeches? Adolf Hitler. We did not know that many of them came from the mastermind of Adolf Eichman. We didn't know at that time about this famous killer. But one thing we knew—there were plenty of them, out to destroy us. In later years I was to find out whose those famous phrases were: Eichman, of course. And here is one of them: "If you want to have a clean garden, the first thing to do is to get rid of the weeds. The Jews are the weeds, of course, and this is what we are going to do with the Jews." So it went on and on with all of their hate propagana. Yes, Eichman was one of their great masterminds, there is no doubt about it, and I hope that by the time I have finished my writing, justice will prevail upon him.[1]

Cilly, I, and books grew tighter together in the world of make-believe. In books, at least, one could find a little peace. How much books helped us through our so-lonesome childhood! We were called the bookworms. One of my favorites was *Heidi*. While reading it, I could really dream of those beautiful green hills, all those luscious fields, as if I really lived there. Oh, how heavenly it was! There there was no *"Juden Eintritt verboten"* in my world of dreams. No one could take away from me my world of make-believe. There were so many nice books to fill a child's little dream world. To tell the truth, I don't know what I would have done without them. Oh, if children only knew how much of a blessing books really are! I remember as we were going to sleep, Cilly and I dreamed while we were still awake. We pretended to be characters from our dream world of books, and our books gave us so many heavenly things to dream about in a childhood so full of hate and fear.

Living in our new surroundings, I became friends with a boy, and of all boys, he was a member of the Hitler Youth. I must have been about ten years old at the time and he was about thirteen years old. His name was Guenther Lichter. How grateful I'll always be that he made me feel in this unholy world like a human being. He was a very gentle and considerate person, not fitting the picture of his idol. He protected me from a lot of sorrow, and I shall never forget it. How could I have been so fortunate to find, in this jungle of destruction, such a friend? He knew my favorite song, *"Am golf von Biscaya,"* so at times he came under our bal-

---

1. Adolf Eichman did face trial in 1961, the year after this book was first written. He was executed in Ramleh Prison on May 31, 1962.

cony and I could hear the sweet music coming from his accordion, which he mastered beautifully. *"Am golf von Biscaya"* means something similar to "sails in the sunset."

One day I asked him what he would do if his leader in the Hitler Youth found out he had made friends with a Jewish girl. He would get scolded, of that I was quite sure. His reply made me laugh; I guess one can call it "censored." I was happy, of course, to have found in him such a dear friend who proved to me that there was still goodness left in some people. But at the same time I feared that, sooner or later, he would get into trouble for his kindness. How many times, when I was frightened to go certain places, would he accompany me? Then no one dared to come near me. There were even times when some of the Youth didn't bother me, for they knew Guenther was my friend, and they were afraid of him. But my fear continued. I knew that it couldn't go on like this; someone would eventually tell on him and he would not be able to get out of it with a fresh answer like the one he gave me, for his father was a Nazi, and a very strict one at that.

I doubt if his father ever knew of our friendship, but if he did know, I am quite sure he didn't know that I was Jewish, for his own father disliked Jews just the same. They had also a man boarding with them who was a big wheel at the Gestapo. He knew that my father was Jewish, and those hateful glances he threw over to our windows made me sink into the ground for fear. But Guenther's mother was different; she was as kind as Guenther. She sympathized very much with me. Guenther's little brother Herbert was a little Nazibrat just like his father. What a sweet little guy he could have been, if not for that. This little guy didn't know that I was Jewish, and he liked me very much.

I remember fun-filled hours that Mrs. Lichter shared with us. Like her own child, she took me to all those places which were forbidden to the Jews. She took us swimming, for she knew how much I loved to go there. On other occasions she took me and Cilly along to the swimming pool, but we really didn't enjoy it too much, for we were in constant fear that someone might recognize us, and in this little town it was quite possible. Once we saw one girl recognized as a Jew, and how frightfully and shamefully they had treated her. This poor thing, she was spit at and thrown stones after, and to my great disbelief the whole place where she sat was disinfected; to top it all off, the girl was punished with a high fine. I think I didn't fear so much for my own safety as for that of Mrs. Lichter.

After going a few more times to the movies with them, I found it was about time to call it quits. But from the day we had seen the incident at the pool, Cilly was frightened and wouldn't go any place anymore with them. After three more times, I, too, decided that it was best to stop, right now. We were grateful to Mrs. Lichter, of course, but when we decided not to go out with her anymore, I noticed Mother giving a deep sigh. My sweet mother, how much fear must you have gone through, not telling us, always afraid to take away a little happiness from us.

How grateful you were that someone was eager to give us a little sunshine in this cold cloudiness! How much did you suffer, never complaining to us! Your old age should have been crowned with joy and happiness, sweetheart of all sweethearts, queen of goodness and love! Now that I look back at it all, I see how much we were rewarded in allof our sorrow, how very fortunate we were to have such wonderful parents. Who of those little Nazibeasts could say the same? With their parents, how awful their world must have been. They thought only hate, not love, and they believed that if they could take care of the Jew, they could go on and conquer the earth. How rich we were in soul and mind, never to allow the entrance of hate into our home. We lived for the day when we would not have to see anymore of this evil, and we hoped that once more the Lord would let us live as free people. At that time, Mother and Father decided that it was about time for us to leave this Naziland. Mother said, "It is about time for us to find a place in the sun." Brother Sigfried urged us to come to Israel. In his letters, he said that Israel was the only place where a Jew could find peace of mind. And brother Max tried to persuade us to come to him in Argentina.

Israel was then still Palestine, under British mandate, and Max told us in his letters about the programs and restlessness that went on over there with the Arabs and their leader, the mufti, the brainchild of the Nazis. The Arabs and the Nazis were buddy-buddy. Max thought that it would be very unwise for us to go there, but where wouldn't we have gone, to the end of the world, just to get out of Germany? For a few weeks, Mother was a little undecided about what to do, and those precious days spoiled a lot for us.

Each day was lost with waiting. The Jewish people saw slowly what was about to come, and when the Nazis started taking Jews of German citizenship to concentration camps, all were faced with the bitter reality—no use waiting any longer. Then it started so quickly; all of a sudden all kinds of accidents started happening to Jews. Some who were today healthy and happy were, tomorrow, dead, so the people started to storm the immigration offices. But it began to get tougher and tougher to leave, and as if the world had come to an understanding, almost all the gates closed for us. Maybe if other things hadn't come in between, maybe if the world hadn't showed the cold shoulder to our problems ... maybe, maybe, such a little word only, but it has one's whole life in its claws.

Everything came so suddenly, one can hardly realize it. To explain it all in one word, it was a nightmare. One day, all of a sudden, Ella stood in front of us. She had left Berlin in a hurry. "A madhouse," was her whole explanation. Most of the time she had passed as an Aryan out of fear of being attacked by those brown hoodlums, but at the academy they knew her race, and she was thrown out. Well, it was not the worst yet, for the worst was yet to come. And how it came.

It must have been the end of summer when, one day, my mother was lucky to get a visa to visit Poland. This had been lately very hard to get. But here she was, visa in her hands, and packing had begun. The coming day, we took off a few days from school, but we took our books with us to study. Well, everything went smoothly—too smoothly, I'd say. Margit, one of our friends, was a little envious about us going again on vacation, and she wished that she could go in my place. And us, we were excited and joyful to be able to visit our relatives again, leaving at the same time this place of madness for a little while.

But when we came to Poland, we discovered things weren't too rosy there, either. Anti-Semitism was at such a peak there that it was hardly a change of pace. It was a little bit different, though, and as Mother told Uncle Jacob about the madness going on in Germany, he tried to persuade her to come to Poland until our papers for immigration could be worked out. And Mother's reply, how very vivid it is still in front of me: "What, from one madness into another? I'd rather die. In Germany the world knows at least of their brutality, but who knows what is going on here? Look how much they have made animals of you here already. Don't you people realize how badly they wait here for a Hitler to come? And then, mark my words, it will be too late. Where will this huge number of Jews run? Oh, no, darling, I want to leave the madhouse over there very, very badly, but for good and not just to change places." If only it had happened that way! Although here, too, we did not have the desired freedom, our eyes could at least rest from those ugly brown Nazishirts, and since I did not understand Polish, I didn't understand the filthy remarks people made about the Jews.

But to a haunted child's mind, it was different somehow. Many things were as I always remembered from the good times. There were those marvelous goodies that only the Jews from the east were able to have: the marvelous ice cream, or *Pinguin*, which I have never tasted once; those bagels, who didn't eat bagels? Really, I didn't know what a real bagel tasted like until I tried those in Poland. No one who ever tasted those goodies will ever forget them. And where but at Nurnberg in Bendzin could one have that delicious bratwurst, from which the juice would burst out when one bit into it? Their marvelous goose sausage, and so many, many other good things to eat? Yes, the Polish Jew was blessed with the best food on earth, there was no doubt about it.

After Hitler's regime took over in Germany, the Nazis wouldn't permit kosher slaughtering anymore; there really were so many good things we had to miss out on. Here in Poland we could at least eat the best to our heart's content. Lately, while Hitler was building up his army, there had been a shortage in food in Germany, and those good things that once were so common over there slowly disappeared from the market. Always when visiting Poland, we would bring home a few things to eat. We had our fun out there in Bednzin; for us kids it was fun, anyhow. Those nice *droshky* rides, with those beautiful horses, who could ever forget them? I think it must have been more fun for kids then, than today's car rides are. When the horses had to fulfill a certain need, how hilarious we thought it was. How many times did we kids wait just for that to happen?

We enjoyed seeing the family, too. Little Pinjush, Uncle Jacob's son, was at that time two years old already and he was a most adorable child. He was the biggest joy to all of us. The thing that bothered us kids in Poland was, most of all, the restroom situation. Why, I could actually hold my breath for the whole time, for to take a breath, one would have to take a whiff of some of the most undesirable scents, and this was catastrophic. Most of the time we would come back home with bad stomachs from holding it for so long.

Mother's mostly wanted to go to Bendzin to visit her mother's grave. The grave was kept beautifully. Going there had always been a great ordeal, for Mother just never could leave it. It was all so heartbreaking. I had loved Grandma so very much, and when I stood beside her grave, all those wonderful memories of her would enter my mind. It was as if Grandma was standing there beside me with her smiling face. How sudden her death had been! She had been clenaing up for the holidays and had been in such an awful hurry, for we were to come and everything had to be spotless and she had to make all that delicious food that she only had been able to prepare. In the middle of her joyous preparations, she ran outside the house screaming for help. A blood vessel had burst in her head, and by the time the telegram reached us, she was on her deathbed already.

Mother went right away to her bedside and was there until the end. "Geniale, my feet are so cold," was my grandmother's last complaint, and when a happy smile came over her face, everything was over. She had an easy death, but for Mother it was the worst day. Between them had been such a wonderful mother and daughter relationship, and my mother had been the only girl in this family.

But it wasn't just my grandmother's death that made everything seem different this time we visited. Uncle Samuel had been lately always sick; it looked as if he would never be his old self again. That time, he was again very ill. As we were to leave, Mother was so worried about him. He was such a wonderful person, but luck somehow was not with him. Although he had been blessed with five lovely daughters and a good-looking wife, he had always had setbacks in his life. He owned a butcher shop in Bendzin, but always had it tough, and the most trouble was his ill health. This time it was so bad with him that it made Mother so worried, but the time came when we had to go back to the brown shirts and *"Deutschland, Deutschland ueber alles."* Mother was so very sad at leaving that she cried a lot, for she was not too sure if she would ever see her brothers again. How very mistaken she was. She saw them sooner than she thought she would.

Our immigration papers were almost ready, and we thought that it wouldn't be long before we would be able to leave Germany. After many hugs and kisses, tears and waving, the train rolled from the station, and back to Gleiwitz we went. Father had for us a big surprise, which he hadn't mentioned when coming to pick us up. While we were in Poland, he had redecorated our entire flat; even the floors had been given a new coat, for now it was very bad back home and Father thought it would make us feel better to have the house redone, if even for the short time that we would still be here until our immigration. Dear Papa of mine, how sweet he was! How, oh, how can such be destroyed? For what? He wouldn't even have let harm come to a fly. And his eyes, how they shone with honesty and goodness! He was the inspiration of mankind. Always thinking of somebody else, he was the most unimportant person to himself. How much I loved him! I can recall him getting mad at me only once; he never tired of my endless mischief. And those times when he would feel like scolding, he just couldn't bring it over his lips to really get mad at his nestling. However hard life was already, his pockets were always filled with goodies. Mother at times scolded him slightly, "You're spoiling the children." But Father came never home empty-handed. And lately how hard it had been already to keep his existence, but he would never let us feel it. Who else can say he had such a wonderful father?

As we came home from Poland, the daughter of the landlord was sitting up on the windowsill. It was already late at night, and I just couldn't understand what she was sitting there and grinning about. Even though she was the aunt of Marianne, neither Marianne nor I liked her. She herself was a year younger than Marianne, and her being a kind of show-off eliminated her from the list of my friends right from the beginning. As I saw her sitting there, well past midnight, because she had heard from Daddy that we would come home that day, I just couldn't understand it. That night I could hardly find any sleep. But soon I was to find out what it had all been about; and when the news reached me, I felt weak in my knees.

Father didn't want to worry us that night, and the next day I heard that Marianne was gone. I knew that her father had left for Israel quite some time ago and he was to bring his family over, but who would think they would be gone so soon, and so quickly? It was all in such hurry. I knew that he was supposed to come back to liquidate his business. Everything came as such a surprise to me; he didn't dare come back and he asked the family to come right away and to leave everything All of a sudden, life without Marianne seemed hopeless. Our ray of sunshine was gone, and I hadn't said good-bye to her. We had been such a happy threesome. I wept.

Mother tried to comfort us with her words of hope. She said that it would not be long before we, too, would leave this hell. "Who knows, maybe we'll even go to Israel, and there again you will meet Marianne," she said. (I want to mention right here that I met Marianne nine years later in Israel). Thinking about it made me feel much better. We would be reunited with brother Sigfried again, and our family could somehow be together. Of course, we had heard of all the pogroms that the Arabs inflicted on our people, but we felt that at least on our own earth we would be able to defend ourselves. And it was worth fighting for, to fight for our peace of mind, our freedom—which meant our survival. "Erez," as we called it that time, was the land of our forefathers, the land of milk and honey, the land that had been promised to us by the good Lord. But the British felt differently about it. They made it so difficult for us to get there. Why, oh, why was the whole world against us? Why did everybody close the door in our faces? What crime were we guilty of, that everybody showed the cold shoulder to our pleas? Even in our promised land, those who had the power and weapons in their hands stood watch and forbade us to enter, even in our most morbid hours. With all our pleas, they still wouldn't let us enter. And how much I shall always despise those with power for going against the weak. Would someone let a building burn where children, helpless creatures, are trapped? Of course not. Then why did they do this to us?

Once again as I write all of this down—oh, Lord, forgive me—pain and sorrow enter my heart, and when all is said, I shall find the peace I long for, and all the sweetness and goodness of my so-dearly beloved ones shall forever live in my heart.

Now to go back to our return home. Things were even worse than before. By now it had become a real witch's kettle. First of all was the sudden funeral of the father of one of my girlfriends. He died, as the Nazis always explained, of suicide.

But we knew better. Then, in the building where we lived, one of the Jewish tenants was taken without any explanation to a concentration camp. So my mother would hardly leave the office for immigration, she was so desperate to get the papers ready. To Palestine or Argentina—whichever came first, there we would go. She always came home exhausted—again, nothing—and so many people were trying just like Mother to get away that the office was full. She pleaded with the officials, saying, "Take all the money, but let us get out." By that time it was already 1938 and everything was real tough. But Mother was promised that, before the year was up, we would be able to leave Germany.

At school, things got even worse. At recess time we were not allowed to go out in the yard with the gentile kids. It was as well, for we had had little fun out there together with their hostility and insulting ways, and if there were a few that were friends with us, it was strictly forbidden. They were afraid of being scolded by their own friends. At times when I saw Guenther, he threw sorrowful glances at me as if he wanted to say, "I am sorry!" To me, he was the only decent person in all of this Naziworld, and I shall always look back on those moments with respect and admiration for him. He was the one who showed me what Mother had always tried to teach us kids: even in the hours of great despair, Mother said, "Don't look at the evil; always try to find the goodness in people, and you shall always be happy. Go and find goodness in people when you can't find around you anything else but evil."

How little goodness there was to find in my childhood! But Guenther made up for a lot of the evil. Never would I see him being fresh or indecent. He was always so kind, and yet he was the son of a mean Nazi. One day as I was coming home from school, the atmosphere around was awful and it looked as though something was brewing. I don't know how, but always before a big storm is gathering, one can feel it in the air. Somehow it felt like that, so as Cilly and I were coming home, Mother told us, "Let's go out and be extravagant, let's make today a festive supper." At first we stopped at our favorite shop, the Fleishers, where we picked up some delicious tortes, and at one of the Jewish delicatessens we bought quite a bit. Loaded with all of those nice delicacies, we came home and started to prepare them. When Daddy came home, he would have a little surprise waiting for him. We hoped he wouldn't notice that heavy feeling that had come over us. In spite of it all, in spite of those hoodlums who were out to destroy decency and happiness in us, our happy home—no, we wouldn't let them take it away from us.

I remember as if it was yesterday. Mother asked me what I would like, and my wish was first of all, "Let's get roses."

My mother said, "What would you like to eat?"

My favorite, of course—shellfish. But the bones from the smoked fish were soon to choke our throats, for as soon as Dad came home, he told us how bad his coming home had been. Why, a person was not safe anymore even in broad daylight. He had to take the back streets, in fear of being attacked by those beasts. "But let's forget it," he said, happy to be at last home. Giving a big sigh, Father said, "Let's enjoy our evening.!" and he started to sing one of his favorite songs, a Jewish version of "Sunny Boy," the song he had always sung to Sigfried when my brother was still a little boy.

Tears filled my eyes; how much did he miss his sons! Although he always said that to have daughters is like money in the bank, a father just needs a son. Mother joined Daddy in singing one of her favorites, "My Yiddish Mamme." And soon all the outside world was forgotten—we were happy and had each other. In all of our happiness, the doorbell sounded so loud and sharp, so demanding. As I opened the door, my heart stood still. A *shupo*, a member of the Nazi *Shutzpolitzei*, was outside. *What evil is he going to bring?* I thought.

My knees were shaking, my throat was dry, and all of a sudden he asked me, "Where is your father?" As I stood there glaring at him, unable to catch my breath, awful thoughts ran through my mind: *Here it comes, they are going to take Daddy away*. And in a split second, I wanted a little time for Dad, so I answered, "I am sorry, but my father is not home."

Then, to my great horror, I heard a voice calling out from the dining room, "Lydia, who is it?" Oh, the agony of life, it was my dad.

As I quickly tried to explain to the *shupo* that I had misunderstood him, he stepped in, and his voice brought me back to reality. "I didn't come to pick him up this time. I have just brought some papers for your father to sign."

He gave Father the paper, and after getting my parents' signatures on it, he left. With him our gaiety was gone. I saw my mother weeping, and she said to Dad, "No, we will not get out anymore." We had been told that we had one week to leave Germany. Being Polish by birth, my parents had been left the choice to go there, or be forced to go there—unless, of course, we could escape another way. My mother knew that our papers were on their way already, that in a short time we could emigrate to one of the countries where my two brothers were. "But Poland," Mother said, "is the end of our dreams. Not only is it hard to emigrate from there, but how will we get along? Everything will have to be started all over again for our emigration? How will we start a new life in this anti-Semitism infested country?"

My father was not so young anymore and Mother was at the end of her strength. "What are we going to do? What future lies ahead for the children?"

Ella tried to comfort Mother, saying, "If it has to be, let it be. It is as well; we are not sure of our lives in this rotten Naziland and our papers will work out from Poland as well." How much Ella tried to comfort our parents, but in spite of my youth, I could feel how little she herself believed it. For her, having to go to Poland was a nightmare. For me and Cilly it meant only parting with our nice flat, our nice friends, and our nice teachers. What did we know? But later I saw what Mother had feared so much, for to emigrate from Poland was so very hard—all the red tape and so forth. But what can one do? Once the devil gets you in his claws, you must swallow everything and do as he says, or else!

And so Mother started to pack. Of course she tried at the immigration office so very hard, and with the papers already on their way, Mother tried to get another week from the Germans. There was so much to settle: our business, what little the Nazis had left still to sell, and boxes to be ordered for our furniture and clothing, and there was plenty of it. Mother had for us three girls a perfect dowry. So many and such beautiful things: silverware, lovely china, and the beautiful cut glass, those huge vases which were in better times always filled with flowers. "The first son-in-law that you girls will bring home will get this golden watch," Father would say. It was a breathtaking watch on a long and heavy chain, studded with glittering diamonds.

Well, poor Mother's hands were more than full. How can one squeeze a lifetime into one week? But Mother tried so very hard. It was decided that Cilly and I were to stay at school until the last three days. The first thing Mother did was prepare everything for washing. Everything was to be sorted for packing, so it was naturally a big mess. For us kids, Mother said, the best solution was to be out of the house. When we came home from school the next day, Mother had quite a bit accomplished. She had been in the office and was promised that things would be talked over for another week, to get our emigration granted. But to be on the safe side, Mother had ordered everything for our baggage, and those things that needed to be washed were soaked. With most of the things taken care of, Mother was a little bit more relaxed. The next day she had put aside for washing only. Margit stopped by our house, and not knowing what was going on, she burst like always into our home with the words, "How lucky you guys are!" To me and Cilly, she said,"You just came back from your visit and are going again, how lucky can you get?" but when she saw how everything was in an uproar, and Mother was going around with tears running down her cheeks, she felt that there must be something wrong. As we told her what had happened, she left, not so gayful, and with tears in her eyes, too. This was the first time that I had seen tomboy Margit crying. Of course Cilly and I, we had a lot to do. There were our friends to say good-bye to, and, of course, our autograph books got filled quickly with all the well wishes and so forth.

Today, after all those years, I still have it among my cherished possessions. Our beloved principal, how wonderful he was to us kids! The Nazis wouldn't let him emigrate, for they had need for him still in Gleiwitz, and later they destroyed him with the rest of my people. All of my wonderful teachers, how much I always enjoy reading the few words they wrote for me in my sorrow. Next day at school there was hardly any learning, only good-byes.

The day came closer and closer for us. Our English teacher, Miss Kathy Enrlich, was touched to tears, for she had liked us so very much. And there I stood and felt my childhood was shattered; here lay the end station of it all, the end of all my hopes and dreams. How was I to know that this all was not the worst yet? How was I to know what horror lay ahead? Not wanting to show the rest of the class my great unhappiness, I went around and asked everyone for their autographs. I didn't even care at that time which of those kids I disliked. I wished everybody to have a space in my little book of memories. In the middle of it all, sister Ella burst into the classroom. Her face full of tears, her dress soaked wet, her hair crumpled, she looked so frightened.

Behind her, two Gestapo men were walking. *Oh, Lord, what has happened?* I thought. My so proud and neat sister—no man had ever been good enough for her, never a hair out of place, everything had to be just perfect all the time. And here, how awful she looked. Soon I found out that those miserable Nazis, they wouldn't leave us the satisfaction of letting it go the way they had demanded. No, they wouldn't even give us the one week they had promised. Oh, no, they had to have their fun and see our dismay. In broad daylight they came to take us from home in their green *minna*. That's what we called the wagon which had always been used for their criminals.

The wagon was an open one, so the whole city could see who had been caught. Mother had been promised a permit to stay for another week, but after only two days, and Mother in the middle of everything, they came so soon, so all of a sudden. The wash was soaked, nothing prepared, but we had to leave right away. They dragged us through the city, the city to which my father had given the best years of his life, as if we were the worst criminals.

When Ella came to pick us up from school, always with the Gestapo in back of her, Mother meanwhile threw a few pieces into the suitcase. Only one suitcase a person was permitted, and Mother wanted to use her own suitcase to take along some food. The real big one Father was going to take. We weren't permitted to take money, they said, just a little unmentionable amount. As we left school in such a big hurry, the last thing I saw was the tear-soaked eyes of my dear friends, and even in teacher's eyes I saw tears. Accompanied by the Gestapo, we went home. When we got there and I looked at Mother, how old she looked, her face ashes, and her eyes as if they wanted to speak, as if they tried to say, "Forgive me for having brought you into this evil world. Forgive me for your rotten childhood!" How little Mother really knew about how very rich my childhood had been! It was the best family a child had ever been blessed with, and they were the most wonderful parents. No, my childhood, with all its sorrows, had been so very, very rich. The only regret I have was that it had to end so soon. All the songs written to honor a mother would be too poor for mine. She was a ray of sunshine in a cold and cloudy world, and my childhood was blessed so very much in having her.

Her first words as we stepped into the house were, "Children, take anything you want with you." Cilly and I had each a little suitcase. Mother didn't make us take any clothes or such—never will I be able to forget it. "Take only what your hearts desire," she said. But how, how can one squeeze a whole childhood into a little suitcase? All my lovely toys and books, so many of them. The first things we thought of was our Shirley Temple doll. Then came my books. *Heidi* had always been one of my favorites, and to leave her behind would mean to leave my whole dream world with her. Then I took many other nice books, not realizing how heavy books could get. Later, on my way, I had to throw some of them away. Mother hid some of our jewelry in her clothing, and Father tried to stuff some money into his socks. After half an hour had elapsed, the Gestapo rushed us to leave. And here we were to leave all of our proud possessions behind. Mother left the keys with another Jewish family, and they promised to take care of things, as much as possible under the circumstances. Anyhow Father left some of our money with them, and they promised us that they would send it to us if possible.

As we left the flat, the place where we had known so much happiness, I felt like my heart would break. Looking into Father's face was like looking at a mask. And my mother's heartbreaking cries! We were not the richest—Father had always tried, together with Mother, to give us children a proper education and they had always worked hard. We were always dressed in lovely clothes and we had always a proud home. Mother had always tried to save for their old age. For us kids, only the best had been good enough. And here all of a sudden, everything was broken to fragments. All their hopes had to stay behind with all of our possessions. The doors had closed to their dreams, I am sure. And as the doors to our home closed behind us, it was as if a thousand fine needles were going through my heart. Here I felt I had buried my childhood forever.

This was the end of it. I was a child no more. All of my carefree life was gone. Seeing how broken my parents were, I felt all of a sudden, with all of my youth, that I had to grow up, to help ease the pain of my so very beloved ones. And I was only ten years old. Childhood, dreamhood, in what an ugly way you were taken from me! But in my memories, you will always be precious.

MY YOUTH

When we said good-bye to our landlord and went downstairs, there was a mob waiting outside in front of the prison wagon. They welcomed us with less than friendly words. Those hysterical shouts of, *"Jueden raus,"* and their hands clapping were like applause to a command performance. For whom was this all meant? We, of course, were the celebrities. Stones were thrown, dirt hurled into our faces, and at whom? Three broken-down grown-ups and two little girls. My mother stepped on the filthy wagon with a smile, and so went Father, which of course was answered with all kind of dirt. "Whatever happens," my parents used to always say, "just don't show them how much they tear your heart out."

Oh, Ella, how courageous she was! And Cilly and I? To tell the truth, we weren't so brave. We were pushed onto the truck crying heartbreakingly; to my regret, we gave those big heroes on the outside so much satisfaction. In the middle of the mob stood our maid, who had always been treated like a member of our family. She came from a broken home where her father was a drunkard and her mother a prostitute, and her boyfriends were always in trouble. But she was a nice girl, and not too dishonest. She was clean, and Mother had always felt so sorry for her and had helped her so much. Mother had always given her food and clothing to take home for her younger brother and sister. Later, when it was strictly forbidden that Aryans should work for Jews, she would still come twice a week, and Mother had still given her help. Here again was another example of the Nazi way. She looked as if she had just hit the jackpot. She joined the audience in their applause.

Not all were applauding. A few Jewish people stood nearby; in their minds the thought must have entered, "When are we next in line?" And in the middle of growling and screaming, I saw a Nazi youth. Once again I tried to raise my head, and as I looked up, there stood Guenther, tears running down his cheeks—the only decent person in all this disaster. "Good-bye, Guenther!" my heart seemed to say, and as if he understood, a smile glanced over his face, a smile so full of helpless pain. Did it really mean so much to you, I only ten and you almost fourteen? Or was it all disbelief at all that was happening, and you, not able to do a thing about it? Whatever it was, it will always be an inspiration for me of goodness and kindness in a lost and evil world, and I shall always be grateful to have had you as a friend! Another glance over the place where I had spent so many happy dreams, another look at my friend, and good-bye, Gleiwitz, it was. I sent my thoughts to Gleiwitz: *How good good life could have been in your arms; you were such a nice and peaceful city, but fate did not want it to be. Will I ever see any of you again?* I did not notice the hostility around me as we were dragged through the city like the worst criminals. I want to mention that, at this time, only those were deported who had no German citizenship. As my parents had come to Germany from Poland as the first World War was about to end, they had never been granted German citizenship. At the time that we were deported, many of our friends stayed in Gleiwitz.

As the wagon drove by the school, classes were out and the kids were leaving, and there in a group were many of my friends. My teachers were outside. Here again, it cut through my heart. And so the truck drove toward the prison gates. Prisoners we had become, and in jail we had to stay, never having done anything dishonest in all of our lives—there was always only honesty and goodness in our home. Prisoners: that awful feeling as the creaky doors of our cells closed behind us. Mother started to scream and I was afraid that she was going to lose her mind. "Kill me but let my innocent children out!" Mother screamed, throwing herself against the cell doors. And Father, my darling, how quiet he was, as if everything that had happened only had been a bad dream. And Ella, trying to comfort Mother in her agony, explaining to her that it would be worse for the children with her behaving like that. The children, always the children, Cilly and me, me and Cilly, that was their only thought, always.

My sweet family, how much I loved them. I went toward my mother, tears streaming down my face, and I begged, "Mama, please stop it, we are all together, and no matter what happens, we will stay together."

Mother, getting up from her faint, hugged me and kissed me. She squeezed Cilly and I close and whispered, "My big girls, how quickly you grew up!"

Although my heart was nearly broken, I fought the tears back, and I promised myself never to cry again. So what if they took our possessions from us, so what if they ran us from our home? Our love, our deep affection, they could not touch. The more agony they would try to make us live through, the more we would grow tighter together!

Together with us on the same floor were mostly people who shared our fate. The Nazis had brought them from all the neighboring cities, and a few families were also from our town. But the other guests were criminals. I remember Mother giving one of the guards money so he would bring us something warm to eat, for we hadn't eaten yet. Anyhow, who could eat? Mother gave him some money to bring some other things, always double the amount it would really cost. Mother was glad that he was willing to do it, but he never showed up, neither with the things he had promised to buy for us nor with the money. Slowly night came. In broad daylight things really didn't look so gloomy, but when night came, an unknown fear came over me. What would happen to us?

Mother tried to persuade us to go to sleep on those prison cots, but she herself stayed up, whispering with Daddy. And with all of my tender age, my youth, I finally was rescued from this misery as I fell into a restless sleep. But it was no rescue at all, for the dreams—or better said, nightmares—were almost worse than the bitter reality. All of a sudden, it must have been around midnight, Mother woke us softly. We had to prepare to leave. We had to walk very quietly, for we were to smuggle ourselves into Poland. And so the journey, those awful days and nights, into "nowhere" had started.

Late in fall, the night was very cold, and it seemed as if everything had turned against us. The rain started to pour, but that was even better for our torturers, because there would be less danger of our being discovered making the illegal entry into Poland, and they would be rid of us quickly. That there were little children among us, and elderly and sick—that didn't bother those sadists. How much easier it could have been, but they wouldn't leave us the satisfaction of making it "easier." The more they could make us suffer, the happier they were. If those beasts only would have given us the week they had offered, we could have gotten our visas and would have gone legally to Poland from the fascist heaven of modern Germany. We would have been able to take our possessions along with us.

If, this little word *if,* that always made such a big difference. No, they didn't want us to got the normal way. First of all, they could rob us this way, and, secondly, they could enjoy making us suffer. This is what *Nazi* stands for. Yes, they had the power to destroy the little, helpless guy in their hands. *What a proud country*, we thought, *so full of culture, yet with only one goal, to conquer the world and to enslave everyone who didn't belong to the superior race, the race of murderes and torturers.* Even their hymn—to hear it makes a person wanting justice and peace sick.

Every hymn that I have ever heard from all over the world, I have respected and been inspired by. But theirs only speaks of being above each nation of earth. Their songs had just one refrain: tomorrow to us shall belong the world. What I am writing is not hatred for a people that destroyed everything I once cherished and loved, it is written out of my heart. How can you hate someone you despise? And I shall always despise everything they stood for. Those very little ones with us on our way cried at being disturbed in their sleep, not having had their warm milk or food. The bigger kids were shaking for fear, looking into the dark and rainy night. My dear and gentle father had the worse of it yet.

His suitcase was so heavy, he carried it on his head all the time. Now that I look back at all that, I can't understand how he had the strength. As we wandered day and night, he never complained. Sometimes he took it down from his head to catch some breath. How forlorn he looked, trudging into the cold, dark night, never saying a word. When others were ready to give up—and some drowned themselves on the way—Dad stayed mute. My sweet little darling. How little and skinny he had always been, but so strong of heart and soul. Until the last day when they tore me from his arms, he had a big blue bump on his head from his suitcase. After all the horror and anguish had almost been forgotten, it always reminded me of those nightmarish days and nights, and I would kiss on the bump on Father's head, and Daddy always smiled at me. After we had been chased out of German territory by the Nazis and their police dogs, and after an endless night of struggle through the rain-soaked night, we could see the dusk coming.

We were in the middle of nowhere. Some of my people had their litle ones on their backs wrapped in blankets; some men carried the tiny tots in their arms, and one could hear their weak cries. We had been divided into two groups. One group was to go through Swiebodzin and the other, among which we were, through Poznan. Sometimes as we were wandering, our feet stuck in the deep mud and we paused for a few moments to change our socks. Anyhow, we were soaking wet and muddy up to our knees. I was so frozen I wept quietly to myself. Cilly was so quiet and Ella, she shouted at those sadists, as she would always call them. And Mama, she wasn't worried about herself.

She had always suffered from rheumatism; she had to take mud baths in Jaschtchemp; one time she wasn't able to walk anymore, but at that time I think I must have been very little. I couldn't recall it, but had heard Mother speaking about it. And here, somehow, Mother had been given the strength; her only concern and worry, as always, was for her children. My sweet and precious Mammale. Seeing all that misery, I tried to complain as little as possible, but I guess that with ten years, one can't be taken yet for a grown-up. As much as I wanted to be strong, I just couldn't go on. I remember Mother begged the leader to stop for a little while, for getting lost from the group was like getting lost in the desert. But they just couldn't wait, for they feared that the day might break and we would be caught. The Polish patrol might get wind of us, and what would we do then? Ella said it would be all the better; then the Germans would have to let us back in, and we could settle everything legally. How naïve she was!

Finally we were told that we would have to sit down, and the man that had showed us the way asked a few men from our group to join him. He said that a train station was nearby, and that we had come through the Polish border. As they went to find the station, we changed our clothing. Daddy went with the men to the train station, and it made me so frightened. *Why is it taking so long?* I thought. So many thoughts entered our minds, such horrible things that could have happened. What if the Germans had lied to us? What if the men had been taken to a concentration camp? And what if the patrol spotted them and shot at them? I was shaking like a leaf. Mother's face looked so sad, so empty, so hopeless. She took me on her knees and put my head on her shoulders, and wanted that I should sleep a little, but through her clothing I could hear her heart beat. How fearful it was, and how much Mother shook!

What went through her mind? But finally the men came back. We had to be very quiet, and we were not able to go all together. We had to pretend that we didn't know each other, every family for itself, and so, finally, we came to the train station. I didn't care anymore what had happened. My only wish was to get out of the wet clothing and get fed and warm. I didn't care anymore that we had left everything behind. I only wanted to have my peace, that was all that counted for me right now. After going through such an ordeal, who cared about anything else? Just to have a roof over one's head again and a bed to sleep in! But things did not turn out the way we had hoped, for we had not suffered enough yet.

At the train station were only a few lonesome passengers. The time could have been four o'clock in the morning. Soon things started to liven up at this tiny station. They must have never seen so many people at once at that station. The sleepy lady behind the ticket counter asked us where we were going. As all the people slowly started to fill the station, she told us to wait for a while. I think the grown-ups knew by then what was going to happen. It did not take long. They came after us with mounted bayonets. After who? A broken-down people—and how meanly, utterly mean, they treated us. I shall never forget their fierce faces, so full of hate. We had to make the whole way back, this time not with dogs behind us, only their bayonets right in back. And if some of our people fell down, heaven forbid, the soldiers hit them with their bayonets. Such was our reception from the Polish side.

At the German border, the Nazis were waiting with their hounds. On one side the dogs, on the other, the mounted bayonets. Which way was there to go? And the cold wind and rain went on and on. A few died on that journey, for after three days and nights of uselss wandering, the grown-ups said, "Here we stay. Let the dogs rip us to pieces. Do with us whatever you want. That is all, no more back and forth."

The thing I still remember most vividly was that I was a wet mess. How we lived through such an ordeal is unbelievable, but truth is stranger than fiction. A few men from the group said that we were Polish citizens and we had rights. We were walking towards the border patrol, and on the way was a farm. A Silesian woman came running out, tears streaming down her cheeks at seeing the mess that had once called themselves people, and seeing the children, how very near to death they were. She called the Lord as her witness. She came out with a pail of hot milk for all of us. After the little ones had been taken care of, we all got some. I had never liked milk, but never before had anything tasted more heavenly than this cup of it. While we were sitting there, the men tried to come to an understanding with the officials. After a long wait as calls went back and forth, the men came finally out with the news that those who had passports could enter Poland.

Those who had none were to go back to Germany, to which the Germans not very willingly agreed. A very small number did not have the passports with them, but finally Dad came out, his face full of joy, waving his passport with its new visa. The group with visas was taken towards the border through Poznan. In a shack, a few rooms had already been prepared, for word had gone around that we were on our way, and the committee of the Jewish help organization had been busy preparing everything for us. Soon there was warm food, dry clothing, beds, and even medicine, everything donated by the Polish Jews. From rich to poor, they all had opened their hearts. It was so heartwarming to know that people cared about us. After our night's rest, most of us got a little bit of our strength back, but a few were taken to hospitals right away. We were taken to the train station, and from there we went to our destination, Bendzin. A short time ago, we had left that station not thinking to ever see it agin, and here we were again, but so different this time! The last time we left with so much hope and now we came so broken-down, like vagabonds.

Uncle Jacob, with whom we would always stay when coming for a visit, didn't know this time that we were coming. We sent a messenger to his house, and right away he came with his wife, Auntie Ester. She was flabbergasted. She asked, "Why are you crying, and why are you already back?" As we explained everything, she only could shake her head. And so we went to Uncle's place for the night. The next day we had to go to a special place with all the deportees, and there the warmhearted Jews of Bendzin had donated what was possible. A big hall had been filled with many, many beds and there was a kitchen for meals. In the beginning, some cooks were hired, but later men and women were taken from the group for kitchen duty. Big halls with tables for dining were already prepared. To me, the huge beds seemed like a gift from heaven. Worn out, we were beginning to undress when we heard a knock at the door, and there stood Sally Reich from Pogon.

She is now my sister-in-law, but then she told us, "I came to take the children to us until you people get settled." I begged Mother not to let us go. I wanted to stay with them, and it was so much fun in the hotel room. But Mother and Sally tried to explain that it would be wise to go; the place was so small and so crowded, and how would the five of us get rest? Mother said we couldn't possibly impose on Uncle Jacob; he was already doing more than in his power. With us so worn out from the journey, Mother said, we should at least go rest a little in Pogon, where the air was nice and fresh, at least until things were settled. In Pogon the Reiches had their own house and bakery, and most importantly, there were so many kids. We would have fun and hardly miss our parents. "Sally is being so kind and thoughtful. You really should go. We will try to see you as often as possible," Mother said.

Finally, with a little bit of aggravation, we got dressed and went with Sally. At Pogon we had a nice room and a soft bed. In the morning Sally always brought breakfast in bed. She was so kind to us, and her parents were the same. Although we were only very distantly related, they treated us very much like their own kids, and maybe even better. I'll always be so grateful to them for how they opened their hearts to us. If they were only alive today, they would be my in-laws. I married their youngest son, Jack, who was then so bashful he hardly ever looked at girls. He was so good-looking, even as a child, and how I adored to tease him and play tricks on him. I was at that time a little over ten, and Jack was around thirteen. At times if I got too fresh with him, he took some drastic measures. I tease him, "Weren't they a little too drastic?" and he replies, "Not for the way you made all of us crazy!."

He liked to play with their big mother cat, so I always tried to hide the cat from him, until one day his grandfather said, "What's enough is enough, a boy at your age should better study the Torah, not play with a cat." He took the cat and carried it away. Grandfather wanted to play it safe so he took her in a big sack and drove way out with her. But what a surprise awaited him as he returned home; he just shook his head in disbelief. "How did this happen?" he asked, twirling his long beard. The cat had reached home before he arrived. And so it went on and on for days, but he never did succeed. I think that in the end, he gave up. He was such a lovable old man. I think he must have been around one hundred years old. He was such a dear. How we used to enjoy to tease him always.

When you are young, what pleases you more than to tease a feeble old man?. Out in Pogon, the folks were very religious. Although we had been brought up to respect the Sabbath, we somehow always cheated a little. In Pogon, we had to be careful. We were out there for two weeks, and they were such nice and memorable ones we had almost forgotten all the nightmares we had gone through. Oh, what fun it was to fly with the speed of a rocket on the beds where Robert and Mark were sound asleep. Robert never got tired of it, but at times we got acquainted with the palm of Mark's hand. How many times Sally teases me now: "When will you pay us already for the couch you broke?". When I recall it now, after so many years, it looks like a whole lifetime. My husband and I feel so close, with all of those nice memories left from a life of horror and despair.

My parents came quite often to visit us, but somehow they always looked so hopeless. How little I really realized at that time how much Mother must have gone through. My proud mother was always be giving, and now she had to ask for help. How hard it must have been for her. But out there in Pogon, we, of course, did not realize what was going on back in Bendzin. One day, Mother came to take us back. With so many nice memories and promises to see each other often, with thanks in our hearts for a family that had opened their home and hearts so freely to us kids, we finally left Pogon for a new life.

Back in Bendzin, Mother had gotten a space for us at the place for the displaced ones. There was one bed for me and Cilly, and one for sister Ella. For herself and Dad, Mother got a bed, too. Those sleeping rooms were in a huge hall where there were coutless beds, one next to the other. For us, what happiness, what joy! For we were all together. That meant one thing for me: we were on our way up again.

Suddenly, one day I got a high temperature, and my back hurt so badly when I breathed. Then I fell into deep coma. My temperature again soared to an all-time high. Yes, it was the result of our wandering in the rain. The doctor pronounced pneumonia. I don't know how many days and nights I lay there unconscious, for one day as dusk fell in the dim daylight, I came to, and there next to my bed were my dear and beloved parents. As I looked about and whispered, "What happened?" I looked into the sorrowful eyes of Dad and the tearful face of Mother. I was so weak, I could hardly move. I will never find out what I said while lying unconscious, but I remember that when the doctor came, he said, "She has gone through a lot, but she is going to be all right." As I looked around at my new surroundings, for I had been removed from the large hall and was confined now to the sickroom, I saw that I had no worry of being alone. I had a lot of company: my sister Ella, with a bad cold; Cilly, with a slight case of pneumonia; and so many cases of pneumonia around me. A few, not so fortunate as I had been, had died. It took months for me to really recover, so slowly did my old strength and vigor come back. At each little thing, I would faint. My feet just wouldn't hold me. Then after a few months, my youth won and I was almost as good as new again.

Ella, Cilly, and I were given a room in Ort just for girls, but it wasn't all roses. The older girls liked to boss us around and were jealous of Ella. She was such a pretty girl, and always dressed herself so nicely. I thought all that time that Ella wouldn't be able to live through it. She cried all the time, and she just couldn't take it anymore. My parents, not wanting to accept too much charity, slept in Uncle Jacob's kitchen, which at times was his work room as well. It was located a few stairs down in the basement. The room was so awfully humid and moist that Mother felt weak and sick. Uncle couldn't persuade Mother to come upstairs to the second floor where his bedroom was. In Poland most of the living quarters left much to be desired. Mother wouldn't listen to Uncle's plea; she told him always that he did more than he could already. Uncle didn't have an easy life. He was a photographer and, not having enough work to support his family, he worked part-time at night at a factory. He was not too well himself, and since he was Mother's youngest brother, she felt always sorry for him.

Pinjush, his little boy, was our darling. I often took him out for strolls. He loved me so very much. At times I was so close with him that people would think he was my little brother. Back at Ort, we made friends with a few nice kids. Among them was a girl named Sarah, whom we liked. She was one year older than Cilly and we got along fine. Although she was much taller and more grown than we were, we understood each other excellently. One day she had twisted her foot and couldn't climb up to her bunk, so Cilly and I gave her our bed. From that day on, we became very much attached to one another. Her name will be very significant in my story later. Although we were getting over our dreadful colds, we were not so resistant to sickness as we used to be. At any little thing, our temperatures would soar . It went on, I think, for the next year or two. We must have been more in bed than up.

Life went on; it had to go on. Never does it stand still. Soon Father had to fight for his existence again and start out of the ruin to build a new life. Father and Mother were not so young anymore, and they had dreamed of a nice and peaceful old age, which no doubt had been earned. Ella had dreamed of a beautiful future; Cilly and I pictured for ourselves a rosy youth, with sunshine and laughter, free of sorrow. Everything turned out so differently instead.

After a few weeks of recuperation, Cilly and I were sent to the public school. Polish could have been for us Turkish at that time. We would have understood both languages just the same. After giving us a test, the school officials decided that, except for the language barrier, we were much more advanced than the grade they wanted to put us in, so we were put into the grade that we had left in Gleiwitz. With the language barrier it was tough.

The kids in school, most of them, did nothing to make it easier for us. At recess time, the kids stood around us like we were the seventh wonder. Me, trying to be cheerful and friendly, I would have them all on my side soon. I didn't go to school much in Poland. First of all, I was sick more than usual. For the first time in my life I hated school. I, who had always been so hapy to attend school. The teacher back home had always talked with Mother about what enthusiasm I had for learning. School had been my life. Here in Poland I disliked school so much it frightened my parents. I remember back in Germany, Mother had wanted so badly for us to learn English and French. Somehow to French I felt such antipathy, and English was my love. Later I regretted badly not having taken French. With Polish it was just the same. From the beginning I said that I didn't want to be forced to learn something I would never understand.

When Cilly and I got home from school, we put on a show of the words we had caught in Polish. At times those words matched some in English and some in German with another meaning, and those words were always the easiest for us to remember. When one is so young, one doesn't realize how blessed one is to be able to learn a language. As Mother used to say, "You never know when you might need it." Polish was one language I needed badly in years to come.

With almost two months gone since our coming from Germany, and Cilly and me still back at that place in Ort, Mother just couldn't take it any longer, and she started making drastic changes.

First of all, Mother spent most of the day apartment hunting. From almost the day we had come to Bendzin, Mother had tried so hard to find a place. Most of the landlords were afraid to rent to deportees; they said we were a bad risk. For Mother, it was like being hit over the head. My mother was always a model tenant, always trusted, always the giver, and here she had to stand in front of their doors begging for a roof over our heads.

We had a little money, and part of our jewelry was worth a quite a bit. Mother tried to explain it to them. Their only reply was to shake their heads. Father soon found work as a painter, and soon we would have a roof over our heads. A painter in Poland! Mother was grief stricken. Most of the painters in Poland had very hard lives and hardly any future at all. Everything seemed so hopeless.

Once again, Ella tried to comfort us. "We won't stay here forever. We will emigrate, and we won't starve," she said. Ella always said that we would make it somehow. But Mother's eyes were so sad all the time, so deep in her face from her daily cry. Our tears she would always kiss away, but her heartbreak, who could take it from her? Now, looking back at those days, it is as though I can feel how hopeless it must have been for them. How fortunate I had been not to be able to understand the whole tragedy. Then a miracle happened. They say that unless it is really dark, it can't get light—how right that saying must be. For in all of our distress, Mother heard that on the edge of town was a new building, and soon an apartment was to be available. The only thing was that the landlord was a Pole. Knowing that many of the Poles didn't sympathize too much with the Jews, Mother was hopeless. But what was there to lose? The building was nice and clean, and, glory, each one had its own restroom. This apartment to be soon available had a large ktichen and lots of room. Heaven on earth! Although we had been used to a very large apartment in Gleiwitz, we had no luxury like that in mind anymore. Getting this flat would mean everything for us now. When Mother went to inquire, we found, to our amazement, that the whole apartment was occupied by Jewish families. The landlord, an old man, got to like Mother right away. His words, how vividly I still recall them: "I look into your eyes and see honesty and sincerity in them." His grandsons and daughter were living with him, and after paying under the table to those people, we were the proud owners of a flat. Thank heaven!

My mother was walking on clouds. Although we had no furniture to put in it, what did it matter? At least we had a roof over our heads and we were all together.

This address consisted of two buildings. One, a new one in back, was where we lived. In the one in front lived the landlord, the baker, and the janitor. Linking those two buildings was a bakery, and across from the bakery was a factory. It was nice and airy, for across the street was a large estate where everything was green. Yes, we had been rewarded for our long wait. Our yard had a huge sandbox and grass all around. Mother fell in love with the place right away and so did the rest of my family. It was a happy day when we moved in.

I remember as if it were yesterday, seeing everything in front of me so vividly. Uncle had given us a folding bed, then we borrowed somewhere a big mattress which we put on the floor, and there Cilly, Ella, and I slept. In the house, a large box was left which right away became our table, and from Uncle we took a couple of chairs. The rest of the immediate things we needed for our housekeeping, Mother bought.

We enjoyed our first meal together under one roof. In the store in front of the bakery, we bought most of our needs, and almost everything was taken care of, except Father's work. We started once again to build our new life. It was hard, though, very hard. Mother was so disgusted at times she wouldn't know what the end would be. Father was not so young any more, and always he had been his own boss, but here he had to go and beg for a day's work. When he got one, finally, it was so underpaid. More than ever, Mother concentrated and worked on our emigration papers. It was now very difficult to work things out, but Mother never gave up. The same I must say of Father. He ran around to get his day's work, for however little it would earn, he just wouldn't sit idle. Then Father tried to work on his own, for as he said, things just couldn't be worse. Father tried everything; he tried the farmers, and in the city; then, after a farmer tried Father out, he got more and more work. Most of the time, they paid him with food, but what did it matter, we had at least made a step forward. The farmers liked Daddy a lot after they saw what a good and honest worker he was. At times he even got paid with money, and so, little by little, things were starting to go up again. My mother's face somehow looked a bit relaxed once more, and we learned to laugh again. Soon Cilly and I had a few friends, but we wouldn't forget the friends we had left behind. Sometimes I heard Cilly cry herself to sleep. For Ella, the beginning was very hard. She didn't make friends easily, but she, too, found her group, and they were nice people.

One day as Cilly and I were playing hopscotch out in the yard, and we were counting in our own language. Our accents were still very German, and kids from the building gathered around to look at us like we were the seventh wonder. Though our language was different, the way of playing is for children the same all over the world, as we were soon to find out. Soon, even the language barrier was forgotten and we played happily together. In a short while, we were all one. There were so many nice kids around. After a few months, Mother got special permission to go back to Gleiwitz for a few days to bring those things of ours that were left. If I am not mistaken, she had it worked out through a lawyer. But what a shock did Mother get when she discovered that most of our possessions had been stolen. The janitor from the building was a Silesian, and he had stolen most of our valuables from us. When Mother saw his son riding my brother's bike, she asked him who had given him permission. His reply was, "The Fuehrer, and if you don't like it," he added, with a grin on his dirty face, "then sue me."

Although most of the things that had been left looked as if a hurricane had struck them, Mother was glad for the little that was left to take back. A little of Father's workshop was left, too, but we had been robbed tremendously. When Mother came back to Bendzin, we were so happy with the little that was left. At least we could start a better life without the bare walls around us. Soon our home was nice and homely again. Everybody could once again sleep in comfort. Mother cried a lot after she returned. Most of the Jews had fled, although many were still left, it was no more the same. The synagogue, our most precious of all memories, had been burned. We had heard of it over the radio when it happened, but to come back and see it, I guess, must have been a great shock to Mother. The stores that before had been owned by Jews, now had been taken over by Aryans, and many of the Germans that had once been so friendly with us would not speak to Mother. This was the least that hurt Mother, for that much we were used to already. I think the thing that hurt so much was coming back to the flat. We had spent so many nice hours in it, and it was destroyed.

For the first time, Mother said, "I am glad, wherever I am, only not to have to look into their faces." But how soon she was to look into their faces again, Mother was unable to imagine. Mother sold a lot of our possessions and went with full speed once again to work out our papers to emigrate. Every day after seeing the awful anti-Semitism that took place in Poland, Mother said, "No, the end will not be good."

One day, we just couldn't believe our ears; we heard a lady say, "Just wait till Hitler comes." So Mother's only thinking and doing was our papers, and out of Poland as soon as possible. To go out alone into a Polish neighborhood at night and to be recognized as a Jew was suicide. So it was not too much different than in Germany. I just couldn't understand it—why, oh, why is everybody so much against the Jews?

One day Mother came home happy and relaxed, for our papers were on their way. It would not be too long before we'd be able to leave this place that we had learned to hate. But, because of a slight error in sister Ella's name, there was a delay until everything could be checked out, changed, and taken care of. But what difference does a few more weeks make when freedom and glory await you? There was really something worth waiting for, and all of our hardship would be twice as easy now, for there in the end awaited salvation! We made plans about our sunny future. It was already decided that we would go to brother Max in Argentina. The British just wouldn't let us emigrate to Israel. So Mother made her mind up, and Father said that the sooner we left, the better.

All of a sudden, Uncle Samuel died. He left his wife and five daughters, so to say, penniless. Mother found it her duty to help as much as possible, and as little as we had at that time for ourselves, she always shared. She had promised her brother on his deathbed that she would take care of things as much as she could. Mother was always so kind and considerate, and however tough it was for us, there were always others in greater need.

Max was all excited at learning of our coming and from then on, his only goal was to prepare a nest for us. Little cousin Pinjush grew each day to be a more beautiful child. I became very attached to him and at times, if he waved to me to come out, my heart would stand still from knowing that he had crossed the busy streets all by himself. I would scold him not to ever do it again. Then I would take him home and apologize to him, and Uncle would have to promise me not to punish him. Somehow my scolding didn't help too much, and as soon as the little guy figured that he had been punished unjustly, there he was again, sneaking in front of my window. This sweet little guy, how much I loved him! If he hadn't been murdered by those Nazibrutes, he would have been a man by now. But more of this later.

Cilly, almost thirteen, and I, around eleven, still liked to play at times with our dolls. But then suddenly, Cilly started to act more grown-up, and somehow we drifted slowly apart. I could hear her whispering, and how she would blush when talking with her girlfriends! To me, loving to always run and jump, this had one name: sissy. So I let her stay with her friends, and I was happy with mine. Until then, Cilly and I had always dressed like twins, but now all of a sudden, things changed. She dressed more like a young lady while I still wore the little girl dresses. But where housekeeping was concerned, things were different. I knew my way around the ktichen—the stove, cooking, cleaning, and so forth—but our weekly cleaning chores were for Cilly just poison. Without Mother knowing about it, I did most of the work for Cilly. I did love her so much, and for me housework was a cinch, while for Cilly it was like a fine. Mother soon found out, and when she saw how much I liked to work around the house, always singing, I heard her say to our neighbor, "I pray to see the day when my little girl will be her own housewife; how blessed her home will be!"

With Ella, I didn't get along that famously. I didn't like her to boss me around, but although Cilly and I were not as close as we used to be, we still were very much attached to each other and understood one another perfectly. If I found out some news from my girlfriends about things Mother thought we still were too young to know, I told Cilly at night while we were going to sleep. Before I could even start, she would ask me if Mother knew I knew it, and I would say, "Don't be silly!" She wouldn't let me speak about it—always the honest little girl! Although our characters were so different, how much we loved one another! I always thought parting from Cilly would be my death, and it was the same with her. I guess we should really have been twins. I can still see her gentle and sweet face. She was always so quiet, but I made up for her quietness. Although I was bashful, too, it still was no comparison to her. I found out very soon that, always being bashful, one just can't come too far. Although I gave respect where respect was due, I felt that things you really wanted were worth fighting for. One just couldn't do that while being bashful. I was always the messenger to places where no one else wanted to go. How grateful I'll always be to Mother for giving me that opportunity, for this is what helped me later in my fight for my own life.

One day we were ordered to prepare together with all of the tenants a shelter bunker. Oh, Lord, what is wrong? Is there really going to be a war? We were soon busy preparing the basement for the air raid shelter. Ella had been chosen to be at hand for first aid, and so were a few of the other girls from the building. Things mustn't have looked too good, for Mother did worry a lot. *There must be something wrong,* I felt right away. Although the Jews hadn't been good for anything, lately, we still felt that it would be good and right to give our lives for the country.

Many newlyweds parted, for their men were called upon to fight for the country. As we saw this, we knew that war was near. But with the army mostly on horses, how could they fight a well-equipped enemy like the Germans? Only a miracle could save them. Although the Poles were not very much favor of the Jew, the Jews still prayed for their survival and helped the Poles so much in this crisis. Most of the Jews were very worried. What would happen if war did break out? Where would we run? What if Hitler really should come? What lay ahead of us? I didn't realize then the darkness of time. Everybody was so busy preparing, but for what? And for how long can you prepare? You can prepare food for a few weeks. You can prepare a few things, but would we be able to stay?

What if we had to evacuate? And for that, too, perparation had begun. Mother was so tired of running already. How worried everybody's faces were. How blessed to still be a child, not realizing fully the danger. But things didn't fool me the least bit. I saw and felt that there was nothing good for us if the war really did come. Just to hear the word *war* made chills run down my spine. At night I dreamed about it. The synagogues were full of people who prayed to the Lord, "Please save us! Save us from the destruction that lies ahead." When Yom Kippur came, I begged Mother to please let us fast. Although she was very religious, and in spite of so much hardship behind us, she didn't want me to fast. "My baby," she said, "you aren't strong enough yet, you have gone through so much, and who knows what lays still ahead of us!"

But I tried to persuade her. "Don't you see, Mother, we all should keep up the holidays from infant to grown-up, for the Bible says that one will suffer for the sin of the other. But if all of us keep up the holidays, the Lord will keep watch over us and everything will be all right!" Knowing how very religious the Polish Jews were, I felt that there was not much to fear of sinning. After a lot of persuading, Mother gave in.

Fasting was not so easy for me. Mother never learned that I fainted. As people were busy making plans for their evacuation in case of an emergency, Mother only shook her head and said, "No, not us, my family and I have wandered enough already. Whatever will happen, let it happen; here is where I live." At times it looked like Mother was ready to give up. She grew older quickly. She was too tired already. My dearly beloved mother—the only thing that kept her going was the thought of her children, whom she loved more than her own life. Those thoughts, it seemed, gave her new strength. How good she had been to us. And dear Dad, how very worried he looked at times. Sometimes I heard them whispering—about what? Now that I look back, I can feel in my heart the pain that they must have suffered. Everybody, but everybody, was sure by now that war was going to break out, and *when* was only a question of days or weeks.

Some of the Poles, like always when misfortune is near, blamed the Jew for it all. In all those years, always the Jew would be guilty of it all. In all the books that I had read about the Jew's misfortune, the poor Jew had been blamed for everything bad that had ever happened. Hitler tried with his hate propaganda to prove that the Jews were provoking the war. Those peasants that had never read anything were the first to believe it all. And here again, like always, it was the Jew's fault. At that time, most of the privileges had already been taken away from the

Jew. Jewish stores were boycotted, almost like a certain time in Gleiwitz. Not far from where we lived was Grobla Street, and near to us on that street was a bridge. One night Polish youth had drowned a young Jewish woman. They took her out for fun and threw her into the river. People, hearing the screams, ran to her rescue, but they just had to stand there idle, for those hoodlums had all kind of weapons, and stood there enjoying her unsuccessful fight for her life. The woman had been a young mother, and for months to come, it was as though I could still hear her screaming for help.

Yes, this was the beginning of my youth in Poland, and me not even in my teens yet. Oh, there are many more horrible things that I could tell—how those hoodlums set the beard of a religious man afire, for example—and so it went on and on, and all the while by their doorstep was their own destruction, Adolf Hitler. All the Poles weren't that way, by no means. There were a good many nice ones, at that, and I would unjustly accuse all of them by not saying so. If there were some who didn't like us, they didn't show it openly. Some of them just shook their heads in disbelief at their fellow man. How could they be willing to sacrifice their own country, just to see the destruction of the Jew?

When the anti-Semites kept saying, "Just wait until Hitler comes," many Poles just couldn't believe their ears. We had in the building where we lived many very nice neighbors. Next to us lived a young couple with a little baby. He was a tailor and their name was Goodman. All of a sudden he was called for duty. It was so painful to see him go. Oh, if the Jew had been appreciated, at least. But here it was like fighting two enemies: first of all, the German, and then his fellows. So many Jews in the army tried to hide their identity for fear of being mistreated. But it didn't help much, for the first thing that was written in the papers was their religion. Mother, as always ready to help people, tried to comfort Mrs. Goodman. I think that in all of her misery at seeing her husband go, she was blessd to have my mother for her neighbor. Mother hadn't only been a neighbor to her, she was like a mother and sister. To everyone, Mother was always a great comfort, except to herself. Her eyes, how deep in her head they were already from her daily cries.

In the front of the hosue, as I mentioned before, was a bakery. Mother had always felt so sorry for them; business was slow there, and they had two little girls. They were Poles and it was hard for us to understand each other. Their older daughter, Sepka, was my age. She tried so hard to become my friend, but the language barrier kept us from undernstanding each other. With the Jewish kids it was different. Although I didn't know Yiddish then, I could understand more or less and I soon got used to it. I couldn't complain of lack of friends.

One day Father brought home a nice hen as payment for his work from a farmer, and the hen was clucking. Mother put her on eggs, and soon we had a nice chicken family. It was great fun. How this mother hen got attached to me! Why did it run after me just like a dog? We kept this hen, of course, with the permission of the landlord. I brought nice green grass, extra special, for the cute chickies. It brought me such joy that at times I even forgot the worries I had seen in the grown-ups. A year had elapsed since we had come to Poland, and I looked back with melancholy in my heart at all the wonderful times I used to have. Funny, the bad things I had gone through in my homeland never entered my mind. I just wanted to recall the nice things. I thought about my friends; if I came back all of a sudden, would they still remember me? That most of them were gone never really entered my mind. How I yearned to be back in that place where I had spent so many nice years of my childhood. I didn't realize that it, too, was gone and could never come back.

Years thereafter I read a letter my sister Ella had written to my brothers. "Yes, my beloved brothers, that what we have had we will never have back again. We have been robbed blind." How hard life was for her in Poland, for the Polish language was so hard for her to master. Ella, who had known a few languages quite fluently, and had given English lessons to people we thought would once enjoy life in a free world—she just couldn't for anything on earth get this language under control. She did speak a little, though, but who was able to understand her? She was so pretty, always dressed as if she just had hit the jackpot, and meanwhile always busy working over most of her old clothing. She was always busy making new designs; she had been such an artist. And what good was it? There was hardly anybody to appreciate all of it. Most of the peole we came in contact with in Poland had to fight for their daily bread, so who needed luxury? Of the rich ones, who would emply a newcomer who was hardly able to speak the language? So she took to knitting to at least earn a tiny bit. Of course she wasn't paid much, and at times she sat up until four o'clock in the morning to earn those few piasters. Ella, who had studied at Berlin at the academy of art—for what? For all that? But she took it all in stride, and she used to always say that the sun would shine for us sometime again, and that all our suffering would not be in vain. "Meanwhile," she said, "let's be happy with what we have." And she was grateful to be able to even make those few piasters. Those letters that my brothers had saved, however, way after the war, they told me a different story.

In one she wrote, "They take so much advantage of us here. They gave me some work in Sosnowitz, but the pay is hardly enough for the fare. It looks right now as if the world really has come to an end for me. I don't want to show it to

Mama and Papa, they have enough worries as it is. But I am about at the end, and only the thought of leaving this place soon is keeping me going, and prevents me from giving up." Poor Ella, what had you gone through, still going about the house singing? Now I know that it wasn't you speaking in your sleep; you were crying in the night, and I, with much laughter had misinterpreted it as sleep talking. Who would have believed that your heart was about to break? You hid it so well.

By the time I was twelve, I had many nice friends. In the building where we lived, I had Jadzka L. and Motek; we did quarrel a lot, though, but we got along great. I guess that the more you fight, the more you get to know each other; anyhow, this had always been my motto. I think we must have driven our neighbors crazy with all of our antics. One day all of a sudden Uncle Jacob came so earnestly, and I was sent out in the yard. Through the window I could hear Mother crying. Yes, the war was at the door. That day was the end of October. Over the radio we heard the Polish freedom song of Chopin. The Polish anthem sang, "Poland isn't lost yet." People had been taken over by the fever for evacuating, and everybody, it seemed, was busy packing. Mother ran to the immigration office and pleaded that they hurry up with our papers. But the tiny misspelling on Ella's birth certificate had held everything up, and now with the war at the door, they had greater worries than that. "Sorry, a few more days."

That was all they would say. Oh, these few days, what have they done to my family? Mother was so desperate, she sold some more of our jewelery. She went to the main official and pleaded with him, "Take whatever you want, just let my family go." But his reply was only a shake with his shoulder, and to wait a few more days. Meanwhile, everybody prepared feverishly. Everybody tried to get potatoes, flour, and oil, as much as possible. But those three items were suddenly hard to get. One had to pay fantastic prices for anything similar to food, but in this panic, even the poorest had money. Everybody bought as much food as possible. Hunger—the fear of this was in everyone's mind. The air raids, well, we had prepared shelters. The grown-ups did worry about this more than we kids did, but they knew to hide their fear in front of us. Some of our neighbors were a little funny, though, or so it seemed to us. Some were very grouchy, and among those was an old maid, a very old one, I must say right now. Was she ever a grouch, oh, boy! Did we ever tease her. She had a fast tongue, and at times for us kids she had a fast hand. There were some grown-ups who just hated kids, and for some reason or other, they believed that kids were just created to bother them. That created a lot of disturbance. When an air raid was rehearsed, the kids had a jolly good time playing hide and seek in those long, dark hallways down in the basement at the shelter. All of a sudden one of us had the brilliant idea of putting something crawling on the old maid. Things really did liven up; it was just lucky that the enemy was not above us or the commotion would have been heard for sure. The child haters were, of course, on the side of the old maid. The non-child haters were on our side, and soon there was an exchange of words one could hardly find in the dictionary. Let it be mentioned that those non-child haters all had children. Anyway, the best part of it all was that soon the cancellation of the air raid sounded, and then spanking went on in some of the flats. That was like music to the child haters. We called them child haters, but they really weren't that bad. It was just that they didn't have any patience left for us.

My girlfriend Sarah often came to visit us. She was the girl we made friends with when we first came from Germany, up in Ort, the place where we had slept. She had it real tough at home with her father being sick most of the time. Here again was Mother, lending a helping hand. How many times would Sarah tell Mother how very grateful she was. She told Mother she hoped that someday she would be fortunate enough to repay her kindness. She did it, all right, but of this I will tell later.

The kids went about with our fun and worries, not fully realizing that war was going to break out any minute. It was the end of October 1939, and a most beautiful autumn. It looked as if heaven wanted to cheer us up for what lay ahead.

All the young men in the building had been called to the army. In the nice warm sunshine, it looked and felt something like a warning. As the evening approached, I think the day was October 28, almost all of the neighbors gathered outside our window and called, "Mrs. Rychner, look at the red sky, there is going to be war, all right!" War, war, war wherever you looked, whatever you did, and wherever you listened, war was in everybody's mouth. I did not even realize how much bitterness this war was about to bring. This was the first war that I lived through, so I read about it constantly. It was something like history to me, a subject you study and get grades for. To live it myself I had never imagined. Even while reading about war, I had never really realized that war really could be that bad. It was a thing of the past, when people were still uncivilized. Here, now, in modern times, with culture so advanced, war really couldn't be as bad as the history books said. When I saw how people shook with fear, the story of the Crusaders came to my mind, and I thought, *What do those grown-ups really know? That was a time when people really suffered.* Now, in modern times, I tried to persuade myself, things like that would never happen. But fear is like a contagious disease; one just catches fear from the other. One just can't help but start being afraid. I didn't realize myself, then, what it was that the grown-ups were so afraid of, but the only thing I could hear was, "Where will we run?" All of a sudden, fear got a hold of me, too. When I thought of war, it was as if something was getting hold of me, deep, deep inside me, and twisting my insides around, and my heart beat wildly. In the midst of all of my thoughts, the sirens started to sound, so fearsome, in such a horrifying way that I held my ears—it was the first of November, and war had broken out.

MY LIFE IN WAR-TORN POLAND

As the sirens sounded louder and more fearfully, I ran into the house, threw myself on the couch, and fell into a deep faint. When I came to, my mother was kneeling on the foor next to me and crying, "Don't worry, baby, we are all together, and nothing will ever tear us apart." How good those words felt. Dad came home right away, for there were plans to be made. The men kept busy preparing the shelter for the night. The girls with the knowledge of first aid had to assemble, and the kids were told to behave, not to create havoc. Who could think about havoc? Most of the kids sat in corners shaking like leaves. We had to take some tools to the shelter in case we had to dig out. Food had slowly disappeared from the stores. In the bakery next to us, butter was prepared for some bread. We were told to just be patient and wait.

Many of our neighbors prepared for evacuation. Mother asked them where they thought they were going to run. They just shook their heads in disbelief. What a silly question, where? Anywhere, as long as it was as far as possible from the German border. Mother told them, when they were astonished at her question, "If you want to run, run! I am tired of running, and we are staying right here. Why won't you understand?" Mother said. "There is no place for us to run. Don't you see? Disaster will strike everywhere. Whatever will happen, let it happen right here, but we are staying." A few neighbors agreed with Mother, but many of them prepared to leave. How thankful those that stayed later were to Mother, for so many of those that ran away were murdered.

Mother was so tired of fighting already that when the sirens sounded, she sent us down to the shelter but she herself wouldn't budge. She just sat there in the darkness and tried to think, think of a way out, out of the grip that took hold around our throats. How much did Mother really forsee? I shall never know. She always knew that nothing good lay ahead of us. She was like a bird in a cage, struggling to get out, but now that the war had started, who knew when the papers for our emigration would come through? Still, at least we had something to hope for. Outside, soldiers marched by, some on horses, some on foot, and some in trucks. Seeing us kids outside, they threw candies and chocolate over the fence. They comforted us with their hopeful smiles, and called, "Poland isn't lost yet!" Such nice young man they were. Poland isn't lost yet! I still remember their proud words. For this was the first day of war.

The second day, we didn't see any soldiers, but everybody ran. They didn't know where to, they just ran. The bakery was open and the batter that had been prepared the previous day had all run over and gone sour. A man in the bakery told the neighbors that whoever wanted to could get some batter and bake themselves some bread. We had all been without bread for a few days already, and soon the bakery was full of life as everybody ran for the sour batter. After being baked, the bread tasted just like vinegar, but we were hungry, and this, too, was eaten up. Somehow, the quietness around killed everybody's mind. It just was too quiet. And so came the third day of war, and with it destruction, evil, and horror.

Suddenly Ella burst into the house, her face white as a sheet, a mask of horror. "The Germans are here!"

"No!" It came from everybody's mouths. When we turned on the radio, we right away felt what we were in for. Those murderers came into Poland with murder and slaughter on their evil minds. One could hear the screams and shooting from far away. Mother pleaded with us to stay in the house. Still now I can hear in my tortured ears and see in front of me the people lying in their blood and dying with their words, *"Sehmah Israel!"* I still feel the blood sticking to my shoes, I, who had stepped, not willingly, over the blood of my people on the concrete which had become a bath of blood at the entry of the Germans into Poland. "Are you a Jew? Then you must die!" Here they lay, crumpled bodies. Just yesterday they might have given the name of their fathers or mothers to a newborn. Here they were mutilated, slain, destroyed by the Nazi culture. Still now I can see how the Nazis had tortured them, torn out the beards of those religious Jews. They took away their prayer coats, put them on horses, bound the beard of one man to the horse carriage and drug the man along through the streets of horror to a symphony of screams and laughter. Even some of the Poles stood there and applauded this performance, while others stood as if they had just been turned into stones. Still now I can see all of this so vividly in front of me, and it seems as though I can still hear the screams in my tortured ears, I, who have heard so much sorrow and shame—screams of the children, dying of people, quiet, and then all of it over again. To whom can I tell this, when all of these gruesome memories come back to me again? Only to you, white sheets of paper, you shall be my comfort. To you I shall turn in my despair, you do understand me! Between you, white sheets of paper, I shall empty my heart, and I will give you life. You shall find justice for it all. Oh, you are so good and kind, to everything you listen. All of my heartbreak I can pour out to you and when my heart is full, then I shall take you in my hands, and I shall read you!

Those murderers stormed into Poland and made themselves right at home. Although Warsaw was not defeated yet, the Nazis got all they could get hold of, all they could steal out of this country. From food to raw material, they kept on hauling it out of this country, not caring if the rest of the population starved to death. Yes, these beastly murderers were on the loose. They plundered Jewish possessions from the day they set foot into this country. It was not too hard for them, though, for they had helping hands from many of the Polish population. I wasn't able to understand, ever, how people who themselves were so shamefully defeated and sold out couldn't feel with us just a bit.

After the Germans had been with us for two days, Mr. Goodman came home from the army. Some people kept him hidden for those two days. He had gone as a Pole, for if the Germans had found a Jew in uniform, he would have been shot on the spot with no questions asked. He came home in rugged civilian clothing, and his wife, seeing him alive, became hysterical from happiness. How happy were we for her! Seeing his little girl, not two years old yet, running towards her father and hugging and kissing him, we cried bitter tears. He told us stories that made our blood turn into jelly. He said that he believed that Mr. Goldstein, the husband of the other young woman in our building, had been shot. When Mrs Goldstein learned the news, her screams and cries were heard all through the night. She had loved her husband so very much. They had fallen in love so very young. They, too, had a little girl, a little over a year old. Their marriage had been such an ideal one. Our hearts were about to break, seeing this beautiful woman going about the house with the little baby in her arms and weeping. Then suddenly one night, a big commotion went on outside in the hallway. Everybody jumped out of their beds. What had happened? Only on sad and happy occasions were there things going on outside so late at night. This time it was a very happy occasion indeed. Mr. Goldstein was not dead; he had come home. Everybody had to keep quiet and not mention a word about it to anyone, for the Germans had known him for dead. He had come home in a torn, muddy, bloody uniform. This nice tall man was a complete wreck. Later what we heard from him was unbelievable, unheard of. Everybody could clearly see that there lay a reign of horror ahead of us.

After the Nazis caught the battalion where Mr. Goldstein was, he said, they shot many soldiers, as many as they could lay their hands on. Then, wanting to give a little zest to their slaughtering, they took all the men, stood them against the wall, and declared that every tenth man was to go free. After every tenth had been freed, the others were shot down and buried still half alive. They had to, of course, dig their own graves before they were shot. Then the Germans took those who they had freed and culled the Jews out to kill. Among those had been Mr. Goldstein. Mr. Goldstein had been hit in the chest and had pretended to be dead. After the Jews had fallen to the ground and nearly all of the burying was finished, the soldiers doing the work had come to Mr. Goldstein. Luckily, there was among them one of Mr. Goldstein's buddies, and he hid Mr. Goldstein beneath a tree. When everyone left that place of slaughter, his friend snuck back with the price of death riding upon his head. Then he dragged Mr. Goldstein away. They came to an abandoned shack, and here his buddy cleaned his wounds and took him from farm to farm, always giving him out as an Aryan, for most of the farmers would have been afraid to hide a Jew. But somehow they made it and this was the night that his buddy had brought him home in a wagon of hay. Here he was, to tell us of the fate of most of the Jewish soldiers. If the Germans hadn't found out who was a Jew, there were always those anti-Semites, the great Jew haters, in the army who would turn in their own buddies. Any Jew found in a uniform would be shot in cold blood. All of this was still only the beginning.

Not far from where we lived was a Jewish bakery, the proprietor a very religious man. He was elderly but very kind. After the Nazis rationed bread, the price changed almost daily, until it hardly reached any stability. At the beginning, no one really knew how much it would cost the next day. Mr. Katz, the baker, had that fateful day sold the bread at the unlucky price of the previous day, which had been a penny more. I want to mention right now that this was by no means any fault of Mr. Katz. After a Polish woman purchased that bread, she ran as quickly as she could to the authorities, her own enemies. Mr. Katz was taken the same day and shot. This woman had a bike storage on the corner of Gziehowska and Grebla. How very frightened I was from then on to go past her stand. Such a beastly woman, how vicious she looked.

With all of this misery surrounding us, changes took place in me. I felt that I was growing up. I was becoming a little lady. This precious time, which should have been so holy for a young person, so wonderful as all of those wonders took place in my body, here was made so ugly. At a time when a girl should feel how important she is to herself, as well as to her parents, when boys should start noticing her, here I was nothing but a worm. Still, in my own world, I felt important, and with all of it, I sometimes even forgot the outside world. Oh, I wanted so badly to grow up already, to share the burden with my so-dearly beloved ones. Only twelve years old, but what a lifetime of despair lay already behind me. And what lay still ahead? Mother's words always were, as far as I can remember, "If Germany loses the war this time, never will they get on their feet again!" If she had known how wrong she was.

Shortly after the Nazis entered Poland, they established a *Judenbann*. These were certain streets where Jews allowed to walk and live. Most of the other streets were prohibited for Jews. Those over twelve years of age were forced to wear arm bands over the left arm: white, with a blue star of David to discriminate us from the others. Now the soldiers were starting to look for weapons everywhere, including the shelters. Any digging tools they found they interpreted as weapons against them, and many grown-ups were held responsible for them. Many of the tenanats were shot. When they came to look into our shelter, we were very lucky, for the day before there had been a strong rain and, the house, built on water, always flooded. When they came to check, the basement was flooded and us kids were having a ball floating on washtubs. Usually the janitor scolded us for it, but we wanted so badly to have some fun in that darkness, while we were still young enough for it. Many people had lost their lives for having hacksaws and spades. But they left us on account of the flood and didn't find a thing that day. There wasn't a thing that one did that could ensure one's life anymore. The Nazis could interpret anything as being against them. The result of any minor infraction was death. If one crossed the street, the Nazis would find a fault because you were on the street. The result was either the black list, which meant deportation, or other most horrible punishment, and if one was lucky, very lucky, one simply had to pay a high fine. The armbands had to be kept nice, white, and ironed at all times, for heaven forbid if they were not. In every little thing one did, danger lurked. Mother begged us to stay in the house as much as possible, but when the grown-ups left, we shook for their safety. When school was again to open, Mother decided it was best that Cilly and I didn't go. Many of our neighbors did the same, for very often kids that left in the morning for school never got back again.

Around me was all that disaster, and me becoming a little lady. "Cilly and Lydia are not children anymore, they are now little ladies," Ella wrote to Max in a letter. "For me they will always be the children," was his reply. Yes, we had always been the children, and how much bitterness and sorrow our childhood was.

Our bread ration was less than a loaf of bread daily, but I always went for the ration, and the lady from the store, the mother of Sepka, knew me well and felt sorry for me, so she gave always a whole loaf. What joy it meant for us at home—an extra piece of bread for each of us. Most of the time, I brought home the bread ration because Cilly was to bashful to go. I didn't mind. I got used to it, and after all, I didn't beg for it. I put up my helpless face and there it was again, a whole loaf. We did mind going hungry. Father hadn't worked for quite some time, and with all of our selling, we still had to economize, so we could hardly afford the black market. At least with those few chickens we had, we had a few eggs daily, and that really meant something at that time. Seeing all that horror outside, hardly a family left where misfortune had not struck, we at least were all together, and that was the most important thing of all. So what if we ate frozen potatoes, so what if we went about hungry? At least we had each other.

To those main streets from which the Jews had been thrown out, the Nazis brought the families of their officials and gave them the nice houses and apartments once belonging to the wealthy Jews. They made those streets restricted for us, and in that neighborhood they opened a few German stores for their people. Then they made a German mayor of the city. As I saw those two girls, the daughters of the mayor, I couldn't believe my eyes. Who else was it but those two girls Cilly and I had made friends with on our last visit to Jasehtchemp? Their mother had been so friendly with us and would never eat other food but kosher, for as she said, kosher meat is much cleaner and much more appetizing. But, here I saw them all of a sudden as the big shots of the city. I was a little excited; maybe their mother would help a little (I still have a picture of them with their mother, together with Cilly, my mother, and me, in my posession today). I called out their name, but when they saw me, they had such hate in their eyes; they had been two such nice kids before, but what evil was in them now. "Don't bother us, Jewess, if you know what is good for you," was their ugly reply. Whenever I saw them again, I hid out of fear and shame. The Nazis started a campaingn to search for the houses of people who had run away. Those homes were locked up, and those people who had listened to Mother were glad they were safe. Many who had run away came back home unexpectedly, but death lurked everywhere searching for them. Just a few had been lucky, but their homes and possessions were gone. Those who survived told gruesome stories from their evacuation—

how the German airplanes had bombed them, and how slaughtered people lay on the road by the thousands. Many Poles woke up to the fact that nothing good was waiting for them after the Nazis finished with the Jews. They had a feeling that they were next in line.

It was already late in December, and the days grew shorter and shorter. One Saturday, Uncle and Auntie came over with little cousin Pinjush. I took little Pinjush in back of the house where there was a little creek. In winter when it was frozen, with all of the danger outside, this was about the safest place for us kids. To skate was my life. There, gliding over the smooth surface, I could pretend to be anywhere in the world. Life recovered its zest again, and the nerves could relax from all the strain of the tight situation around us. We raced, and although a few were missing from our group already, life still went on. We forgot, while playing, all of the darkness on the outside. So, when little Pinjush joined us, I was busy teaching him the first steps of skating, so I did not notice that the other kids left one by one. Somehow time flew and I realized that no one was around anymore only when I saw the deadful darkness around me. With the blackout, there were a few poorly lighted lamps out on the street, which really emphasized more darkness than light. I took Pinjush as quickly as my shaky hands and feet would go, and we left. On our way home, I heard bootsteps in back of me. Who never went though such a thing just can't imagine the horror of it. As I spoke softly to Pinjush not to answer a thing that I said to him now, I prayed that the little boy wouldn't say anything that could cost both of us our lives. Those little kids already knew how hated the Nazis were, and a child, not realizing, might say what he thought—and who could blame him? My little angel, how smart he was. As I spoke softly in German to him he kept on nodding with his little head. He didn't know any German, just Yiddish, but the little guy just kept on nodding. My hand was holding his hand so tightly he must have understood my fear, for he looked up to me as if he wanted to say, "Don't worry, I won't spoil it!" As I continued walking slowly to show whoever was back of me that I was not afraid, that I had nothing to run away from, the steps came nearer and nearer until they finally reached me. As I heard somebody saying, *"Guten Abendm, Fraulein,"* I thought that the earth was about to open and swallow me. When I looked up, there stood a *shupo* in front of me. "What are you doing with that little boy out in the dark?" he said.

"I am taking him home, I have given him a lesson in skating," I replied in German, meanwhile praying that Pinjush would not speak a word. I don't know what the *shupo* thought, perhaps that I was a German girl, for nearby us on the big estate, Germans with kids had taken over. Maybe he was the one in a million who was not as rotten as the rest of them. I shall never know, but someone watched over me that time, I am quite sure of that. The *shupo* took us up to the gate, knocked his boots together in a salute, and warned me not to be outside at that time of the day. Then he disappeared into the night. When I came back into the house, Mother was pretty worried, but after looking into my face, the scolding words hung onto her lips. There was no other way out but to tell the whole story, which made my parents as well as Uncle and Auntie shiver. After that, I was never outside in the dark again, even in the yard.

After the Nazis set foot farther into Poland, they wanted somebody to speak to the Jews. The Jewish population, in hopes of saving some lives, and glad to have someone to speak for them, opened a committee which would deal with our problems. Thereafter, if the Nazis wanted something like clothing, money, or human cargo, they let the committee know about it, and the committee was to take care of it. The Nazis still did not like the humane way the committee went about it, so they still helped out with all of their might. At night, we got surprises: the Gestapo would visit us, turning the house upside down searching for food bought on the black market. Woe to those where something would be found. Having the few eggs from our chicken and a few homegrown tomatoes made us die of fear. From the Nazis there was no hiding place; they found everything. Every trick in the book was known to them. One just had to pray that the day they came to one's home, one would be lucky and have nothing to hide. We lived from one day to the other with just one hope—that they would soon lose the war, and we would be saved from the evil that grew worse and worse from one day to the next. Uncle Jacob, knowing that the end was lurking somewhere in the dark, fled to Russian-occupied Lemberg. He wanted to prepare a small place where his wife and son could follow him, along with us and Auntie, the widow of Mother's older brother, with her five daughters. A good many people I knew did escape at that time, but with so many people escaping, the situation in Lemberg was real bad. But at least there were no murderers behind one. When free, one had the greatest chance of all. So Uncle came back and begged us, he begged his wife, "Please, let's leave everything, and go back to Lemberg." My mother, too, all of a sudden was all for it. No, there was no sense in staying here one more day. Just to leave this disaster would be freedom already. But this time, Ella did not want to go.

"The Germans are losing the war, and soon," she insisted. "And what will we do there? Again lose everything, leave everything behind? We can't take anything along, and hunger and disaster we will suffer there, too." If we only hadn't listened that time! Of course, those people running away weren't handled with kid gloves—they were sent off to Siberia—but most of the people I knew that ran away are alive today. Poor Uncle, he tried so very hard to persuade us. He told us that all of his friends had stayed there. He said, "It is hard, I know, but all of us together, we will make it somehow, I feel nothing good coming, please let's go back." Those were his words. But when he finally persuaded the rest of the family, including his wife, there was no chance any more to run away. The Germans were watching, and good. We had been robbed by stupidity of a chance for survival.

With all the disaster around us, those Poles that had given Father work before became afraid now. After a lot of persuading, they still gave him work, but Dad had to work nights, and he had to leave in the dark. They feared that someone would get wind that they employed a Jew, but they did like Daddy so much, he was such a wonderful man. I remember going evenings with Mother, taking some warm food along. I think the food was just a pretense for Mother; she went only because she was worried. From the frozen potatoes, Mother made such nice cakes; they tasted better than any torte I have ever eaten since. For one thing, the frozen potatoes were very economical. First of all, they saved on sugar, and who had this luxury? Even saccharin one had to purchase on the black market. Day in and day out, we went to see Dad at work, then, on those long nights, we waited for his dear footsteps to assure us that he had come safely home. He had to have a schedule because of the curfew. My sweet and wonderful father, how hard he worked, and under what circumstances. No matter how, nothing was too hard for him, nothing impossible. The only thing that mattered to him was that we wouldn't be hungry. Working for farmers, he mostly brought food home. One day he got some work from a farmer who lived outside the city in a little suburb called Gzichow. Those people were a young, nice couple. This man had gotten so friendly with us, he told Mother that if things got too rough, we should come to his house to hide. He had an attic into which one had to crawl. The best part of it was that from the outside it was not noticeable, and no one would suspect there was an attic space. Whenever he advised us to come, Mother always said, "Not yet." I don't know, Mother was somehow scared, she just wouldn't trust. I do think that he really meant it. He had always been so nice and so kind to us. We paid, of course, enough for the food that he brought us, but after all, we understood that it was very dangerous for him.

Mother told him that, when the time came, we would make plans, and then he replied, "What if it is too late?" But we had seen so many Poles that people had thought were trustworthy who turned out later to be spies for the Nazis. After taking away the possessions of those people they sheltered, they gave the people to the Nazis, and got paid another time. So Mother was very careful and just waited, maybe to get to know him better, or maybe just for a miracle to happen. And with this, our second chance for survival escaped. Mother said there was still time to wait a little. Oh, if we only hadn't waited! Maybe this Pole had meant it, and just because there were some bad ones among them didn't mean they all were that way.

One day Ella came home excited; she had met on the street a German girl we had known in Gleiwitz. They had lived under us on the Kronprinzenstrasse. Just to see someone from home made my heart beat fast. She had been with her husband, who was a soldier with the occupation, and she told Ella that she would love to come see us. She was about Ella's age, and Ella had known her quite well. At that time, already so desperate, we would grab any blade of straw for help. A few people we knew had some acquaintances that helped them get out of the country—for high pay, of course, but what did it matter that time? Even though Ella hated seeing her friend come to our home, she thought that she might help us. But she came to us only to be able to write back to Gleiwitz about the frightful circumstances in which the once so-proud family Rychner lived. At that time, we didn't care about such anymore. Ella's motto was always, "If at first you do not succeed, try, try again!" One thing we were about sure of was that to emigrate from that island of death now was out of the question.

One day, after Mother was informed how things with immigration were going, she found out that children under the age of thirteen could emigrate to Argentina if said person had relatives over there. How happy Mother was for me, how excited. Me being still under thirteen made them get wild over my opportunity. I objected. "You want me to leave you here in this disaster? I would never find a minute of peace!"

"Don't be silly," Mother replied. "The war will end soon, and at least one of us won't have to go through all that hunger and bitterness."

"What if we have to smuggle ourselves out of the country? You are still so weak from our last journey you will only hinder us!" Ella said, trying to persuade me.

Well, they finally did it, and with stones on my heart, I agreed that whatever they decided was the best, I would do. My thoughts were already on Max and that happy moment when I would be able to see him again. But things did not work out, for the Nazis soon switched the age to twelve years, and even this I think was a lie. I could relax again after I knew that I wouldn't have to leave my beloved ones behind. "Whatever will happen," I told Mother, "I don't care, as long as we stay all together." Then I saw how happy Mother was that I had not gone, for most of the kids that left later were drowned by the Nazis. I could see how Mother shivered when she had learned of it later.

One day, everything happened at once. Cilly got a high temperature all of a sudden, and the doctor said her tonsils would have to be removed. The next day, Ella got sick. She had to have an operation to have polyps taken out. She decided that when Cilly got back from the hospital, she would have it done at the office by the physician. Too many from one family being registered at the hospital wasn't too good. On top of that, Mother didn't feel good at all. All of a sudden she had become so skinny, and she just wouldn't touch any food. She had such bad cramps in her legs, it seemed as if her rheumatism was coming back. What could we do? Dad looked so worried, so old in his grief. To crown it all, he had been out of work for quite some time. When Mother came back from the hospital with Cilly, everything at home looked so hopeless that there and then I made myself a vow; I swore to myself and the Lord, and here is my promise: "I shall steal, I shall cheat, and I shall lie to help my dearly beloved ones in this bitter fight for survival." My parents never knew about it, but in my heart, toughness and readiness to fight had entered, and no matter how, I knew I had to be strong so that the weaker ones could find a bit to lean on, even if they did not realize it.

One gruesome day, the Nazis ordered two fathers to be hung in the middle of the town. The crime? Somebody had brought to the ears of the Nazis that there was some sabotage in the works. In order to show the people how they would be treated for such thoughts, the Nazis took two completely innocent Jewish men and ordered them to hang. This wasn't all. The whole Jewish population was ordered to come see it, adults and children alike. The soldiers came in the homes and forced the people at gunpoint. Those poor children whose fathers were taken, and those wives, had to stand in front while it happened, seeing their loved ones struggle. Never, as long as I shall live, will I forget this most horrible picture. With the screams of agony from the children and their wives kneeling and begging, "They are innocent!" those Nazibeasts enjoyed every bit of it. Those men had to hang on display for three days as a warning, before the wives were permitted to bury them. Yes, this was the peak of the Nazi culture.

On the street where we lived were two little cute girls. They were very shy and always stuck together, just like Cilly and I. One day as they were walking together, I saw a car full of soldiers drive right into them. My heart stopped beating. The littlest one was dead right away, and the older one, crying out in agony for her little sister, was badly injured. I just couldn't belive it. How could they do such a thing to two innocent little children? What had those girls done to them? Their mother's heartbreaking cry brought me back to reality. I thought, *What if this had happened to me and Cilly?* I would have died right away, for Cilly and I were one. After this gruesome incident, Cilly and I became again closely attached to one another.

With all of this disaster around, youth wants its laugh and fun sometimes, too. This is the one privilege of being so young. One just wants to erase those ugly pictures that haunt one day and night. In the big yard that connected the two buildings where we lived, *droshkies* were parked all the time. There we kids would go at times to dream. We gossiped about other girls, and how badly we thought they behaved. Across this yard was a handsome boy, two years older than I. His parents had come at the same time that we had come from Germany. One day—how proud it made me—after I had thought he didn't notice me, he whistled a song after me: "Oh, You Beautiful Doll." In the evening when I came home, I told Mother proudly of my conquest. Mother smiled so wisely. How happy she was for me and how much she wished that I would be able to enjoy my youth, to have a little sunshine! But I really never did become friends with this boy, for, as I found out later from some of my friends, he belonged to a too-fast crowd. I did make friends with another boy from this crowd, though. He was such a nice boy and very good looking. One day we accepted him among my friends. I was at that time about twelve and Szymon was about fourteen. He was such a gentle and kind fellow, but in the beginning I didn't like him, for he had belonged to that other group that had not a very good reputation. This showed how wrong people really could be. He was one of the kindest people, and we liked him a lot. His father had been the manager of the department which supplied the stores with vegetable rations. In the beginning, my main interest in him had really been to get better rations. As I remembered my vow, I looked away from the reputation he had. How very ashamed of myself was I later, for he went with me for our ration, and at times I really did get better and nicer merchandise. When I saw how wrong we had been about him—why, he was even better and nicer than many of my own friends—I felt so guilty. Our friendship was such a nice one, and I had started it with advantage on my mind. I tried to make it up to him. I always defended him, everywhere, and from then on he became a regular and good friend of ours. Poor Szymon. He left from Bendzin a year before I did. He was killed in Buchenwald. I gave him a picture of mine as we said good-bye, and tears were falling on it from his kind eyes. But life did go on.

In the summer we would go in the back of the building where the little creek was. There was a little hill with grass. The place being cut off from the outside, there was no noise of Naziboots, no fear from the mouths of our grown-ups. There we would take some food and something to drink and pretend that we were going on a nice picnic. We took blankets and bathing suits into our world of make-believe. One day we noticed that our favorite spot, our dream world, had been taken. Some ladies had decided to do some sunbathing of their own. We didn't like that idea at all. What else could we do but go to the rooftop? I still don't know how we could have done it. We actually took two pails of ice cold water, and the rest one can imagine. For the next couple of weeks our favorite place was ours again. How funny, how funny life really is. For no matter how bad things are, a person will always find a bit of laughter. If not for this, a person wouldn't be able to go through as much bitterness as we did. Just like a flower, one never could live without his sunshine. This is probably one of the most precious gifts a human is given in his cradle. Even in the darkest hours of our lives, I always find something to laugh at. There was always something to make fun of. "My ray of sunshine," my mother always called me. So, life kept on going—if one really could still call it life.

The Nazis created all of that horror by going into Jewish homes, but the Jewish Committee tried to come to an understanding with them. They formed the Miliz, a Jewish police force. They had to wear white and blue uniforms. Of course, as everywhere, when they had power, there were a few wise guys among them, but we really weren't so frightened when they entered our homes instead of the Nazis. They, of course, had to do what they were told, but some were real nice guys and they would try looking away. A few of them were mean, though maybe they didn't want to be, but they were scared for their own lives. It did make a difference, though, to see one of the Miliz come into your home instead of a Nazi. It was a little improvement. What I am writing here is only my view, and I am speaking myself from the view I had as a child. I don't want to say that everybody shared my opinion. Maybe people shared my opinions and maybe not, but all that I am writing here is strictly my opinion.

With all that gruesomeness around us, the Nazis started to take youth out of the ghettos for slave labor camps. Those were later called concentration camps, but of that I'll write later. Meanwhile lists were made of the best youths of the ages fifteen years and up. The raids on our homes at night had therefore begun. At first, they sent notes to the homes, and the person wanted was told to be ready with everything to go. In the beginning some went by themselves, for they thought that by going they would be able to save the older folks. Later, when we saw what they meant by "going to work," people hid when such notes came. What was there to lose? Those camps, we had found out, were awful, even in the beginning when they still didn't want to show how they were out to destroy all of us. In order to be safe, one had to have a certain card which proved the person was employed and working for the Reich. The best card was the color blue, for any other color, though better then nothing, was not sufficient. There were all kinds of firms that employed Jews in the city—for small wages, of course. But who cared then how much the pay was, even if was nothing, as long as one could get that certain blue card? As soon as the Nazis set foot into town and brought over their own families, they were out to squeeze out of us anything possible. They brought over some white Russians from Ukrainia. Those were the worst yet. They had become *Volksdeutsche,* and after the Jewish businesses were taken away, they were given to the *Volksdeutsche* to manage for the Reich. If the previous proprietor was lucky, he would be able to get a job in his own firm. There were many, also, from Silesia and other parts of Europe who never did like the Jews in the first place. They now could satisfy themselves by seeing the Jews suffer badly. There were some who were Germans by birth, or whom the Germans wanted to have on their side, and all those were given Jewish businesses to manage, as well as Jewish wealth and riches. Those that had before despised the Jew now had somebody to admire for taking everything away from the Jews and giving it to them. They took anything they could get a hold of, and when they were through robbing the businesses, they started to rob us at home. The Nazis told the committee that if the Jews wouldn't give all up of their valuables, they would start drastic measures. With this, deportation began. At first, they took the older people—they wouldn't have much use for them anyway—or those on relief. Those were the first ones to go. Where to, no one had the slightest idea. From then on, Mother kept on saying, "When will be the line for us?"

So the committee asked. In order to prevent bloodshed, or worse (and still what could have been worse we were soon to find out), we were told to bring our jewelry, at least a certain amount. Also, our furs were demanded from us. After Ella had turned in her fur, and Mother hers, they were really heartbroken. But Mother kept on saying, "At least it will be for a good cause, and if it will save lives, I am real glad to have given it."

Ella said, "You are still so young, and you will have much more beautiful furs than this one." We saw them joke over all this even though so very little had been offered. They somehow couldn't take it to heart after all that had happened. They even seemed relaxed when it was over.

Mother had also given part of our jewelry but they weren't satisfied and demanded more and more. Then, they wanted a certain amount of money. Whatever they asked for, however poor the people were, the beasts always had their wishes granted. People sold whatever they could, just to keep the Nazis satisfied. They were just like the blackmailer; once started, they just couldn't stay satisfied. They demanded always more and more. If they did not get what they wanted, they did horrible things. They somehow didn't trust the Jewish Miliz. "You are sticking together," they used to say to the Miliz. "We will smoke you all out, and then perhaps you will know what obedience means." So, day and night, we had still the Gestapo as our visitors, which made us tremble. We lost our voices just to hear them coming. With all of that, one still was able to find an Aryan willing for a small fee to buy one's valuables.

We had some Polish acquaintances who were willing to buy some of our possessions, for only a small price, of course, for they themselves were frightened. We had still left our beautiful bedroom set. Mother being such a great housekeeper, everything looked all the time as if it just had come from the showroom. Mother had accumulated through all those better years in Gleiwitz many most precious Meissner figures as well as breathtaking china. Although we had been robbed tremendously, our Jewish neighbors had taken those things to their own apartment when we left, and at Mother's return, they had given them back to her. They had been very nice people and saved a few very valuable things for us; otherwise, the Germans that had heard we had been taken away would probably have stolen these first. Those things once had been Mother's pride. How she did adore beauty. But with all of the hunger and fear around us, Mother started to sell it all slowly, piece by piece. With each piece she sold, I saw how a piece of her heart went with it. She always smiled at me, if she saw me noticing it, "Don't be sad, Lydilein, once this gruesome war ends, you'll see, we will have much more beautiful things, we will live in our little house outside the city, and have a nice beautiful garden, just like we used to have, remember? There we will have chickens, lots of them. Every day will be a holiday!" Those were the words Mother told me, comforting me with them while her own heart was breaking. And me wanting to scream, "Mother, it really doesn't matter, we are together and that counts for me more than all the most precious things in this world." Poor Mother, how happy she would have been to see her youngest almost fulfill her own dreams.

The Polish baker, located in the house where we lived, had not been too well off when we moved in, but now all of a sudden, he started to prosper. What wouldn't one give for a piece of bread? Especially if it was your children that went about hungry? My mother started taking some of our nice dishes over to the baker in exchange for some flour and bread. Sepka was the baker's daughter whom I had felt so sorry for when first we had moved in. She had always been so poorly dressed and had wanted all the time to be my friend, but now she didn't care about it anymore. She was dressed now in copies of Shirley Temple dresses, and how much I envied her for this. She, too, wouldn't play with a Jewish child anymore. They later became *Volksdeutsche*.

She had always been an ugly duckling, but in the midst of all that misery for us, she grew out to be a beautiful girl. How much riches do change people was clear to see. And then her parents received from the Nazis a nice Jewish bakery, and those Jews who had owned it moved into theirs. It was by no means owned by the Jews, of course, but the Polish bakers had been given it to manage. In this family there was a girl my age who later became a very good friend. Together with those bakers, many other families moved into our building, for the Nazis started drastically clearing the Jews out of the streets. From all the neighborhoods they took them and squeezed them into ghettos.

By that time they had already taken the kitchen away from us, and we had to share it with a mother and daughter, so the five of us had the one room. But we were glad that at least the street we lived in was still for Jews. At least we hadn't been thrown out, but we had gotten a lot of new neighbors, for the Poles had to move out and the Jewish families were moving in. For me it couldn't get better than to get rid of those fresh anti-Semitic kids who only knew to insult us. With new neighbors moving in, we would make new friends, and this could only suit me.

The factory which linked those two buildings had been taken away from the Jewish proprietor and given to a Ukranian who was half German. This was the worse drunkard ever to imagine, but he did like me, and he always told Ella that I reminded him of the daughter he had lost during the bombardments. I was the same age and had the same name. He even proposed to Mother once that he would take me out of Bendzin, and no one would know that I was a Jewish girl. Maybe if he hadn't been such a drunkard, we would have thought about it. But who could trust them?

Who really knew what went on, deep in their fithly minds? He even gave me a pass that would prove I was working. It was a white underage card. Only grown-ups, mostly, could get blue cards, and they had to be fully employed, but getting a white card at my age meant a lot at that time. Mother was grateful to him, of course. He wanted to show his good intentions. With the fear of deportation and all of the requirements to have a blue card, everybody started feverishly to get jobs. To be employed anywhere, for anything, counted the most.

The blue card was the only thing. The blue card was, we thought, our passport for survival. Ella, with her good knowledge of German, got a job as a secretary at the factory in the building next to us. There, everybody just loved her. She had always been so fresh and cheerful, always lending a helping hand wherever possible, and through her, a good many found employment and their so badly desired blue cards. She was always ready to help someone. Mother was forced to have a blue card, too, or face deportation, but at what could Mother work? She was so sick all the time, and so weak. So Ella asked the Ukrainian, her boss, to give Mother the cleaning chores at the office, and assured him he wouldn't have to pay Mother, so he agreed.

With Daddy and Cilly left, we were looking to take precautions. Cilly was given a job at the factory, too. It had been hard work meant only for men, but it was better than having to face camp or deportation. Father had gotten work through the Jewish Committee at a firm of a *Volksdeutsch* in his own profession. With everybody more or less taken care of, we once again started to adjust to this miserable way of life.

Mother's card was green, which meant part-time work; Cilly's was yellow, I think, the youth card; mine was the white card, the children's card. And so we went on, trembling through those days of that gruesome war. At times when the Nazis found me in the street, they took me to clean out their filthy living quarters, which always stunk from alcohol, and always their horrible filth nauseated me, but we were grateful to do even this, for we were all together and not many were left who could say the same. With all of the family going to work, I had to take over the household chores even though I was not thirteen years old yet. I was in charge of everything, from washing to ironing, from cooking to cleaning, from shopping to doing almost anything. Here in the ghetto, like everywhere else, there were those who collaborated with the enemy, and though it is my biggest disgrace to say it, there were even two of our own people. But how very much despised they were. Such cheap traitors. What did they known about decency, coming from the gutters and never having been taught anything decent? I guess they just didn't know any better. I had known many people who had come from poverty, but never and by no means did they ever do anything indecent. On the contrary, most of those people were the nicest ones I had known. But Mother said that traitors, even in the best of families, could happen. They were everywhere at any time, especially in war time when it was the means to save one's own skin. To me, such was just not understandable, me who could see just goodness and kindness in our home. Where decency was king and humanity queen, I just couldn't understand that people would stoop that low. I couldn't even keep up the vow I had made to myself to help in the bitter fight for survival. To steal and lie I thought was just impossible, even though it meant to take from the enemy who had robbed us blind and would torture us so badly. Even here I had been taught never to repay evil with evil.

But life was so very miserable, with my parents away at work, and myself alone home keeping track of everything. There was no coal, no potatoes to cook, nothing at all, so I decided, without my parent's knowing, to take things into my own hands. First of all, coal was brought to the bakery, and there it lay in such a heavenly pile, just waiting to be taken away—just a tiny bit, who would know the difference? And who would it harm—the Nazis? So at night when everybody was sound asleep, I jumped out of the window and took some pails. Having made some previous arrangements with a few of my friends, we met by the coal pile, and we took just a little bit for each of us. Somehow my mother never found out about it, but she must have been suspicious when she saw that we didn't run out of coal. She just begged me not to endanger myself, but me being under age, I somehow had the feeling that even if I was caught, I wouldn't be severely punished. Anyhow, we were real careful. All that, and me not thirteen years old yet.

At times I removed my white armband and went into the German district to get some food, and how much would it hurt me to see those other kids free and going with their loaded arms, carrying their food rations, which looked to me so heavenly. My heart cried, *How am I different from them?* I had had long and beautiful braids since I was a little girl, and I combed them to the side so everyone would think that I was a German girl. It helped me sneak into their neighborhoods, which were strictly forbidden for us. Somehow I always got away with it, and sometimes when my parents and sisters came home from their dreadful work, I had surprises for them—the most heavenly food for all of us.

When Mother found out about it, she was so scared she begged me to quit doing it, but somehow it was like a magnet. I just couldn't resist it, and I usually went back until it became too dangerous and I decided to quit. Bringing home those fresh vegetables and sometimes even fruit, and seeing their eyes glow, was, for me, worth all the danger. At times I went to the Polish places as a German girl to get butter and milk. However bad times were for us, Mother always shared with others. She always helped those that were more in need, as she used to say. Father still went at night to some of his old customers to work in exchange for potatoes, oil, and flour, and Mother always shared with others. She wouldn't have been able to swallow a bite, knowing some people had nothing.

In the building where we lived, there was a very unfortunate family with a little baby. Those people, as far as I can remember, always had bad luck. Mother knew that those people hungered and so she took part of our own food, which was so very hard to get, and sent me in to them with it. The thankful and tear-filled eyes of this young woman told much more than thanks. Here was the fight for daily food, and on the outside was death and destruction lurking for us wherever we went. One night, Cilly and I were sound asleep, my parents, like always, sitting in the dark till the morning approached, and waiting—waiting, for what? Waiting for the devil who would strike like lightning each night at a different home. But this night was different from all of the other nights, for this time I woke up to horrible screams, and my parents weren't in the room. The night outside was glowing as if the city were on fire. This was what had woken me up so suddenly, and I heard shooting and screaming. Among it all, I could hear German commands. I came right away to reality. Cilly and I jumped quickly out of our bed, and as we were looking into the hallway, for our door was wide open, we heard voices coming from the upper floor.

The hallway was lit from the outside with the glow of fire. We ran quickly upstairs to where the voices came from, and there were all of the neighbors, standing unbelievingly, looking into the night and whispering, wondering, looking out the window with horror on their faces. And those awful screams from the outside continued. As I leaped toward my mother, she begged me to go down and back to bed but I wanted to find out what was going on. And what I saw, oh Lord, my blood in my veins froze. The temple was burning. From the back of the building we lived in one could get a good view of everything that went on that night

The temple was not far away, and near it were the Jewish warehouses and stores. As I understood later, here is what happened. As people went into the temple that night for their prayers, the Nazis set the temple alight, not permiting anybody inside to escape the inferno in the hosue of worship. As the fire became more severe, the people that were inside slowly smoldering begged them to please let them out. But they were pushed back by those brutal beasts into the flames. The wives of those trapped inside came running with their children and begged those murderers to please let their men and fathers out. But the Nazis only asked if those were their kin and when the women quickly replied yes, they wrote their own death certificates. For those Nazis replied, "If those are your kin, that is where you belong," and hurled them into the flames. The screams of those who were burned alive was unbearable. The Nazis even took some people out of those masses and poured fuel over them, lit them, and threw them back into the buildings and warehouses. Never will I forget the gruesome picture of that night. But that wasn't all that happened, for as we went out in the morning, there by the temple lay, next to many burned bodies, a young woman with her breasts cut off, and next to her in her blood was a little baby. Those beasts had pulled this beautiful woman out into the street by her long black hair, even as she nursed her infant in her arms, and there in the streets of horror and death, they murdered them both in such a gruesome way.

Yes, I saw all this before I was thirteen years old. I saw this and so much more, for the tale of horror is just beginning. I just wonder where those men are today. They certainly weren't forced to do what they did. Are they fathers of children, too? And how do they feel after all those years, after they did such proud deeds in the name of the Fuehrer? For they try to wash all of their guilt from their souls by saying they were just following orders. Oh, I know a great many of them are alive today; a few I have even seen after the war—but this is called justice.

That night, we were all shaking and asking ourselves when they were coming for us, for our building was not far away from the scene of horror. We didn't know what to do. It was like being caught in a net, unable to escape. A neighbor said, "What can we do? What has to happen will just have to happen. What can we do? If they decide that it is our turn, well, then it just will have to be." Mother didn't want us to hear it all, and the grown-ups forced us back to our beds. But we just lay there shaking. I cuddled up closely to Cilly, covers us up over our heads, and said, "How lucky we are to still have a nice and warm bed."

She answered me with tears choking her words: "For how long?" Oh, if I only hadn't hear those awful screams—still, now, it is as though I can hear them in my tortured ears, those gruesome screams which told of torment and horror. They'll always be with me, and I will never forget them. After that night, just to hear a step outside at night was enough to make our hearts stand still. With all of that going on, day in and day out, nobody was sure of anything anymore, especially at night. For the coming nights from then on, we decided to go into hiding. Even those with blue cards were taken lately by surprise at night from their homes to slave labor camps.

We found for each night a different hiding place. One night, while we were hiding in an attic across from our apartment, they came looking for my sisters. We were shaking. I was so scared that they would be able to hear our heartbeats, but after they made sure that no one was home, they left. The next day Ella found out that they had been looking for her, and the manager promised her that he would have her taken off the list. But still things weren't the same. Once they had you on their list, they would give you a little time before they came again, but we knew they would be back. So even with all of the promises from Ella's manager, we wouldn't trust, and we kept on going into hiding. Those nights were full of nightmares.

One night in a coal bin, one night in a chicken barn. One night in those wooden restrooms, or one night at the bakery on flour sacks. One night they came into the bakery to look for some people and they searched the whole place, but luck was with us and they didn't find us. They weren't even looking for us then, but their suspicion would have been aroused and that would have meant bad luck. All of us had to hide all the time, for if the person they were looking for wasn't home, they took somebody else from that family. We hid a few nights at the factory where Ella worked, shivering on the cold floor. The man that had owned that factory before got to keep track of it now, and he had the keys so his kin and a few of our friends, together with us, and a few neighbors that were on the list for slave labor, could hide there for quite some time

Although they would never probably have suspected to search there at night, one still couldn't be too sure. Besides, the Ukrainian that was the boss could come some night. Who could be sure that he would not? One night—I still don't know what made us skip that night—sure enough, the Ukrainian came. From then on, we were afraid to go into hiding at that place again, but life had to go on, and we had to continue our nightly rounds if we valued our life together. One just wasn't safe at night at home anymore. And the deportation continued. We didn't know at that time about the crematorium and the gas chambers they had been busy building in Auschwitz, but when they continued to take people out of the hospitals and people on relief, as well as the oldsters, by then we imagined already that their destination was death. Many people kept coming to my sister Ella for help in getting their sons back from their imprisonment, for Ella was the secretary at the factory and they soon found out what a wonderful, unselfish person she was. Even those who had declined to give her a job came to ask her for help so that their sons could work for that firm. And Ella, as always, lent a helping hand. If there wasn't any place at that factory, she tried to find someplace else for them to work. When some of the boys were taken to Dullag, the place where one was taken before being taken away for slave labor, she took her white armband off and went to the authorities to plead for their return. Dullag was in Sosnowitz, a few miles out of Bendzin, even though she was endangering her own safety. She said that the boys were badly needed at the factory. When neighbors asked her why she did it, saying that those people didn't deserve it and asking "What did they ever do for you?" she replied that she hoped if ever she was in need, people would do the same for her. And she just kept on doing it. One time Dad had a job at the prison which was to take a few weeks. There were many Jewish people there, some waiting for deportation, some with death sentences, and some heading for camp. I don't know how, but people soon found out about Dad working there. They came to our home bringing letters, food, clothing, and all kinds of things for Dad to smuggle to those unfortunate ones.

And Dad, this dear, sweet, lovable dad, smuggled those things in with his working material, always endangering his own life. Never would he turn anybody away. I remember bringing food for Dad there while he worked. It really was only a pretense, for what I really took was food and such for those people imprisoned there. At times Mother was scared to death, but what did it matter? At least we were able to help those poor unfortunate ones.

Meanwhile, at home, new neighbors moved in every day. I made new friends. There was the daughter of the new baker—her name was Ruth—and the daughter of a new neighbor, Jadzka. We became good friends. Jadzka had another friend whose name was Esther, so she and I became in short time very good friends. Esther was a very beautiful girl with shiny long black braids that reached down to her knees. She went always nicely and neatly dressed. Somehow, from the first moment that we met, we felt great sympathy for one another, and so our friendship started to bloom. Together with Motek, Jadzka L., Jadzka M., and Szymon, we were a real nice group. One could even call our friendship ideal. Soon Ruth joined our group, and so, in spite of all the darkness outside, in our world of friendship we shared a good many hours of happiness, forgetting the cloudiness around us. Having boys in our group was the best excuse to have someone to boss around. For what thirteen year old girl would like to be bossed around? But with boys it was different, one just could do with them what one desired. They were really very ncie sports, and we all got along just marvelously.

Sarah came to visit us quite often. At her home things looked real bad. With her father sick all the time, it was so dangerous, for if the Nazis got wind of him being sick and unable to work, he would become a target for deportation. Mother always tried to comfort Sarah. Later on I didn't see her and we thought she had been taken for deportation or slave labor.

There was a family from Glewitz that had come to Poland a little while ahead of us. This household had been fatherless; their father had died back in Glewitz. There was a girl and three boys. This whole family had come apart. One boy emigrated from Glewitz, the girl had gone to Israel, and two of the boys had stayed. One of the boys was named Salo Haberkorn; his name is well known by the partisans, for he died as a great hero. When the partisans started to form, he was one of the first ones to join. He must have been no more than fifteen years old, but those heroic deeds he performed were just unheard of. He was later shot by the Nazis near the ghetto. I heard of it years after. As I have heard, he accomplished a secret mission and knew too many secrets, so instead of being captured alive, he ran from them when he was ordered to stop. He died with the song of partisans on his lips: "Never tell this is the last way that you go, for blue skies will push away the days of gray, for it will come the day of freedom that we pray for, and when our boots step proudly, you'll know that we are here."

This was the wonderful song of the partisans, never to give up hope. Did anybody ever honor those heroes? Those unknown ones, who died on that big battelfield of humanity? Those men and women who wouldn't sit idle and look at the slaughter that went on. Those that fought with the odds against them, but the big advantage with them—humanity, freedom—to them I shall always look up and pay my highest respects to their memory.

As time went on, German families took over the nicest flats, those that had once belonged to the Jews, and after they took over the Jewish businesses, they still weren't satisfied. They had already taken the furs and the jewelry, and now they asked for our warm clothing and for our shoes. The Jew was stinking, the Jew was filthy, but their possessions weren't filthy; their clothes didn't stink. As as the fight for Stalingrad began, they really got crazy. They feared the cold more then anything else, so they just had to take whatever they could put their bloody hands on. They demanded, and we had to give. It was just like a well, never running dry. They would take our clothing off our backs, if they saw us on the street still a little bit decently dressed. Shoes had become such a luxury, our footwear at that time consisted mostly of wooden soles. But this wasn't all. Since they brought their families to the city, they had to have furniture. After taking it away from the rich families, they didn't care what it was, they had to have it and we just had to give. The officers had to have the best. They went around houses to check who still had some good furniture left. And here Mother had again something to fear. Although it was only furniture, one still was glad to have it. We had at that time our precious bedroom set still with us. This suite of furniture was a source of pride for Mother, after she had been robbed of all the nice things she had saved for in better times. It was always kept like it had just come from the store. Mother had seen it once on an exhibition in France, and having fallen in love with it, she bought it. It had cost a great deal of money, and now Mother feared the Germans would take it away from us. She had been afraid to sell it, and for the little amount of money offered, Mother wouldn't have brought it over her heart anyhow. Each time the doorbell rang, we sat quietly and did not open the door. But we knew that was no solution; here, too, it was only a question of days until they found us. After the gentiles had to move from the place to make it a Jewish ghetto, a neighbor became janitor. He was the father of one of my girlfriends. He was very nice person, and I want to mention that what happened now was not his fault; although it was his guilt, he himself didn't know that it would happen.

One day two civilians came to the building and demanded to see all the flats. They said all they wanted was to do some counting. When Mother saw them outside, she quickly locked the door. They hadn't noticed Mother, but the janitor saw Mother quickly lock the door, so he called to her not to fear, that she should open because this was only a survey. What else could Mother do but open the door? Somehow, Mother didn't trust those two men from the beginning. She just had a feeling that they didn't mean any good. What glances they had thrown at the furniture. It didn't mean any good, all right. Their main purpose was, like Mother had suspected from the very beginning, to look for some good furniture. And Mother's pride was confiscated. Mother was brokenhearted. What would we do? Where would we sleep? But by then we were used to so much already that it somehow didn't hurt so much anymore. We somehow got along, and we bought someplace some filthy beds, infested with insects, which Mother, of course, took care of very thoroughly, and we made the best we could of it. When they came to take away the furniture, Cilly and I stood in each corner of the closet and made some hex wishes over it. Even Ella joined us. When they carried it out, it was just like a piece of our own flesh. Mother wept. People in the streets stood and were surprised—who had still such? Who was crazy enough to still keep this? Who could understand how many happy memories were connected to that beautiful furniture? Ella ran after the truck which carried our furniture to at least see where they took it. It went to a house at the edge of the ghetto, and in the evening when their curtains weren't drawn and the light was still on before the blackout, we walked by there to get a glimpse at it. But to the janitor Mother said, "I shall never forgive you as long as I shall live." And he looked at Mother with such a guilty expression and said how very sorry he was, and how he never imagined this would have happened. The poor fellow, he just couldn't believe it himself. Mother advised him that next time he shouldn't push his nose into things that didn't concern him. Mother forgave him after the first hurt was gone, seeing him always so guilty. After all, he didn't mean any harm, and if not this day, they would have found us another day. As Mother said, "I wish that the worse thing that could have happened with it was to let it take all the evil from us."

But life became more dangerous with each day. With all the wandering around at night from one hiding place to another, I couldn't remember a good night's sleep. Ella went to the director of the factory and told him to settle once and for all for her to be completely removed from the list for slave labor. He promised to do so, and one day he told her that all the danger was over and she could be assured that nothing would happen; we could relax. For a short time we enjoyed the comfort of our home and beds again. One day Mother came home very excited. She had found out that, for a high price, of course, we could escape to Switzerland by plane. Mother said that we would have to sell all of the valuables we still possessed, and the rest of our possessions we would have to leave behind. First of all, it was too dangerous to sell them, and secondly, we didn't want to arouse susupicion. Mother said that by getting out, even though we sold all our jewels, we would still have our lives. Then, she said, we would just have to start all over again, but what would it matter as long as we were out of that disaster? This time Ella wanted to be the smart one. If we only hadn't listened to her. Oh, Ella what did you do, why did you take away our last chance for survival? After we heard that the Germans were defeated at Stalingrad, she told Mother that the war would come to an end soon and we would be able to save at least a bit of our possessions without having to run, which was a big chance to take, for there could be some fakery involved. Mother listened, and with that, our last chance for survival was gone.

For Chanukah or Sabbath, we lit the candles on a brick that we had gotten from the destroyed temple. It was among the Polish Jewry an unwritten law then. I still remember so vividly the day I went with Mother to choose the brick from the ruins. I wanted a whole and nice birck, but Mother said that it really didn't matter as long as it was brick from our holy place, which buried so many innocent lives. What a proud death they had died, Mother used to comfort me, in their place of worship, which meant for them more than anything else in the world. For to die in the temple is one of the greatest honors ever to happen to a Jew, Mother explained when she saw my young mind wasn't able to get it. "What was there to be so proud about, to murder people in their holy place? And the Lord, why did he stand idle, what did he have to say about it?" I asked.

Mother replied, "Don't worry, the Lord's mills grind slowly, but they grind thoroughly! You are now too young to understand everything, but the time will come, and justice will prevail." Justice, what justice was there? I could still see that young mother, lying in her blood with her breasts cut off and her little darling baby, it must have been about four weeks old, that baby with a smashed head, in her mother's arms. What justice could be found on earth to punish a people with such an evil hatred that it wouldn't even stop for a thing? What justice could prevail upon such monsters? Today I am much older, so many years have passed since then, but they have not the pain taken away, and I am still searching for an answer twenty years thereafter—where is justice? Do we have to punish such acts with kindness? Is this justice?

One day Mother saw that things really didn't look too sure for Ella and Cilly at the factory, for a few people had been taken away. Although Ella tried to get most of them out, still it wasn't too sure that once she got into their claws there would be someone to save her. She always went as an Aryan to save those workers, but if the time came, who would go for her? So Mother gave our sewing machine, which she called her second pair of hands, to a shop that had the very good reputation that people weren't taken from there. The name of it was Rossner's. This shop employed a big part of the Jewry from our town, and one could even say that, under the circumstances, one could feel safe working for this shop. This work was exlusively for the Germans, and since they were very much in need of clothing, they didn't bother those people having a card which proved they were employed there. But to get in there was another act of art.

First of all, it cost a certain amount of money to bribe those high officials, and secondly, one had to give a sewing machine in very good condition for each person meant to be employed there. So Mother parted with her sewing machine to save her children. At that time I knew already very well how to sew, and it did hurt a lot to have to give the machine out of the house, but it was worthwhile. We received a reciept for it, of course, and as soon things were settled, we were to be notified that my sisters would be able to start work there. The managing director of the firm where Ella was employed didn't know about it all, for he would probably not have liked the idea of Ella wanting to leave. As soon as things were really settled, Ella was to break the news to him. Anyhow, him being a drunkard, we couldn't rely on him. A rumor had also started that we would have to go outside the city into a very strictly guarded ghetto, together with people from the neighboring cities. There, it was said, things would really be bad, for we would have to share one room with a few families. But what was there to do but to wait and see, and be grateful for each day that we could still be together? For, as we thought at that time, each day brought us nearer to the end of the war, and with it came salvation. There was no question about it. For how long could we go on living like this, in constant harrassment, fear, hunger, and death, and the worst of it all, horror? For not one day would pass without something horrible happening. With each day that dawned we asked ourselves, *Who is going to be next in line? Where will the lightning strike this time? Which house will it be?* It was soon to come to our house.

One day Ella came home very excited. "They have brought the German Jews over," she shouted. As she passed the street which led to the border of Beuthen, buses had passed her and she heard her name. Looking into the buses, she caught glimpses of some of our friends from Gleiwitz. Well, the day had certainly arrived when they had fulfilled their promise to clean the Jews out of Germany. "How lucky we are to have a home at least—where will those poor people go?" I asked.

Mother cried. She knew so much more than my child's mind was able to imagine, but Ella, with hatred in her eyes, quickly let herself go. "Where?" was her disdainful answer. "To the gas chambers, of course." We already knew that the Nazis had built gas chambers to destroy the Jews, but with all of our hope that the war would come to an end soon, we had hoped so badly that they wouldn't be able to fulfill their dreams to destroy all of us. Some day those who survived would demand answers from the Germans for everything. "It just can't go on like this; the world will hear about it all and it just won't sit idle," Ella said.

MY SORROWFUL TEENAGE YEARS

In all this misery I turned thirteen. Those years which should have meant for me sunshine and flowers were instead filled with destruction and death. Those wonderful years I had yearned for were marred with darkness and fear. But how happy and fortunate we were to still be together and have hope that someday we would see it through, all of us together. "And then your life will again be sunshine and roses!" Mother would say, always thinking about us, never for herself. That she grew older and weaker with each day, and more hopeless, never entered her mind. She was in her late forties, and although still in the prime of life, it seemed to us as if she was so old already. For herself she demanded nothing from life, but her children she still wanted to see live in freedom.

On the day that the Jews from Gleiwitz had passed Ella on the street, we found out that they had been taken to the Jewish Committee, and there no one was permitted to go and see them. But somehow Ella got a permit to visit them, but it was just too heartbreaking. There she saw many of our old friends and neighbors, who begged Ella to get them out, to allow them to stay in Bendzin for work. Poor Ella, how badly she wanted to help, but her hands were tied. How could she? She herself wasn't sure of her own life anymore, and here were our old neighbors and friends from the cigar shop on Kronprinzenstrasse. We had been friends with their two daughters, and the parents begged my sister to at least get their two children out. Ella promised to try her best to help, for as she was aware, the director at her factory liked children. Ella speculated that perhaps he might help her, but it took too long. Too many procedures had to be gone through, and when Ella got back, all of them had left. She saw from afar their crying faces, and their handkerchiefs waving good-bye. "Good-bye, dear friends," she cried aloud, for Uncle stood next to her, and her body was shaking from their heartbreaking cry. She said, "One chapter of our lives destroyed." None of those people were ever heard of again, except for their clothing and pictures, found in the huge storehouses of Auschwitz, the death factory and symbol of the Nazi culture, that was the only witness of the fate of our friends from Gleiwitz. Those monsters of modern Germany, they wouldn't kill anymore by the hundreds or so, oh, no—now they had a new system, and their killing went on a big production basis. To get the people from their homes one by one was too slow for their masterminds, so they searched all the time for newer systems, and they found them. Soon they found a way to get rid of us quickly and cheaply. The memory of this will always stay with me, and whoever lived this through will, like me, always remember those gruesome hours of hell. At that time we had to change from the white armbands to the yellow star of David, with its inscrpition, *Jude*. This had to be sewed on the left side of the chest. One day, the Nazis decided they had to take some new, quick action to clean the city of the old, young, and very young—that meant infants and pregnant women as well. They would leave in the city only the middle aged to produce in the factories for them. The youth they sent to the slave labor camps, and the children they sent to Auschwitz with the sick and pregnant and the old people. And how could they organize this?

The best way was by concentrating all of us from the city in a place of assembly, which was a place of horror. We didn't know what the murderers had in mind, for they said that everyone had to come and have their passes stamped. And we, blind people, went, not realizing what was behind it all. We, who had lived through so much desstruction already, and had heard so many lies from those brutes, we went just like sheep to their slaughter. The Nazis said that whoever didn't come would get shot right away, that they would find these people and whoever didn't have their passes stamped would, without any question asked, be sent to Auschwitz. So everybody thought what was there to lose but to go, get our passes stamped, and get it over with. It was such a lovely day in summer; the sun was shining and it looked as though it wanted to cheer us up. The day was August 12, 1942, five days before my birthday. Oh, how I will always remember this day, for the Punkt, the point of no return, is now well known. I just can't understand how the people, who through those years had been tortured so badly by the Nazibeasts, how could we have gone so quietly, why did we trust them? Or is this only the thought of a child's mind? For there was no other way out but to go into the arms of the devil. Yes, it was a trap and nothing less. Our orders said that we had to be at the Punkt at five in the morning. As we walked there on that nice summer morning, the birds were singing in the trees and the air felt so good. It was so good to be alive and to be able to enjoy it. But what started as a promising day soon was to turn into the biggest nightmare ever to imagine. People, inclined by loveliness of the morning, made plans for what they would do when the war ended. And who wouldn't be inclined to make plans on such a nice and peaceful morning? For those monsters were hardly seen on the streets, and one could really say that it was peaceful. Some people started to speculate: maybe the Nazis had to leave occupied Poland, maybe they had finally been defeated, and so that we would not see their defeat, they had ordered us here. And then there were others that said, maybe they have taken us here because they are going to burn our homes. But my mother had a bad feeling. She said, "I feel nothing good coming; it is too quiet around, as if it foreshadows something." And was Mother ever right.

The Nazis had to prepare, all right, for what they had in store for us. At eight in the morning the Nazis closed the big gates of the place where we were, and with that, Mother sighed very heavily and said, "I hope that this time my feelings cheat me, for I have such a spine-tingling feeling." The sun started to burn down on us mercilessly as though it wanted to burn us alive. People had imagined they would come and have their passes stamped, and then they would be able to go back home, so many hadn't brought along even one thing. Mother had taken a little food laong, "just in case," as she said. When Father took his raincoat, Mother asked what for, and Ella made jokes, for the day looked so promising, and soon we would be home, anyway. But Father said that it paid to always be prepared, and what harm could it do to take the coat along? So when the sun burned over us, with no place to hide, we took Father's raincoat and hid underneath. There were so many sick people who had been taken out of the hospitals—people who had just undergone surgery, and women who, just a few hours ago, had brought children into the world. There were old and young, sick and very gravely sick ones, but they all had to come. Even if they were on stretchers, they still had to be there. Seeing the awful sight of the sick and those infants lying there in the hot sun and crying, we saw that nothing good lay ahead. Next to us was a neighbor of ours, a woman around the age of thirty; she had two days ago brought a little boy into the world. This woman had always been so gentle and quiet, one could say that she was a model tenant. She wasn't able for years to have any children, but ten years after her marriage the happy event had happened, and she went around on clouds. But the poor little guy, here he had to smolder in the hot sun, so we took him under Father's coat, and he hardly cried. He was such a precious little thing. Mother gave the woman a helping hand, for the birth had not been an easy one. She hardly could stand on her feet. But Mother took care of them as if they belonged to our family. Those eyes, so sad, how they said thanks. All of a sudden, as if the sky wanted to cry with us for what was about to happen, the sky turned dark and gloomy and the rain came down. It came down so fast, as if it wanted to drown everyone on the earth. And here without a roof over their heads, in the open field, were thousands of people, sick, and children. Those poor little infants, drenched to their bare skin, those poor mothers with tiny infants in their arms, hardly had they opened their eyes into this evil world. And so the rain continued to pour without end, mercilessly. I asked my mother how the Lord could see such, and be quiet. Or did the Lord turn away from us? How did those tiny infants sin? What have they done to deserve such? Why? And why? One question, never to find an answer. How lucky it was that Father had brought his raincoat along. We were able to let a few people under it, and at least we wouldn't be so drenched. Father, of course, was soaked, for he had let somebody else go underneath the coat in his place. It was the same with Mother—never thinking about themselves, always about somebody else. Now that I look back on it all, I know that the sky wanted to cry for the big disaster that was in store for us. Oh, heaven knew what was to come, and did it ever come. After the rain stopped, when the sun came back out again, this time it was a blessing, for we could dry out. It was not noon yet, and already there had been a few casualties, a few deaths, and dying people. But what did it mean in this jungle? For already a life didn't mean much anymore. Remembering back, how hopeless it looked to liven up that place, for as if an army that was to conquer the earth, those murderers burst through the gate with shooting, screams, and horror. The horror show was about to begin.

People started to run us over. They ran who were able. Those who weren't able to run had the worst of it. Bottles flew over our heads and chairs until it looked just like an earthquake, and in the chaos mixed screams of anguish and pain. But that still wasn't the worst of it, for the worst was yet to come. Kutschinsky came through the gates, ready with his adjutants, his assistant butchers, for Kutschinsky was the man in charge. He sent the people wherever he found fit, to slave labor or to Auschwitz for extermination. He was one of Eichmann's men, all right. And so the selection began. Uncle Jacob was forced to take care so that people wouldn't panic, and he got his family somehow out among the first. He tried to help in getting us out, but it was impossible, for once you were in this trap there was no way out. The only way was back through the gate, and to reach that, you had to go through the selection and Kutschinsky, and here again the odds were against us. They were against us especially, for we were five, and hardly a family was left together. Those already over middle age, or those who were young or sick, had one future—Auschwitz, extermination. Those healthy ones and young ones had another thing to look forward to—slave labor camp. All of a sudden, we couldn't see Uncle anymore; he had disappeared. For there was another Punkt for the people from the neighboring cities. There, I heard later on, it was even worse than it was for us, and there Uncle was taken. I think he must have known we didn't have a chance, for when I caught glimpses of him, I noticed the heartbreaking expression in his eyes. *What will be, what will happen to us? What will they do to Mother and Dad? And me and Cilly, my so-dearly beloved sister, will they tear us apart?* Those thoughts ran wildly through my mind. "Oh, Lord, please save us!" I prayed quietly to myself. I just knew that I wouldn't be able to live if I was parted from my so-dearly beloved ones. All this was on my mind while the horror show continued. I looked with disbelief at those sadistic performances, which were very much enjoyed by those evil sadistic Naziswine; as a matter of fact, the more havoc they created, the happier they seemed to get, and nothing could satisfy them more than the screams from the tortured ones. I know that I am writing down as much as I can, but let me say this: no paper in the world will ever be able to tell of all the horrid deeds that were performed by those filthy Nazis. They put up big pillars with the numbers one, two, and three posted on them. Number One was to go free—free until the next time they got hold of you, but at least for the time being, free from this one disaster. Number Two meant to go to slave labor camp, which was not the worse yet to happen, but bad, still bad enough. And Number Three, so very well known and feared, was deportation. It was the ticket to death.

 The rain poured again and wouldn't stop. I can't recall anymore when it stopped raining, for what happened from then on was all in a haze, just like a nightmare where you dream and don't seem to be able to wake up. You feel that things are choking your throat, or somebody is pushing you off a bridge into a dark nowhere; you want to scream but you are paralyzed, you just can't do anything about it. And at the time, everybody was so numb already that each of us looked like a robot, with our hair hanging down in wet strands, our clothing drenched—there we stood, a helpless people, letting everything take its way. Oh, why couldn't a typhoon come and wash us all off the earth? I asked Mother, "What good does it do to have to suffer so much? And, please, Mother, tell me, where is God, whom you have taught me so much about?" Next to us stood a very religious woman—I knew her from seeing her often on the street—and she wore a wig, for the very religious woman only wore wigs. She heard me asking Mother that question and she answered in my mother's place. "Dear child, when the angel of death is loose, there is no help, and when the devil roams about the earth, then he is the master. Just keep on believing in the good Lord, don't lose your patience, and you shall see that the good Lord has not forgotten you." Later I saw how they took this woman and kicked her brutally toward Number Three, deportation. Her children were torn from her and pushed toward Number Two, slave labor. As she went toward her goal, or rather was pushed toward it, I still could see her looking back to me, waving with her head and throwing a smile back to me as if she would say, "Don't worry, the Lord is with us!"

As they tore the families apart, so sadistic, with such murderous attitude, I thought to myself, *How heartless.* Suddenly I felt like laughing out in hysteria at the word—heartless. From whom did I expect a heart? From a people full of murderers? Those screams from the tiny infants, it is as if I still can hear it almost twenty years thereafter, as though I still can hear their little whispers, I still can see the agony of their mothers' faces when the babies were torn from their arms, their faces deformed from horror and disbelief. Those little ones, how thirsty and hungry they were, or those little ones already able to walk, how the Nazibeasts hit them with their guns over their precious little heads if they wouldn't let go of their mothers' hands. And how the Nazis would kick and push back their mothers, who screamed in agony, "Give me back my baby!" The Nazis let some children go free, taking instead their mothers and fathers, or one parent, and those children cried out of agony: "Mammele, why do you leave me? Mamale, come back to me!" Those sadists stood there with their happy faces and laughed at the children's agony, saying, "They are only going on vacation, they will get nice and brown in Auschwitz the Crematorium!" Then there were the screams of the infants they stuffed into sacks and threw toward Number Three: their merciless screams would go up to heaven. I stood with horror and disbelief in my eyes at what went on and on—I, myself, still a child a little over thirteen years old. Those for deportation were squeezed into a little corner, just like sprouts, one on another, as though they couldn't give them before their death at least a little freedom. Poor mothers, poor fathers, and those oh-so-poor little ones. Now that I myself am a mother, I just can't bear thinking these thoughts. Every time I think about it, I feel their pain and agony on that fateful day, and when I look into the eyes of my children, I just can't believe that this all is true, it really did happen, and I am the witness to it.

All of a sudden Ella said, "I think that our neighbor goes toward the selection, how foolish! Why at least wouldn't she wait until the night when it will be dark?"

It was the lady with the tiny infant. The infant was drenched so she feared for its life, and it was so hungry already. She took the infant under her coat and left the buggy behind. I don't know what happened from then on, for everything went so quickly in such a nightmarish manner. I don't know if the baby started to cry underneath the coat, or what happened, I just saw it all in a split second—how they tore the coat from her, tore the baby out from underneath her, and it looked as if they tore it apart, limb from limb, and threw it on a pile where there was already a great number of lifeless, beaten, mutilated bodies of infants. From there, people had to stuff those little bodies, some still alive, some screaming, some dead—they stuffed them into sacks which were thrown on a truck. As the woman saw this, she tore her hair and screamed, "Give me my baby back, murderers, give my baby!" She, of course, half beaten to death, was taken for the slave labor camp. Her husband, who stood stiff like a stone, so lifeless, as if all that had just happened wasn't true, he was given the luxury of freedom. He later joined the partisans to avenge the death of his little boy, this little guy who they had been fortunate to get after all those years of praying. But they were not lucky enough to see him grow up; just a few days of being in the world, and he had found such a gruesome death. But thousands of infants shared his fate. They were thrown into open pits of quick lime, still in the sacks they had been stuffed into. A few days before, how happy their parents had been with them. Some would have shown their first smiles, some their first teeth, some would take their first step, and now their parents had to stay helplessly and watch as the Nazibeasts brutally murdered them right in front of their eyes, to see and feel their agony as they cried, "Help me, Mamale," but there was no mamale to help, there was nothing mamale could do. And I kept on asking myself, *Where is God?* And the rain continued to pour.

There were some lucky families, though, that were not torn apart, but we dared not dream about it. Although drenched to our skin, we somehow didn't have the guts to go to the line which held our fate in its grip. Seeing how those people, squeezed tightly together at Number Three, were severly beaten, my stomach just couldn't take it any longer. And then one fearful question came to my mind: *What will happen with us?* As if Mother read my mind, she said all of a sudden, "Come on, kids, let's get in line. What has to happen right now, let it happen right now." But her voice was ony a whisper from the unshed tears choking her throat.

She tried to tell us where she had hidden the valuables but her words cut like a knife through my heart, and I wouldn't listen, I held my ears. All of a sudden it came to me, the grave situation we were in, it all stood in front of my eyes.

Mother didn't believe she would get out alive, and when I looked at Daddy, I was sure that neither of them believed we were ever to get out again. For them it wouldn't matter, as long as they were sure that nothing happened to us. Yes, such were my beloved parents. When I saw Mother speaking seriously to Ella, Daddy, my darling of a father, took me and Cilly into his arms and said, "Children, we have had a nice family, and whatever happens, wherever fate might bring you, just remember this: that we have loved you more than anything in the world. Yes, we were seven together, we had our rough times and happy times, but please be grateful for what we had. You kids were our biggest diamonds, and I will always cherish the thought of you!"

Then Mother came to talk to Cilly and me, but I just couldn't go on anymore. I broke out in a heartbreaking cry, threw myself on Mother, and said, "What? Do you believe just for one second, if heaven forbid, they take you away from us, that I will just stand there? No, they will have to kill me first and I will never let them tear us apart." I just couldn't realize a life without Mother and Father. I loved them so much I just couldn't think of it. Mother tried to talk some sense into Cilly and I, for Cilly shared my opinion completely. Mother tried to explain that going on Number Three didn't mean to always going to death. There was always a chance to get out of it still, for as long as one is alive, there is still hope. She told us that we shouldn't try any nonsense, but Ella's voice brought us back to reality.

She said, "What are you all excited about? You will see, we will get out of it." But she couldn't hide the big lump that was stuck in her throat. She was always the one to cheer us up. Even in this disaster she found some jokes to tell, some gags, and she reminded me of those tricks I used to play, but it didn't make me feel beter, for they left here a bitter taste in my mouth. It seemed so much like a lifetime away. Those screams and cries and shouts around us didn't help much to boost our courage; somehow courage had left us. I didn't realize we had entered the line, for as if in a dream, I saw myself standing in front of the murderer Kutschinsky. As if out of the fog, I heard Ella's courageous voice say firmly, "Five persons, all employed!"

He looked with murderous eyes into hers and said, "Is this true? All five of them? What if I check?"

In a split second her proud reply was, "Please do so!" She was the first to take her blue card out of her pocket, then Dad took his card out, and with that the color blue came to an end, but we pretended that all of us had the blue card. We pretended to reach into the pockets to take the blue cards out—this all took only a few seconds—for those other cards were worth nothing anymore. For Cilly and I, it meant slave labor camp, if we were lucky, but for Mamm it would mean deportation, the gas chambers. My feet felt so weak, as they were any minute to give under me. It felt like I was standing on a island and all around me was quicksand; I felt like drowning any minute. And in it all I can hear his voice, as if from far away, the voice which held all of our lives. Beneath disaser and death, I could hear words which seemed like music to my ears: "All of you to Number One." Is anybody able to imagine what we felt? As if dreaming, we ran toward Number One as quickly as our feet could carry us. Fear made us run, the fear that he might change his mind, for we were actually free. After our passes were stamped and we left this gate that harbored so much horror and sorrow, we hugged each other and cried, but this time we didn't cry from fear. They were tears of happiness, for once more fate had been good to us and we were still all together. The time was exactly twelve midnight; we were soaked, but who felt it? We were so happy. How could we hear the screams that followed us home, those screams of anguish and sorrow? Although we were free, I knew that never in my life would I be free of the vision of the horror of that day. Even at my tender age, I had seen so much horror. The burning of the temple was bad enough, when I had seen with my own eyes how they made human torches from people. But nothing, nothing compared with the picture of Punkt. And then I think it entered my mind that if anyone was fortunate enough to live through this terror, the whole world should learn about what had happened. Although I had always kept a diary of my own, Mother was frightened for me to write down all of those details, but I had hidden it, and as much as the mind of a child could, I had written down everything that happened. I said to myself, *If I should be fortunate to live through this, I myself will never rest until I have told it the way I really saw it, until the whole world, even to the least little corner, will be taught what happened.* That night as we walked home from that disaster, we had mostly eyes for ourselves. How could I really feel, deep in my heart, the sorrow that followed us? I was so grateful and happy that we all were together. But deep down inside me, the pain for my fellow men kept eating at me, and this marred our happiness, for this choir wouldn't leave us. Those screams of pain from those that had lost their loved ones followed after us.

Deep down, I feel, the world just can't believe what happened. Many now even say that it is exaggerated. But if they only knew how little they really do know. Some say that such horror just isn't possible, but if they knew how wrong they are! They just can't believe that such atrocities happened, but there was so much more. "Oh, Lord." I always pray, "just do justice for the death of those innocent little darlings that those beasts murdered so brutally." Some had been torn from their mother's arms, and the Nazibeasts had torn them into halves right in front of their mothers' eyes. How the Nazis committed shame over shame, murder over murder! Oh, how can I ever write down all that really happened? It would take a lifetime.

As we walked home, we stopped at Uncle Jacob's house. When he saw all of us together, he broke down and cried terribly, for he couldn't believe that here we really stood, all of us together, alive. He hugged Mother, and after a very heartbreaking scene, we went on home. But coming home was like coming to a ghost town. A few neighbors were home, but most of them were not back yet, and many were never to be back. After that awful day, there was hardly one night that I found sleep, for always the sorrow was in front of me. At least we no more had to make the nightly rounds of hiding, for we were told that at the Punkt, the Nazis had sifted the population very thoroughly. Those who had been fortunate enough to get out alive would from now on be able to stay in the ghetto—but we would have to work for the Germans. They promised that life from now on would become more peaceful. How wrong they were, we were soon to find out.

The horrible events at the Punkt had taken until morning, and slowly through the morning hours, life started to form again in the hallway outside our door. We heard the grown-ups whispering about those who hadn't come home. It was then that we realized that we would never see again a good many neighbors, especially the infants—the Nazis had cleared the city so well there were hardly any babies left. I still wonder how those who were left got out. Two of my girlfriends had been taken for deportation, and I just wouldn't believe it when I was told that my girlfriend Edzia was among them. I cried and cried and just couldn't believe it.

And here is what happened to those who were taken, soaked through and through, from the Punkt to their goal. The little infants, as I mentioned before, most of them, unaccompanied by any of their kin, had been taken in the sacks they had been stuffed into and thrown into the clay pits. The rest of the people marked for the destination of death were taken to a prisonlike place, but it was much worse than prison, for they were thrown one on another, with no washrooms or restrooms around, no water, nothing. So many died before even reaching their destination at Auschwitz, the crematorium. Some did break out, though, and they told us later of all that. But many weren't successful and were shot breaking out. Into those few small prison rooms, hundreds and hundreds of people were squeezed on top of one another for days. It was just the foreshadowing of all of the gruesomeness men ever dared to imagine. Many of those poor victims were poisoned with carbon monoxide in the big wagons which were to take them to the crematoriums, but it took those poor, helpless victims quite some time to die, for those beasts had even saved on the carbon monoxide. With so many people pushed into one place, one can only imagine the horror of it all. From the twelfth to the seventeenth of August, the Nazis kept those poor victims imprisoned under the most cruel conditions. And when we saw how they kicked those so-badly exhausted ones into the trucks, just like animals, oh, what am I telling? It was much, much worse than the whole world can know; it was just unbelievable, even to those of us who witnessed the horror.

Those chosen for slave labor camps were treated a little bit differently. They were taken to Sosnowitz, to the Dullag, a place to wait until someone came to buy them. This was an awful place, filthy, with all kinds of noxious insects. There in a few rooms were shelf-like beds made out of planks, and on each level they crowded together fifty or sixty girls. In other rooms, on another floor, it was the same for boys. Each room had about four levels, and there were hundreds of people crowded together. When they got to the camps, they were more than exhausted already, and treated worse than animals. But to all of that I shall come later, for I shall describe it from first hand experience, how I myself lived it.

A few people that had someone on the outside who could intervene for them would get free. One day as I was walking on the street, tormented by thoughts of my dear friend Edzia, I thought my mind was playing a trick on me, for as I passed the place where all of them had been taken, I saw Edzia with her parents. She, as well as were her parents, was a sight—my gorgeous Edzia looked as if she had just stepped out of the grave. Her face was a mask of horror and as I called her name from far away, she just looked through me. Edzia, always had she been singing and laughing, but here, what had they done to her? Her beautiful ebony black hair, her gleaming braids, was all loose and halfway torn out of her head. When I came home and cried, telling Mother all about it, Mother said, "Just give her a few days to snap out of it and to come to herself and soon she will be the same." And after three days, Edzia, my dear friend, came back to me and she told all the gruesome stories I never tried to ask, but soon we tried to forget. Like youth, we soon tried to be gay again, but never was the innocent happy gaiety with us anymore. Something precious had been stolen from us, together with all that we possessed; the Nazis had taken everything holy to us, never, never to return it. And we knew that a new page had opened in our lives.

After that awful day, fear stood in everybody's face, and one question was in everybody's mind: "When will the line come to us?" That there was nothing good waiting for us, that was one thing each and every one realized. Mother hid the few valuables we still had, and if we wanted it or not, we just had to be prepared for any emergency that arose. But if we thought that the Nazis would be satisfied for the time being, we were very much mistaken. Again the deportation and the raids for slave labor camp began, for those taken to camps had it so tough there that many died and many were driven to their deaths. Some were taken for experiments and put to good use by the murderers. For instance, there was an artist who made lampshades out of human skin; Miss Ilse Koch was an expert. Or they made many other experiments, like the death baths. Why should they bother to experiment on animals if they could have humans to test all of their cruelty on? They had so many uses for the Jews in their experiments, and the added satisfaciton of seeing their victims suffer in their agony. They even had a good name for the soap we were given on ration. It was called RIF, which mean *rein juedishes fett*, or in English, "clear Jewish fat." There was no end to the inventions of their evil minds. Those diabolic brains worked day and night, night and day, they just kept on working overtime. And after all, they had so much to do to figure out the quickest and cheapest way to destroy a whole people. This was their only goal at the time, no matter how they did it, as long as they could get their full enjoyment out of our despair. No life was life anymore. If some help didn't arrive soon, we knew that we were doomed and that our days were counted. Oh, they had taken everything away from us, even our good spirit. At times it seemed that they had taken our hope from us, although we tried so hard to hold on to it, but it seemed that even here they had succeeded. We thought hope was gone already. But if we had not had at least a little hope, I am quite sure that life wouldn't have been worth fighting for anymore. If we knew that the spirit was still with us, we could be strong. They had taken everything away—they took our shoes, they took our socks, they took our coats, anything—nothing belonged to us anymore, for everything belonged to Reich. But this is nothing compared with what they took from me later.

 My beloved mama, beloved papa, my so-dearly beloved sisters Ella and Cilly, all have fallen to those brutal Nazibeasts, murdered in their prime of life. This book shall be dedicated to you, with all my heart and love. For there is no other way to ease the pain that keeps burning in my heart. You, and only you, showed to me the path of happiness, and without you I would have been nothing. How dearly I loved you and always shall. The dear memory of you will be a shrine in my heart. And while I am writing down what lay like a stone on my heart through all those years, ever since I lost you, I promise to you that with each word I write, I will search for justice for all that was done to you and my people.

 Yes, one night it came—what we had feared. Although having been assured by Ella's boss that no one would bother us, Mother had still taken more precautions. She had taken out a card from Rossner's so that when everything was arranged, Cilly and I would go to work there. Since Ella was assured of her safety, Mother worried about me, so even though I was still under age, she arranged for me to work at Rossner's instead of Ella. With this plan, we thought that the one fear that lay over us was at least taken care of. But everything happened so differently than we expected. Who would have thought of it? Cilly, still so weak from her last operation and from being undernourished, had to have certain vitamins, but how could we get them? One night a strong bang on our door brought us to reality. We were shaking from fear, for we felt right away that outside that door was nothing good waiting for us. And here they stood. The Nazis sent the Miliz in advance, but they came right after them. The horror of that night struck just like lightning. They had come to take Ella and Cilly. Everything I can still see, so vividly in front of me, as if it all just happened yesterday. Until now it had always happened to someone else, but this time it was different, for this time it struck at our home. And how unbelievable, how painful, when you see that those so-dearly beloved ones torn from you, and you just have to stay there helpless, unable to do a thing about it. You wish that all this was a bad dream and you hope that any minute now you will wake up, but you start to realize that it is no dream, that it is the whole and bitter truth. My so-dearly beloved sister Cilly, never had I gone to sleep without her. We had always so much to chat about. We had always been so sure that we would never be parted. We had made so many plans about life in freedom, and were so much like one another. No wonder that everybody always thought we were twins; we were always together, always adored. And here I stood, shaking with helpless and tormented anger, realizing they really were taking Cilly away from me. She was so young, still a child, so skinny, so weak that Mother just wouldn't let them take her out of her arms. She wept, "My baby, my sweet little girl." For nothing else did I have an eye at that time, just her. I just couldn't stand the thought of us two being parted. *What will I do? And when will I see my darling sister again?* Ella, seeing us cry so awfully, tried to comfort us. She made jokes, took her time with getting ready, and laughed and sang. No, she wouldn't give them the satisfaction of showing them her heartbreak. "Don't you see?" she said. "I am protected at the office. They had no right to take me in the first place. But never mind, I will go, and tomorrow I will be back home. And Cilly, she is still too young for slave labor, they have better uses for her right here. So there is really nothing to worry about." But one thing Ella didn't count on was that with her gone, there was no one to get her and Cilly out, for she was the only person always to get people out of it. She had always endangered her life and gotten people taken back. Going as a German girl, her star of Jude removed, somehow, she always succeeded. Now, with her in the Dullag, who would go and do it for her? This was one thing she probably hadn't counted on. Or did she? Maybe she just didn't want to show it to us, not to break our hearts anymore. She pretended only to ease our pain. This is also a question I shall never find an answer for. After a brief good-bye, tearing my heart out at Mother's heartbreaking cry, I covered my head in the pillow. As they left, I tried to ease my pain in a long and silent cry. That was the last I saw of them, my proud sister Ella and my angel of a sister Cilly.

And so they came to the slave labor camp Lichtwerdenueber Freudenthal, in the Sudetes. Freudenthal means "Valley of Happiness." They should have named it Valley of Sorrow, for it destroyed so many young lives. While still in Dullag, Ella sent a note home expressing her hope that she would soon come home, together, of course, with Cilly. But I think she didn't believe it herself anymore. When the Nazis prepared the girls for camp, Ella arranged that Cilly would go with her. Ella was chosen as the eldest Jew, and the girls at camp were very happy, for many of them knew what a wonderful person she was. They thought that with her as their supervisor, life would be bearable. But she soon gave it up; she just couldn't do what the Nazis demanded, so she became the secretary for that camp. When Mother learned of that, it made her relax a little bit; she had a feeling that Ella would somehow see it through, and it was a relief to us that Cilly was in the same camp. Oh, they had it tough there, I know. I understood so many things written between the lines that came from Ella, for in the beginning they were permitted to write home once in a while, and we were able to answer them, too. Most of the mail got lost, but those few cards that came brought home all their sadness, sunshine, and hope. How Ella hoped to soon be permitted to come back home! Maybe she just wrote that to us to make us feel better. I will never know; everything was so very heartbreaking. Ella said Cilly didn't feel too well, but it was only a question of days before she would have everything taken care of for Cilly to return home. Later she told us, "No worry, we will be all together again." Such and similar were all of her postcards. She was so courageous, always with a nice appearance, and always gay until the last minute, till they took her away to the chambers. Even then she had her head up high and proud; never would she give them the satisfaction, those who had stepped over her, however much they tortured her and however much they hurt her.

No, there never could have been another one like her, for there was just one Ella, and she was my beloved sister. When the Nazis started their horror campaign back in Poland, she, like the rest of us, had to change her name to a biblical name, and we called her Estera Ruchla Sarah Rychner. As a matter of fact, we all had to have the name "Sarah" after our first name, and the men had to have the middle name "Israel." But changing our names to biblical names had really been the least thing that bothered us.

Now back home, with my sisters gone, life was so gloomy, so very quiet. In the beginning, I cried myself to sleep. How much did I long to see Cilly again! It just was unbearable for me. But life had to go on. With all of the agony of having given away two of their kids, my poor parents were just shaking from fear that now the line would come to me. And this, my mother said, she wouldn't be able to live through. At night I heard her praying to the Lord, "Oh, Lord, they have taken from us everything, just don't let them take my baby from me." I could see her crying in the dark, and I could hear her weeping. If I stayed out with my girlfriends for a few minutes longer than expected, I could see Mother's red eyes when I came home. "Lydilein, don't do this again, I feared that something had happened to you!" she said. Wherever I went, whatever I did, there would always be Mother's fearful eyes as a warning in front of me. It got so that I would hardly leave the house. "My sunshine," as Mother used to call me—and how hard I tried to bring a little sunshine into their grieving hearts. I sang, although at times it pinched like tiny needles through my heart. I joked and laughed and tried as much as possible to fill the emptiness that my sisters had left.

One day, Mother was made another offer to smuggle us out of Poland into Switzerland. But this time Mother only shook her head no; she would wait until her kids were back home, and then, the first chance given, she wouldn't wait for a second, but we would take that chance and run. But without the children, Mother wouldn't leave for anything in the whole world, for her children were the only thing she lived for. Our Polish friend came to our house again. He warned Mother not to wait until it was too late, but to come out to his place to hide now. He tried persuading Mother with these words: "Don't you see that your hours are counted?"

But always came the same reply from Mother. "I am not going without my children; first they have to come back home and then we won't let escape one single chance anymore!" Uncle Jacob was frightened by now, too, and he said that we should really start considering something. For, as he said, as soon as they finished with the youth, they would take care of the rest of us. The youth disappeared now in a great hurry, for each day the Nazis took them from their working places and sent them to the slave labor camps. So Uncle kept on warning, "How long do you suppose it will take for them to get to us?"

But Mother still replied, "If you want to go, do so. I still will wait for my two girls to come back." So we kept on waiting; what else was there to do? Who would have done differently? Of her own safety, Mother was never concerned anyhow, and with Dad it was just the same. Their diamonds were their children, their greatest fortune on earth. This was the only thing that counted, in their great unselfish way. Oh, yes, we went into hiding again. Mother wouldn't take any chances with my safety. I wasn't slated for the slave labor camp, but who could count on it? With those monsters, who coud be sure of a thing? They took anyone whenever they felt like it, and one just had to go. So we started with our nightly rounds again. One day, Uncle came to our house, his face like ashes, and he took me into his arms, squeezed me toward his heart, and cried. At first I didn't know what he was crying about, and my first thought was that something must have happened to his family. When I saw Pinjush and his mother coming toward our house, I relaxed. Mother's screams brought me into reality. Yes, Mother was the first one to guess what it was all about. Uncle had been given the job of watchman in the laboratory of the Jewish Committee so he had a few connections, and he was at times able to find out who was on the list for deportation and slave labor. This way he warned a good many people, of course endangering gravely his own safety. He just couldn't go on watching the misery of those people who were caught and brought to him. He had to see all the misery and heartbreak each day at first hand. So when lists were made up for slave labor camp, he looked them over. This time he had seen that Satan had put out the claws for me, the nestling. No staying at home for us from that day on. How can I mention all of the filthy hiding place we visited to save me? So very many of them. Each and every night it was again another place. One night on flour sacks, one night on coal sacks, one night it was a rat bin, sometimes a little dog house, but it is too hard to run away from the devil; one just can't outrun him. He will come whenever you expect him the least.

We were so very frightened, out of our wits. Mother would have given away anything she still possessed, only to get me off that list. This time, too, she paid for the promise that I would be removed from that list. For with our sewing machine at Rossner's, and this the safest place yet, Mother ran and paid plenty to get it settled that I would be able to start working there. With that, I would get my blue card and I would be safe from the slave labor camp. So far, so good, everything promised, everything taken care of, and we were able to breathe again. Or was it our imagination? Mother wouldn't trust anything anymore. We spent more of the day in hiding than out. Most of the time when we were out, we were preparing food for our next round and making plans for where to spend the next night. Of course, Daddy went from hiding to work and from work into hiding. At times he went in the house to wash up, but what was the use of getting washed up, for we would get more dirty on our next round. Mother was still employed that half day at the office where Ella used to work, but she wouldn't let me out of the hiding place anymore. I just had to stay there alone and wait till Mom gave me the OK to leave for a little while. Sometimes I felt that I just couldn't stand it any longer there; outside, the days were so very beautiful, the birds were singing, and here I had to be all by myself in a filthy attic with the sun burning on the roof. Outside I could hear the heartbeat of the city with its frightened inhabitants, and here, all alone, my diary was my only companion. Oh, there wasn't much to write, only about broken dreams and a torn heart, a youth so full of sorrow and despair. Here again, books were my steady companions. I read whatever I could get hold of, but even with a book, you want to discuss it with someone, and here I just sat alone and waited for my dearly beloved ones, hoping that the Lord would bring them back safely to me. I just sat there helplessly and prayed that I would see them again, and when I heard their dear footsteps, I jumped into their arms and cried for happiness and sorrow. Once again I felt so very rich, for I knew that nothing could happen to me when I had them near me to protect me. When I was alone with so much to think about, I started to search for an answer to our suffering. I read *Ben Hur,* I read about Jews in chains, and all those books about the house of Borgia, but always one thing was written so vividly; always was the Jew condemned to suffer. The Jews always had been hated, and they had always tried to survive in the those hateful times of their persecution. And then the Crusades, when the Jew was forced to give up his faith—those who wouldn't, how badly they were tortured. But that was still nothing to compare with our time. For us, no chance was given at all, and the horrible deeds of our time topped even those of the Crusaders. The superior race, as the Nazis called themselves, those people so full of culture, no, by God, no, nobody could compare with them—they were superior in their evil deeds, all right.

One day Mother was assured we wouldn't have to fear a thing anymore. My name had been entered on the list of Rossner's shop and we could finally relax, stop making our rounds into hiding, and finally be again at home. Oh, how we were taken in. In all of their evildoings, the Nazis wanted to taste our sorrow with all its trimmings. But since we didn't trust them too much anymore anyway, we still were careful. Meanwhile, while everything quieted down, we had at least a chance to relax a little. Then one day came a card from Ella, and there it was written, black on white, that Cilly had permission to return home, for she was sick and they had given her the OK to leave the camp. How very naïve we still were! We had forgotten what those beasts had done with the sick. But sometimes girls really did return home from camp on the pretense of being sick, so if a miracle could happen to someone else, why shouldn't it happen to us? I still can see the tears running over Mother's sorrowful cheeks. Those lovable eyes of hers I had seen filled more with tears than with happiness. How the card shook in her worked-out hands. "Lydchen, *Liebling,* can you imagine this? Cilly is coming home!" Mom said. How much happiness! Her worried face shone with. It looked at though the sun was about to shine for us again. But week after week went by and from Cilly there was no sign. Meanwhile another card arrived from Ella with regards for Cilly, but there was no Cilly and no sign of life from her. Months had passed since Ella had said good-bye to her and was assured that Cilly was on her safe voyage home. She had even been told that they thought Cilly was already home. And Mother twisted her hands in worry. "My sweet little girl, where is she? Where have those bandits taken her?"

I tried to comfort her always, saying, "Mama, you will see; one day, all of a sudden, she will stand in front of us." But I didn't believe it anymore. Mother ran from place to place to try to find out where they had taken her. The committee promised to shed some light over this mystery and we were promised that they would try their best to bring Cilly home from wherever she had been taken. Those sleepless nights were so full of fear and nightmares, for what could have happened to my beloved sister Cilly? It didn't matter to me anymore where I slept. Sometimes we even slept at home, but nothing made me happy anymore, for in my dreams I saw Cilly in torn clothes and barefoot, begging and pleading for me to help her. I couldn't even tell Mother about my nightmares, but she was always near to comfort me. When I woke up crying from my dreams, there at my side like a guardian angel was my angel of a mother, but I couldn't tell her of my dreams; she was worried enough already. And Daddy, he looked a wreck, undernourished, with no sleep, and worried. So what was I to do? I just had to cry to myself and try to be quiet so no one would find out about it, for I wanted so badly to be the strong one. I tried so hard to bring a little sunshine to my so-badly broken-down beloved ones. Now looking back at all those years, I see how blessed I was, me, the youngest one, able to bring a little bit of comfort into their sorrowful lives. I wrote postcards to camp, to Ella, and in those, too, I tried to put a little humor. I don't understand now how I was able to do it all, for my heart broke apart into pieces. When I look back, seeing Mother's and Father's dear faces in my memory, I can hardly remember them other than sad and weeping. I was growing up so fast, but the fear for my beloved mother and father would sometimes choke me. What would the Nazis do to them, when would they be through with us? For inside the ghetto it looked more like a graveyard without monuments. So few of the people I had known were left. Each day, a transport full of all ages of people would leave the city, each group meant for a different place. And here I was, thinking and praying for my dearly beloved ones. How much I loved them, they knew, for I loved them more than my life. They deserved it, for they were the best parents any child was fortunate enough to have. Oh, if once again I could take Mother's tear-drenched face into my hands and kiss it, kiss it, with all of my heart! If only once again I could lay in Dad's arms and hug and squeeze him! What a small man he was, but how big in love and humanity—never could you find anyone like him. And my sisters—once again to be able to talk and laugh with them, to feel them near me! I know that this is only a dream and that those things never again will come true. But in these pages they will live on and on till the day I die. I hope and pray that my children and their children will cherish the memories the way I always will, for this is what is left of a childhood filled with a little happiness and so much sorrow. By having to grow up so fast in all that hustle, I had hardly time left for my friends which still were left. Jadzka K. had been deported from Punkt and on the day of my birthday she had been taken together with her whole family to Auschwitz. Szymon, my good friend, had been taken to camp quite some time ago. There was only Jadzka L., Motek, Edzia, and me left. Sometimes Ruth, the daughter of the baker in our yard, would join us. Although she was a tomboy like me, we never felt like playing pranks on anyone anymore. People had too many worries, and we understood. The grave situation was all around us all the time. Of course, being girls meant sharing secrets, too, but somehow it wasn't important for us anymore. Who were we? What did it really matter that we became ladies? What was life in this jungle? Since I was Mother's whole joy and pride now, for I was the only one left in their sad lives, she tried to explain to me how very important these years were for a young lady. I, as the youngest, had always tried to dominate the household, putting my foot down (which resulted in a few spanks on a certain place), but now all of a sudden, I felt unimportant.

When we first came to Bendzin, I had noticed one thing—everywhere in the world kids and grown-ups alike had one thing in common. The higher-ups looked down on the middle class, and the poor were no people at all. Here, all of a sudden, us deportees were the poor ones. I never cared much for those big shots and tried always to find my friends among the middle class, and some of the nicest kids that I got to know were among the real poor ones. They were never spoiled, always kind and considerate for their fellow men. To tell the truth, after having a few acquaintances among the rich ones, I couldn't say the same about them. If they were good enough to bow down to one, one had to bow down to their shoes, but now here in the ghetto, they were together with us, fearing for their lives the same way we did, and then they came looking for our companionship, but we didn't care for it anymore. Maybe during those first months when we had come to the city, so broken-down, so homeless, maybe then I would have been happy to have some of them for my friends, but now it didn't matter, for I had my Edzia, who was my most cherished friend of them all. We got so very attached to each other, especially since Cilly was away, that I shared all my happiness and sorrow with her, the same as I used to do with Cilly. Her words, so very heartwarming, were, "Lydia, if they ever part us, I think I shall die!" Mother was very happy for me to have found in Edzia such a dear friend. She was such a nice kid and from such a nice home. At home, her family was very religious and she tried to persuade me back into things I had already started to disbelieve since that gruesome day at Punkt and that awful night when they had taken my sisters away. Of course I did believe in God, I wanted so badly to believe in him, but somehow I neglected most of those other things that should be held by a Jew. Mother noticed that change in me, and was now happy that I had found a friend like Edzia who was able to persuade me a little.

One day we decided we would have our picture taken. I remember it still, it was such a beautiful day; the sun was shining as we were walking along the streets of the ghetto. We went to the Goldstein establishment, one of the biggest photographers in the city. Before the war, they used to be one of the richest in the city and now even in the ghetto, they still got along somehow. They still felt among the higher-ups. Uncle Jacob, before the war, used to get some work from them at times. They had a boy, now about the age of seventeen, who, before the war, went to one of the best schools, and he still was a big shot. He was a handsome boy, I must admit. I remembered him hanging out with the high society, and now he was working in the store, taking our order. He smiled at me, which made me blush. After we had our pictures taken, he showed a little interest in me, and I laughed to myself. I never believed it was possible. Here I was, the poor daughter of deportees, when the richest girls had run after him, and now it looked as if he really showed some interest in me. But when we left, I never gave it a second thought again. Outside we laughed and copied those girlfriends of his; if they knew what we thought of them, what they would say! Forgetting most of it, we were reminded a few days later when we returned for our pictures. Those pictures came out so lovely, and here he stood again, big, handsome, and beautiful, handing us the pictures and smiling softly to me. Later I found out that he wasn't really the one to hand out the pictures, only he had waited to see me again. He had them on top, waiting for us. But I still tried to get it out of my head. I was still so young, what did I care if a boy smiled at me? I could still remember, for many days, those nice brown eyes smiling at me, but soon I had forgotten the whole incident. I really wasn't interested in any boys, and especially not snobs. A fight for life and death was going on, and this was for me more important than anything else.

One night, we heard a quiet knock at our window. Mother looked out and there stood Salo Haberkorn, the boy I mentioned earlier who had joined the Partisans. We hadn't seen him for quite some time, and we were very happy to meet him. He, of course, was most of the time out of the ghetto wherever duty would call him. And here he was to tell us things that made our hair stand up. The partisans were well-informed of what was going on outside the ghetto. They knew everything that went on all over. He told us about the death pits of Maydanek, Treblinka, Buchehwald, and all those other gruesome, murderous camps. How well-informed he was about Auschwitz! The partisans had planted their people all over. Of course, many of those things he didn't tell us then, we were to find out later. We learned that many of the people we hated because we thought they were collaborators for the Nazis were really spies for the partisans. Many of the Miliz boys we had despised had joined that force for one purpose only, to help to the partisans. And then he told us what happened to those people taken to Auschwitz, especially those taken that fateful day from the Punkt. Those who hadn't died on the way were taken out of the wagons and another selection began, women and men separated. Everyone had to undress, their belongings taken from them. Children were taken right away to the gas chambers on huge trucks, but not before those beastly murderers robbed them of anything still useful. For instance, some of those children had beautiful long curly hair; the Nazis had good use for it. Toys and such were taken from the children, their last precious possessions before they were murdererd so gruesomely. And the screams of those children, screaming for their mothers! The agonizing cries of the mothers whose children were taken to the chambers! And then the crematorium, how it worked day and by night! There were huge storehouses filled with the possessions taken from the victims, but the Nazis had good use for even these. There one could find everything from children's clothing to all kinds of clothing, toys, and loads and loads of human hair, which was very precious for these monsters. There were even warehouses with gold and silver taken from the mouths of the victims. Those poor victims had even been robbed of their teeth so the beasts could search for gold in them. This is not even to speak of the jewelry that was the first thing the Nazis searched for. Many good-looking girls were forced to work at the brothels, but many of them finished their lives on the electric fence as they tried to escape. Those that were spared to work for that monstrous camp of death were undressed, shaved from head to foot, given prison coats, and confined to special barracks until the selection when their fate would be decided: to go to the chambers, or to stay still alive. Some were chosen for *Sondercommando,* and this was the worst task yet, for they had to work directly in the gas chambers and the crematoriums. And how diabolic those gruesome murderers worked! Some were assigned to take members of their own families to the chambers, or out of them. Some removed their own children from the gas chambers and had to take them to be cremated. Some of the victims were not even dead yet. Then there were those who found in the chambers of horror their mothers or fathers, or sisters or brothers, or other members of their kin. What evil mind could think of such gruesomeness? When the victims were taken to the gas chambers, they were told that they were going to take showers. They were given a piece of soap and were told that their clothing was to be disinfected. Some children were still hugging their beloved dolls when they were taken out of the chambers. They were cremated with them, because they wouldn't let go of that last of their precious possessions. When the victims entered the so-called shower rooms and the doors were tightly closed, they felt nothing right about it anymore. When they saw that the soap was not soap, just stones, they banged against the heavy doors of their chambers. The screams and cries were so gruesome that some of people assigned to work there went insane. Then, when the screams had faded, the doors were opened and the victims, many still alive, were taken to the crematoriums. Yes, all this Salo told us. Yes, this, and so much more, a people have done, whose hymn starts and ends, "Over all in the world!" Salo Haberkorn, this great hero of the partisans, told it all that night that was the last time I saw him. As I mentioned before, he died as the big hero he really was. This was about the end of 1942, and what we had heard made us nauseated. It was impossible to think of, it just couldn't be true. This must all be part of a bad dream. No, such just couldn't happen. But it was the naked truth, and the only hope left for us was that the world would find out about it and come to our rescue. Salo told us that wouldn't take long anymore, for America had gone to fight the Nazis, too, and the Germans now had a tough time fighting everyone. It was just a question of weeks before the war came to an end; at most, it would be a few moths. Now I know that the thoughts of our precious freedom kept us going through that life of hell. Our hope let us breathe, and we waited. Each day that passed with us still alive at the end was a winner. Freedom waved to us with all its glory.

After hearing Salo's stories of gruesomeness and horror, I lived only for the day when I could take revenge for it. One day I couldn't hold still any longer and I burst out with hate, telling my mother that I only liveed for the moment of revenge. How sweet it would taste! My eyes must have been filled with hate, for

Mother took me into her arms, caressed my hair, and said in her soft voice, "What have they done to you, *mein Liebling?* You could never do harm to a fly and now I see your eyes aglow with hatred. Don't you know that the Bible teaches us to forgive and love thy enemy?"

And my reply was, "Oh, yes, I will forgive them, I will even love them, but not until I see each of them suffer, each of them dead!" Mother's wise reply was that there was a court high above us all, and there sits the greatest judge of all, for no man can judge. She said the time would come when I would understand it all, and I would see that justice would be done. For no earthly punishment would do, no man could pay for all the gruesome crimes committed by those beasts, the superior race of Adolf Hitler. "Us Jews are a forgiving people," Mother said. "Live with it, and in the darkest hours, your life will be crowned with happiness. I know," Mother continued, "you are too young to understand it all, but wherever you go, you will always be able to find evil if you are looking for it. You grew up in a destructive and evil world, surrounded by so much evil, but keep on looking for the good and remember always the good and you will see, you will always be happy!" Oh, Mother, if you had only known how much evil stood still ahead of us! I am not so sure, but I guess you never would have taught me to hate, even then. Such were my parents, my mamale and pappale. How much I long to see them, how very much I miss them, for each page will tell my longing for them.

One day at the beginning of 1943, Mother said, "You know, it is no sense to pretend, we really don't know what is going to happen. So whatever will happen, let's go and have our pictures taken, the three of us." The day was a nice and sunny later winter day. The crocuses pushed out their heads from the disappearing snow, and spring lay in the air. The day was so promising, but deep inside was such a hurt at not being able to live the whole joy of it, all the joy for a young girl my age that spring should bring. But here we were walking along to have our pictures taken, and the good Lord only knew what was on Mother's mind. As I looked at her from aside, her good face was so wrinkled from all her worries. Her last big blow had been Cilly; we still hadn't heard a word about her.

"Tell me, Mama," I said, "what is in your mind, what are you thinking about?"

Mother sighed deeply. "Oh, nothing," she replied at first, but later, thawing out, she continued, "I was just thinking, where will we all be when this gruesome war ends?" And so, each of us with a different thought in mind, but all following the same pattern, we entered the studio of the photographer. And here he was again, the handsome boy, smiling again, not speaking a word, and I smiled back this time. We took a few pictures and one of them is still today in my most cherished possessions, always in front me. As I look each day at this picture, taken almost a quarter of a century back, it tells me a story. My so-dearly beloved ones, their dear faces, still today I can see the pain in them. It looks as though they want to tell me a story, their forfeeling of what was to come. With all those years, robbed of so many memorable things I had lived with, never has there faded the memory of their great love and devotion.

The raids on the people continued and Uncle's advice again was not to be at home at night. For his fear for my safety was the same as my parents'. Mother was so desperate. Again our nightly rounds started. At Rossner's, nothing happened, just promises each day. "Just don't fear, everything has been taken care of." But until I worked there, we knew very well that promises were worth nothing at all. But what was there to do but to wait? One night, staying in the attic, we saw the yard full of Miliz breaking into our flat. They were searching for me. After being sure that no one was home, they left, but we were warned, for we knew that the situation was already grave. We stood underneath the window shaking like leaves. My teeth must have been knocking together something awful, for Mother took me into her arms, wrapped me into a warm blanket, and tried to comfort me. As I lay on her breast I could feel the warmth of her tears falling on my hand. We were so hopeless, so desperate, and there was no help for us in sight, for our best help, Ella, was gone. I, who used to be so courageous, I broke down under this heavy burden. I wanted to continue being a child, not able to understand it all, especially how gloomy things looked at night when everything looked lost. But with the coming of the next day, I was ashamed of myself. Why did I have to show Mother my fear, just to make her more unhappy and worried? Why had I been so childish, I asked myself. How silly, for Mother had anyhow always read my mind and had always known when I pretended. A mother's heart, who could feel it? Now I know that she just pretended not to know how I felt while I went about the house singing and whistling. I thought that I fooled Mother, but who could have fooled her? Somehow, I guess, as I showed and pretended all of my courage, it gave them a little new strength, too, for they always called me their ray of sunshine. Yes, I was their last ray of happiness left, and they were my all and everything. After that night when the police came and searched for me, things were no more the same. Mother was frantic, and she wouldn't let me go anywhere anymore.

I hadn't seen any of my friends for over a week. I was hardly permitted to leave my hiding place. But we knew the the Nazis and the Miliz usually came looking at night, so I snuck out for a bit of fresh air. The days had gotten nicer with each day that passed. The beginning of spring had always been my favorite time of the year. Now that I am free, my biggest enjoyment is the spring time. Remembering back how dark and frightful those days were for me, I enjoy it now twice as much. As things quieted down a little, I left more and more during the day, escaping my place of detention for a little while. But Uncle was always behind me, warning us not to take any chances, so we tried to stay as much as possible at our hiding place. Mother just left for her few chores at the factory, and Father went to work. On his return he picked up our meager rations and after we prepared some food, we went back to our hiding place. One day Father brought the pictures that we had taken a few days before. I cried when I looked at them. How sad Mother and Father looked in them, my face shining freshness and hope, and their faces sad and forlorn. How deeply the sorrow had carved grooves into their dear faces! It was Friday evening, the time that had always been such happy time for us. And now we were sitting there in the darkness in that dreadful hiding place, reminiscing about the past and remembering those times when all of us were still been together. Mother had baked a cake during the day, and she brought a few pieces of it to our hiding place. She had been in such a hurry that the cake didn't come out right. She knew that one of my favorite cakes was honey cake, so she had whipped up one with what there was on hand. The cake was soggy and didn't rise, but to me it tasted divine. I was so grateful to Mother for having been so thoughtful. In all her rush and worry, she had still bothered herself to make me happy.

The next morning turned out to be the most beautiful day of the year, although it was still in the beginning of spring. Outside the weather was just breathtaking. Father left early for work, and Mother went as usual to the factory. When she came back, she told me to come with her to prepare some food, for, it being Saturday, the hunters usually didn't bother coming. Staturdays and Sundays were the quietest days of the week. We figured it might be safe for a few minutes to go down and prepare something to eat. I was so happy and gay to be permitted to go down a little. Maybe I would see some of my friends, maybe I would be able to go for a stroll outside in the yard—I was so happy, so excited. But soon darkness was to mar my happienss. It was early in the afternoon and we expected Daddy back any minute, when all of a sudden our next door neighbor burst in with a big scream. "Mrs. Rychner, they are coming for Lydia!" We look out the window, and there they were; the house was surrounded by Miliz and Nazis, and there was no way out for us, no hiding or running away. I did escape, but how? When we saw them there on the outside, our first thought was, what should we do? We wouldn't make it easy for them to get me. So Mother bolted the door tightly, and then bolted the door of our bedroom. We had a little round table there which was covered down to the floor. We used it to hide food from the Gestapo when they raided our home. Now we hid under that table, praying that Daddy wouldn't come home right then. When they started to break our door down, it took only a split second till the idea reached my mind. Before they entered the room, I jumped out the window. Although the place was surrounded as if they were searching for a badly wanted criminal, they didn't notice me jumping out. It seems fantastic, I know, but this is really what happened. I slipped quietly into the bakery next door, and there I hid behind the open door. I waited there, praying that no one would close the door while I stood there perspiring, pressing tightly against the door. I could get a good view of everything going on outside as well as in the bakery. A mad search was on. They looked all over, but didn't find me. I heard one of them saying to a man in the bakery that if I was hiding there they must turn me in, for if I was found there, they would get a severe punishment. But no one knew where I had disappeared to. Those hunters, there were so many of them! Every few steps, another one. Looking through that little opening behind the door, I was shuddering. All of them were out there searching for me, a little girl not even fifteen years old yet. It must have been hours, and I thought that they must have given up the search for me, but then, all of a sudden, I heard two neighbors talking to each other. "Well, they certainly weren't able to find Lydia, but too bad, for they are taking her mother instead." Oh, no, this I wasn't going to let happen. Thoughts were running wildly through my mind. I shivered. My sweet loving mama. Me they would take to the slave labor camp only, but Mama—I got all cold and shaky. And as quickly as my feet were able to carry me, I ran out. If only I could come in time, before they took my everything away from me. I ran and put myself into the hands of the Miliz, I, the very badly wanted criminal, my biggest crime having been born a Jewess. At that moment, seeing me in the arms of the Miliz, my beloved mother aged about twenty years. She screamed when she saw me coming. They had been about ready to remove her, and here I came at the last minute. "Why did you come out?" Mother kept on weeping.

And I said, "Better me than you!" She said I shouldn't have come out, that maybe Uncle could have gotten her out.

"Maybe, but if not?" I asked. Oh, Mamale, I still hear your heartbreaking cry in my ears, although so many years have passed since then. You just couldn't believe that the line had acutally come to me, your nestling, your baby! No, Mamale, I don't want to take revenge, I promise you, but this writing I hope will contribute to the justice that everyone wants!

We started to wrap up a few of my belongings, and now I wasn't able to give even a little comfort to Mother. I couldn't tell her that I'd come home soon, that I was anyhow too young still. Those were the same phrases that Ella had used that awful night when the Nazis had broken up our home. What was there to say? Nothing would ease at least a bit of our pain. Each piece of my clothing was drenched with the loving tears of my angel of a mother. And then Daddy came home. My pappale, will I ever forget the look on your poor and innocent face? Oh, never, as long as I shall live! Your dear sweet face, inflamed with helpless anger, your eyes so full of sadness and disbelief, and so full, yes, so full of never-dying paternal love. With your hardworking hands full of blisters, you stroked so very gently over my braids.

MY LIFE IN BONDAGE

And then everything, all of your sorrow broke out of you! You couldn't keep it in any longer, you didn't care anymore if they killed you or not, your life didn't mean a thing anymore. Lucky it was that only the Miliz was in the room at that time, and also that the brother of one of my previous girlfriends was among them. How scared I was that right there they would take you away because of the words, spoken in your sorrow, that you threw at them. Nothing mattered anymore, for your life was gone as far as you were concerned. And who could really blame you? Bit by bit, they had taken everything from you, and you knew so well that they weren't going to stop. You knew that the final performance was coming, that destruction was knocking at the door. And here, while you stood helplessly watching as they took the last away from you and Mother, I know that inside you something must have broken apart. Your screams must have been heard all over the ghetto—my father, whom everybody had known as one of the gentlest people on earth, never, ever did you punish me for anything, never would you raise your voice even when angry, always so quiet, always so very gentle, and here you screamed in your agony into their faces, "You murderers, you criminals, swine, and informers." To all those accusations they kept quiet; they didn't answer a word. "Where do you take her?" you screamed. "Haven't you taken enough from us already? My other two daughters, my whole possession, everything you have stolen from me, and now, for what did you come? Now you come to take away my last, my baby!" And so it went, on and on. I couldn't even stop you. And the languishing glance in your eyes, full of unshed tears!

While in hiding, I had knitted for myself some beautiful costumes and dresses. Everybody used to say that I followed Ella's footsteps with my talent and imagination. And now Mother told me I should take all those nice clothes along. I should take what my heart desired. But somehow I didn't feel like taking all of them, for I felt, somehow, that with them I would take from my parents everything they had left of me. They had always been so proud of my work.

Daddy said, "Why is she taking it all? She will come back, we will do everything, we will see everything and get you out," and to Mother he said, "won't we?" I just could see that, with each piece I put in my suitcase, a piece of Daddy's heart went, too. I told Mother to stop it, that after all, in an emergency, she could send clothes to me. Mother turned to Daddy to scold him slightly, telling him to let it go and to let me take everything I loved. All this was accompanied by cries of despair. I looked into the eyes of Srullek, the brother of one of my girlfriends, who now was in the Miliz. I asked him if he was proud of himself. He blushed and replied, "What can we do? Those are our orders. Don't you see the black hunters outside your window?" By this he meant the Nazis who were waiting outside. "Don't you think that everything he had said, they would have taken against him? I do understand his hurt, but please don't let him overdo it."

Yes, those black beasts outside the window had gotten impatient, and so we went, accompanied by a choir of screams and cries, the searching and disbelieving eyes of my friends and neighbors, those tear-glazed eyes of my girlfriend Edzia behind me, and an escort of Miliz. Behind the Miliz were those black hunters, always prepared to shoot, as we went toward the destination where the committee kept a small prison in a house. And here ended another chapter in my life. As I walked toward my prison, I made fists from my hands, holding them in my pockets while wild thoughts ran through my mind. *Oh, murderers, oh, sons of hell, how much do I hate you and always shall, you aren't even to compare with the Crusaders in your land so full of culture, as you like to call yourself—the great culture of the twentieth century! How much hate have you taught me with your culture that has only brought sorrow over my people!* While those thoughts were going around in my head, Mother held me tightly and Father carried my heavy suitcase. *Oh, yes, I shall write some day about your murders, and millions of people will read it. And they will have to hate you the way I do. Land over all, over all in the world? And it shall be a memory for me, for my children; it shall remind me always of everything so dear to me, never to be forgotten.* As we approached the place of detention where I was to stay for the time being with many others that had been caught that day, Daddy was permitted to come in with me. A few cots were put up and around were boys and girls. Some were smiling, some were weeping, and some were heartbreakingly silent. Daddy told me good-bye, and this heartbreaking moment I shall never forget; it always will be vivid in front of me. For whenever I remember this scene, it pinches like needles through my heart. My sweetheart of a father, how you squeezed me toward your heart, as if you wouldn't permit any power on earth to tear me away from you. I had never seen you cry, and even on the saddest occasions, you just couldn't cry. Sometimes Mother even told you that a little cry would do you good. But never had I seen you cry until that moment when you fell to the floor—and your cry will always be in my ears! I thought you wouldn't live through it; your sobbing followed me for years to come. And then they tore us apart. I suddenly felt paralyzed from all that had happened in those few hours. My life had changed so suddenly; fate had written a new page for me. While I was standing there unable to move, deep in my tears and sorrow, everyone touched by that scene suddenly got quiet; you could even hear the drop of a needle. And in the middle of it all, two eyes looked at me so full of understnading, so full of sadness. I looked up into eyes I had known before. I seemed slowly to awaken to reality, for I heard a nice warm voice say, "My name is Sallek Goldstein! I do hope you recognize me, Lydia!"

And all of a sudden it ran through my mind, *I know him!* "Aren't you the boy from the photographer?" I asked.

"Yes, indeed I am," he replied. *How funny life is,* I thought to myself. In all of my sorrow I couldn't think other than, here he was, Mr. Bigshot himself, and of all the places to get to know each other better, here we were in this awful place of detention. He proved right away to be a good friend. He, having come much earlier, had a cot, and he let me have it right away. Then he tried to be helpful in any way possible. This friendship with Sallek up there on the crossroad of my life was very valuable indeed. He helped me through a great many painful hours of agonizing waiting. He removed his handkerchief and wiped the tears from my face. Then he said that I should rest a little and he kept watch over me. When some wise guys—one can find them in any predicament—wanted to say anything fresh, he knew how to handle them. And then he told me how much he had wanted to get to know me better, ever since I had my first picture taken at his father's establishment. And how much, from the first moment that he had seen me, he had liked me. He said that, of all those girlfriends that he had, no one appealed to him so much as I did. When he was there when I came to pick up the pictures, he had tried to get to know me better, but my ironic smile chased him away. He had always thought about me, about how he could meet me again. He even found out where we lived, and at times he passed there with the hope of seeing me. He took out of his pocket a nice-sized picture, beautifully retouched, and it was me. "And now," he said, smiling, "of all the places to bring us together, this place here." His smile was winning, and I liked him from the first moment. His looks were like a god, so proud and untouchable, but here he was, this boy, and he cared for me. I, too, had thought about him, but had never given it too much thought, for I had too many other things on my mind, and boys were for me unimportant. But come to think of it, I really had cared a little for him. And now I could find out who the real Sallek was.

He came from one of the richest families of Bendzin, and he had a girl-friend—of course, the top of the crop. He had always what his heart desired, and only the best had been good enough for him. His parents would get him out, of this he was more than sure, and then he would get me out. He was so much nicer than those rich kids I had known. He was no snob at all. He was so well-mannered, why, he was a little over seventeen and the perfect gentleman. We liked each other right away and talked the whole night through. As we looked into the cool spring night, so full of a promising future, so hoping to get out and to go into a new future, the day started to dawn.

We were told that we couldn't leave for the Dullag at Sosnowitz before Monday, for on Sundays no transports were going—the better for us. My beloved parents went and sold whatever they were able, only to get me out. This was Sunday, the day was dawning, and through the window I heard coming from the yard tired and slurred steps. I would have recognized them out of a million, for they were so dear to me; those steps had always sounded like music to my ears, and sometimes it is as though I still can hear them, those beloved steps, telling a story of their own. As those steps came nearer, I heard a voice so dear to me. "Lydichen!" it kept on calling. As I looked through the grated window in the dusk of day, I saw my darling father—how poor and helpless he looked to me. And when he saw me, how his face lit up, so full of undying love. He called up that I shouldn't fear, that everything had been taken care of, that they had worked feverishly to get me out. And that Mama was going to Rossner's where she had an appointment, "and tonight you'll sleep again at home," he cried.

With those words and a happy gleam in his eyes, Daddy left for work, and this was the last time I saw my father, for I have never seen him again. Soon thereafter Mother came with Uncle Jacob. They brought something for me to eat. Uncle and Mother told me the same thing that Father had told me in the morning. Mother had just come from Rossner's and things were taken care of. They were confident that, before the day was up, I would come back home. My poor mamale, how strong she held herself to give me more strength so that I would be able to fight it all. What did you have to go through? I shall never know. Mother asked me what I would like to eat, so she could bring it to me. It would be good to have something proper to eat since I had hardly eaten a thing for over a day. Meanwhile, Mother had brought two loaves of bread, their own poor ration for the next week. And when Mother asked me what I wanted, I answered, "Bring me a piece of that delicious cake that you baked on Friday, almost a lifetime away." It hadn't been two days yet, but it seemed to me endless. Mother asked why I wanted that cake, it hadn't even raised, but I answered the same as I had told her on Friday when she first brought it into our place of hiding—for me, no delicacy would ever taste better. Mother smiled so wisely, and she promised to bring me some of it.

Now when I look back at it all, it looks to me as if heaven wanted to grant me a last meal prepared by the hands of my so-dearly beloved ones, just as when one goes to the gallows, his last meal is also granted. Mother assured me that she would be back and bring me what I desired, but suddenly in the middle of it all, Uncle grabbed impulsively at his breast pocket and took out two pictures. And then suddenly Mother gave me six copies of the pictures we had taken a few days before. Then Uncle said that it was foolish of him to give me those pictures, for they hoped to get me out, but just in case, on the back of those pictures he had written in dedication, codelike, the addresses of my two brothers and of Uncle Heinz, his and Mother's brother in Israel. As he gave those pictures to me, he said, "You are so courageous, Lydia. When this awful war comes to an end, I am confident that you will be the one to live through it. Just remember one thing; stay always as clean and innocent as you are, for courage you have been given in the cradle. Just remember the one thing, for freedom it is worth fighting for. If anything should happen to us, just remember our great love for you. Remember our best regards and love for everybody near to us."

How came Uncle just then to tell me that? How came he to believe so much in my survival? Wasn't this, too, a sign from heaven? There I stood, the youngest, giving a vow that if things really should turn out bad, and if it really was like Uncle said, that I wouldn't only tell those near to us, but I shall tell the whole world about it. Uncle still tried to tell me of certain things in life: that I shouldn't trust boys, and that I should always be careful. "You are now a little lady, and a good-looking one at that; be careful that no one takes advantage of you. For you are still too young to understand the earnest of life." After giving me a short lesson on anything and everything, they left, Mother with the words, "I'll be right back." I never saw my beloved mother again.

Suddenly things started to liven up. While my parents fought for my freedom on the outside, not sleeping for one minute as they sold most of their possessions for me, their nestling, my fate was decided by somebody else. As long as one was still at the prison in the committee building, it wasn't too tough to get out. Once one left for the next destination, the pre-step to camp, it became harder and harder to get free. It was only natural that my parents worked so feverishly for my release. Having me still in the city was their greatest comfort. But things did not work out so well as my dear ones had expected, for as soon as Mother left, there came a huge furniture truck and we were chased like wild animals into it. Sallek was the first one to go, and I feared that now I would have to face everything alone. When I was to go down, I could hardly budge with that heavy suitcase. I think it must have been heavier than me. While I was being chased down into the truck, hardly able to drag the suitcase, I heard a heartbreaking cry, and I looked up into the tear-drenched face of Uncle Jacob and my cousin Sally. "Good-bye, Lydia!" they cried. Oh, Uncle, did you give my unforgettable, my dearly beloved parents my last regards? I am sure you did. And you will always be remembered by me, you and your wife Auntie Ester and little Pinjush, my darling cousin. You, too, were swept away by this inferno, you I never saw again. Always will I love all of you!

As I was pushed into the furniture truck, the last thing that stuck in my memory was the heartbreaking cry of Uncle Jacob, the cry of anguish which he felt for his beloved sister, my mother. As the doors of the truck closed, it went like needles through my heart, for the gate to freedom had closed behind me. I did not know that it would be over two years before I saw freedom again. Those years were like a thousand years for me.

Our truck hurried toward our gloomy destination, Sosnowitz and the filthy Dullag. There we had to wait outside for hours until they gave us our place. The place was filled up with girls and boys sharing our fate. At last we were given our room. "Room"—how silly of me to express it that way, for "stables" would have been too good an expression for what we faced. The girls were separated from the boys, and my foolish dream to stay with Sallek burst apart like a soap bubble. I was confined on the third level of that filthy place. Each room had four levels, and on each ledge, about fifty girls had to make their home. That little pigpen where I was seated held about two hundred girls. One can easily imagine the confusion. I felt up there in my filthy confinement like hope was slowly starting to dwindle. All kinds of noxious insects crept around us, putting on a command performance. In this darkness of our young lives, we cried, but at times we even joked and laughed. Yes, out of our grave desperation, we found it worthwhile sometimes to laugh. However unbelievable it might sound, we had lost all our human touch already and had no minds of our own anymore. Whoever has ever seen people laugh out of their desperation has probably seen the most tragic laugh of life, for there couldn't be anything sadder than this.

While confined in my place, I made friends with a girl a year older than I; her name was Topka, and we became very close friends from then on. Luckily, most of the girls I made friends with in the place later on came to camp with me. If misery ever was born, it must have been born in those walls under that roof, for here I faced the first big misery of my life. My yearning for my parents was so strong in me that I thought I wouldn't be able to stand it, but as the days passed and I got to know many of my new friends, I somehow tried to get my yearning a bit out of my system. Anyhow, the Nazis hardly left us time to think. There were roll calls, one after another, every time another fat pig arrived to take stock of us animals, selecting those of us they thought would do the most work for them. Of course, they had to pay the high officials a certain amount of money for us, but doesn't everybody who buys animals have to pay for them? I soon figured out that we weren't considered people anymore.

As I looked about that gloomy place, I met a girl I had known in Bendzin, for when we used to visit Uncle's house in Poland, there were always girls around us, eager to play with Cilly and me. Cilly and I must have seemed to them like we were from another planet, us speaking German and them Polish or Yiddish. When we came to stay in Poland, some of those girls became friends with us. Here now, looking around, I met some of those girls. It was kind of a comfort to me to meet some girls I had known outside this prison. Of course, we kept close together from then on, hoping to come to camp together. I was very worried not to part from Topka, for we had become good friends already. She came from Kattowitz and knew perfect German, so we had a lot in common. From Sallek at times someone would smuggle some little notes to my room. His notes said that he thought in a day or two he might be able to get back home, that his parents had taken care of everything already. No matter what, he would see that I got out, too. But as the days passed, his notes were less hopeful, and one day he wrote that he thought he would have to go to camp if things didn't speed up back at home. He had been lucky so far not to have been selected, for he was a tall and good-looking fellow. I wrote how much I wanted to meet him again, but out in the free world. One day I had a funny feeling and I asked him to please send me a picture. At first he sent me a little one, him riding on a bicycle, but I wanted a big picture to remember him by, so he sent me down a nice big picture, on the back signed, "To my Lydia, a big picture from your Sallek." This picture I still have today. A little later, as we came back from getting our food, I saw Sallek for a second from afar. There he stood, waving to me, always with his warm smile, as if his lips were forming the words, "Don't give up the ship!" I never saw him again, for the same day he was taken to Buchenwald, where he was later murdered by the Nazis. All of that I found out much later. One of his friends found me after the war and told me everything about him. Sallek had asked him to tell me of his great admiration and love for me. I was shocked, of course, to learn of his death. Did I really love him? Now I know that it was only infatuation, for I have found the most wonderful man on earth and I really could have never loved anyone the way I love my husband Jack, for he is the fulfilment of all my deams. And Sallek? He wasn't really my kind of people. He would have probably been much happier with a girl of his kind, but it is still a sweet memory.

Those few friends I had made, out of fear that we might get parted, had written some dedications into my book of autographs. It made me feel good to have found such a nice bunch of girls. One day a Pole came underneath the window and whispered up to us that, if we wanted to send some letters home, he would be happy to mail them for us. How could this good man have done this? His own life was at stake. But one still could find some good and kind people in this jungle of bestiality, for those letters really came to their destinations, one by one. I wrote to my beloved parents, telling them what most of my friends thought: that we were too young for the camp and that no one wanted us and that we would get our return home. For I was always left with those other young kids after a transport was put together. Together with me were kids from the ages of twelve and up. I dreamed for that moment to come when I could be reunited with my mother and father.

One evening my name was called out in my room. As I looked up, there stood a cute girl about my age, with braids, and she spoke to me in German. She brought me the best regards from my parents; she had seen them the previous day before she was caught. She asked me if I realized how very much my parents loved me. How foolish a question. Who would have know their parents better than I did? She told me that my parents were busy working on my release but, after they received the letter where I expressed my belief that I would be allowed to come back home, they were now waiting feverishly for my return. The girl told me that, when I was taken away without a chance to say good-bye, Mother wanted to die. She could hardly pull herself together, and Father went about like a ghost. He wouldn't talk to anyone, just kept on brooding to himself, but the thought of my return put a new shine into his eyes. How well I could imagine all of this, as if I were next to them and seeing it with my own eyes. As we walked down the dark hallway, Frieda—this was her name—told me all of this and so much more. I felt right away very close to her, as if she had brought to me a piece of my home. She was also a deportee, from Czechoslovakia. Frieda was later together with me in camp. She was also among those few fortunate ones to live through this hell. If I hadn't written that I would come back home, maybe my parents would have succeeded in getting me back—*if, if,* the word that made such a big difference. Maybe it was meant to be, maybe it was my luck. Again, maybe if I had been home, I would have been able to persuade my parents to go into hiding and maybe they would be alive today. This was my fate, and I can do no more than wonder.

Two days later came a big fat swine with two of the most vicious, murderous eyes one can imagine, even in one's worst nightmares. He bought anything he could put his filthy fingers on. He got us wholesale, or as rejects, for very little money. As I looked into those vicious eyes of our boss to be, I was shaking. The thought of it made me shudder. My throat was dry as straw. When they asked me about my age, I wasn't able to even open my mouth. He shouted to me to answer clearly or else. *Well, Lydia this is the end of it,* I thought to myself. I shuddered, thinking of the future. No, there was no future for me anymore. *I might as well be dead,* I thought. Luckily, most of the girls I had made friends with were coming with me. Even Topka was chosen among this group; how much it eased my pain. We were loaded into special compartments in the train which was to bring us to the slave labor camp. Of course we were heavily guarded and in front of our train compartments were huge signs with the words: *"Achtung, hier fahren Juden!"* (Caution, here are Jews!) Heaven forbid, some people might not know, and might stop by us—how contagious, what disaster. Those idiots ran past our train like the plague was on their trail. From what did they run? A few Jewish children. When the train stopped on its way at certain stations, the people around, those men, women, and their children, would spit at us. We heard their vicious talk: "Pfui, how it stinks here, one would know without the sign that here are Jews." Today they don't know about it at all; it has elapsed from their memory—no, it just couldn't be, it just isn't the truth. Then, no one would have passed our train without spitting at us and insulting us, but today no one seems to remember such things. Those filthy fascists. One of the girls started getting hysterical. She started to scream, "One day the war will end and I will take those little beasts from them, like they took my little brother from my mother's arms, and I will smash their little heads, just like they have done with our children!" Topka went toward the girl and begged her not to speak such evil. She told her to cry, that it would make her feel better. I didn't take it to heart. Used to the German insults since my early childhood, I felt like it really was not me they meant.

And so we went on, with insults, evil faces, and grimaces, all that on the way to our destination. At one station we stopped for a few minutes, for the machine had to be filled up. *Well, what difference does it make?* I said to myself. *So there will be a few more insults, a few more evil faces.* As the train stopped, I looked up and saw the sign, Gleiwitz. I couldn't believe my eyes. Gleiwitz, my birthplace, the place I had spent the most wonderful years of my life so far. I wept to myself, and as I cried I felt as though I was all by myself, for the girls kept quiet as if they understood what it meant for me. My happy memories came back to me. I saw myself as a little girl again; those nicer days of my life were returning, those happy days when all of us were still together: my two brothers, my two sisters, and my dearly beloved parents. I saw how the table was set for our holidays, and it was Passover, my brother telling the *Manischtanah,* and later on Cilly and me searching for the *Afikoman.* That small piece of matzo was hidden from us, and when we found it, we demanded from Daddy anything that we wanted. Yes, Passover was the holiday I had always liked the most, when everything started to bloom, the holiday I myself had named the holiday of hope. How very joyous was this, and all those other holidays we had always spent all of us together. Now it was Passover again, and I remembered how Cilly and I would go and pick Daddy up from the temple. As all of those wonderful memories arose in front of me, the wheels of the train started to move again and I traveled with my sorrowful eyes, still the eyes of a child, into the darkness of fear, out of the city which harbored my most precious memories. And slowly we came close to our destination, our hell for the next two years.

When the train stopped, we were pushed outside, and I saw the sign, *"Graeben Kreis Schweidnitz"—You are now in the camp of Graeben, near the town of Schweidnitz.* Although it was still daylight, we saw no living soul around, except for our guards, of course. One, two, one, two, and three, so we kept on marching into the camp. Good-bye, beautiful freedom, good-bye birds in the trees—who knows when I will ever be able to enjoy you again? I felt like I was leaving a piece of my life on the outside. Why did I have to be so enslaved? Why was freedom for others to enjoy? What awful crime did I commit in my young life, to have to be punished with the worst of all punishments? My heart was bleeding and crying for freedom as we passed through the big gate which cut off everything I yearned for.

As those gruesome gates close behind me, a new chapter of my life began: my life in bondage. As we entered this awful place, which from now one was to be my home, I thought right away that life here would be unbearable. First of all, our welcoming committee consisted of the camp eldest. This didn't mean she was actually the oldest person, but she was the woman in charge of us, and she was a German. Then there was the Jew eldest; the same with her. She was by no means the eldest, only in charge of us, with the difference that she was also a Jewess. Just looking at those two made our hearts stand still. The German woman told us that, for the time being, we were to go to our barracks and that discipline had to be kept under all circumstances. She told us that if we obeyed the camp regulations, life wouldn't be too bad. And to our luck be it said, she was not the worst yet. Although keeping stict order, she didn't do it in a too bad way. Or if she did, she didn't show it, and did it in a very smart way. Anyhow, after she checked over our hair, I asked her if I was permitted to keep my hair, for to lose my braids would have been too much. I promised that I would keep them neat and clean, and to my great joy she agreed on it. And so we were confined to our quarters. In the beginning sixteen girls were to be in one room, sixteen feet by sixteen feet. Of course the bunk beds were two levels high, and had sacks which we had to fill with straw for mattresses. My room, No. 57, was named the *Kinderstube*, for there were girls mostly my age in it. Only one older girl came into the room by mistake, but we liked her because she was such a lovable old maid. As the oldest, we right away agreed that she would be our room eldest. The room eldest was the one in charge of keeping the room in order. She was to watch that the rations were shared equally, and she was in charge of all other miscellaneous details. It was by no means easy to have that job, for there were girls from all walks of life, and some of them just wouldn't take orders. When the Jew eldest entered our room together with our camp eldest, we had to salute them, and there again it was the duty of the room eldest to start the salute by saying, *"Achtung."* She had to say how many Jewesses were present, or if some were at work, she had to mention that number. If some were at the restroom, that had to be mentioned, too. As we were to salute them for our first time, our room eldest choked on those words. The camp eldest asked us if there wasn't one among us who knew German, and the girls right away pointed to me. It was soon decided that I had to be the room eldest, and what agony I had to go through with this job, I shall tell slowly. Soon we had to go out on roll calls and the Jew eldest got us acquainted with her. We soon found out that almost the whole personnel in this grave consisted of her relatives. There were her two sisters, who did most of the loafing. Then she had some cousins and some friends; this woman didn't care for anyone in this camp. Her mean welcoming speech, which I better not repeat right now, was very degrading. Then we were put up into groups and given the places we would work from now on. There was, first of all, the flax comb department, to which I was confined with most of my roommates. Then there was the department of the living death, for there the material we had to work with was washed in awful humidity, in an inhuman heat. Those girls that had to work in that department had to go down into boiling kettles and pile the flax for washing after we sent it up to them in bundles. Most of the girls working there under the most horrible conditions died of tuberculosis, always hurried, always rushed, with always the whip in the back of them—"You dirty Jewess, can't you work quicker?"—and those girls working with the last bit of strength. After that place the flax went to the ovens to dry out, and from there it was packed to be sent to the spring mills. What cheap workers they had in us. No doctors, for if anybody had an accident, too bad; if any of us got seriously ill, well, this was too bad, too. The nurse was the cousin of our Jew eldest and she knew next to nothing. But I guess that she really, under the circumstances, wasn't the worst yet, one just had to know how to get along with her. In order to stay alive, we just had to pray for our good health. I was put at first at the flax comb machine, which really was a highly dangerous piece of machinery. But what difference did it make, wasn't everything there highly dangerous? Because the flax at our place was coming straight from the fields, the dust in the factory was terrific, and at times it was so bad we weren't able to see one another. After we finished the day's work, we looked like miners. At times girls broke down udner the heavy burden. Then a girl much older than the rest of us was chosen to be our group eldest. She was very sweet and kind and how many times would I admire her beauty. Even those Germans appointed to watch over us would turn their heads when she was coming. She had to run about the place and watch that everything was in order. Then we got to know a few of our foremen, who had been appointed by the Germans to watch over us. And then, of course, each group had its manager. At first, we were divided into three shifts, but soon it had changed into two, which meant twelve hours of work daily. Our foremen were gentile boys from Czechoslovakia and Belgium. Most of them were very kind and considerate, but those managers were devils in person. In the beginning they didn't show it so much, but there were two Belgians whom I especially will always remember. The older one was kind, but the younger one was much much kinder. His name was Alfred. Although I have never found out where he is today, I shall always be grateful in my heart for the sunshine he tried to give to us girls in that dark time of our lives. He made himself look stupid so we could have a little laugh at times. Once he saved my life, which I shall mention later on. I saw him wiping tears from his eyes, which I didn't understand then, for he told us that a speck of dust had gotten into his eyes.

Back at the barracks each of us was given a food card. This card entitled us to two and a half ounces of bread daily, which, of course, was withdrawn in any case of misbehavior. Then we were given inoculations, which we were told were to protect us from contagious diseases. I soon found out that they served another purpose, namely to stop us girls from our development. The end of it was that at first almost all of us got sick, but soon we were used to it, and soon we forgot that we really were girls. Somehow it was as though we were pieces of machinery. If we were caught at the smallest wrong thing, the result was severe punishment, like, for instance, having one's hair shaved off. One day two girls were hung from their hair in the midle of the yard. The memory of this still makes me sick. They had to stay in the rain, hardly dressed, to teach all of us a lesson in case we tried doing anything funny. After the girls were taken in, they were half dead.

One day we got permission to write home. We could write and get mail aproximately once a month. We were told it would be once a week, but the most one really could receive was once a month. Those letters that we were permitted to write hardly ever came to their destinations. I reveived in all that time only two postcards and one package from home, and my parents weren't even that lucky, for they received just one postcard. But from Ella at her camp I did receive more postcards. Once she even sent to me some clothing which she said she didn't have any use for. Thanks to Alfred, the Belgian, I have those postcards still today in my most cherished possessions. Later on, I shall translate them from German one by one. In the camp where Ella was, she was secretary and with her was a cousin of my Jew eldest, so Ella asked my Jew eldest to take a little bit of care of me, and in return she would keep an eye on her cousin. Well, she promised it to Ella, but she was only pretending, for she was the one who ordered my braids to be cut off, although I always kept them as clean as possible. On top of that, I had permission to keep them. Oh, how I hated her for this, and I vowed to myself never to forget it, for as they cut off my braids, there went a piece of my own life, all my innocent childhood, my most precious of all memories. When they cut into them I felt like they cut through my body, and my tears fell constantly. I will never forget the sorrow, which meant so little to her but meant so very much to me. I remembered how I had always been teased with them at home, how my two brothers had pretended to cut them off, and how Mother scolded them to stop teasing me! And now all the precious memories that were plaited into my braids had been cut together with them. But life still went on, if one really could still call this life. Soon I had much greater worries than my braids.

I had been known among my friends as the girl with the beautiful red lips. One day a girl burst into our room and told me to hide, that an inspection was checking to see if any of us used lipstick. How ridiculous! Why would we use lipstick? And where from would we have it? In camp was a girl that was mute and she, too, had nice red lips, so when the inspector of those pigs came to us, they grabbed this innocent girl and shaved her hair off, for punishment, as they would say. When the girl came in to tell me to hide, I was flabbergasted. "How can they do this?" I asked.

"Don't ask any questions, just keep out of sight for now," she replied, so whenever an inspection came, I feared because of my lips. Those lips that had earned since my early childhood so many compliments now meant great fear and danger to me.

In my room I had quite a nice bunch of girls. We shared our happiness and sorrow and still at times had our laughs, for instance, when Hinda, also from Bendzin, started some of her rough jokes about the Germans. She was so wild that at times we just had to laugh at her antics. Her bunk was up on the second level and the day didn't pass when she wouldn't fall down on the girl underneath. With her around, the place really did liven up at times. She was very temperamental and once was caught by the Jew eldest writing a letter home. Somehow, we never asked how, she stayed in contact with home. And when she was caught, she kicked and called names, and somehow got out of it, how, I shall never understand. Even the Jew eldest was speechless from that outburst of temperament. Across from Hinda's bed was another young girl also sleeping on top, and this girl had a worse habit then Hinda, for hers was a wet habit and a not too comfortable one, especially for the girl underneath her. At night we would hear the cries of anguish from the party concerned—which from our side meant an outburst of laughter. How sad it really was, I do understand fully now. Poor girls in a lost world, grabbing at any piece of straw to have some fun in the darkness and to drown our sorrow. Of course, not all of my roommates were ideal, but we tried somehow to get along. There were fights, too, and at times vicious accusations, but this was life and one had to take it in stride. Next to my cot was Topka, and once we even had a bad fight. She threw in my face how silly I was to dream about Sallek, how silly I was to think that he would want me, for she knew him and his girl came from one of the richest homes. As she said, he probably had just been making fun of me. Well, those remarks nearly ended our friendship forever, for I was able to stand anything but vicious criticism. Later on, we did make up and stayed the best of friends until the end.

Tuesday was the day we received mail from home, for although we were allowed to write only that often, the mail could come anytime, but it was kept in the office until Tuesday. Sometimes if we were lucky enough, we would get twice a month mail. Each Tuesday our hearts beat in suspense, and we waited anxiously to hear our names called out. From Ella I did receive mail quite a few times, but from my parents, very seldom. The first card that I received from Ella was dated April 29, 1943. And here is what she wrote:

"My dear Lydia! Impatiently I have waited to hear from you; just now I had a card from home and right away I am writing to you. Dear Lydia! Forget everything that has been, and now do everything as you are told and fulfill your obligations so that those over you will be satisfied. And you will see that you won't have it too bad. Mama wrote that you could keep your braids. Also in our camp those that had their hair clean could keep them. Stay clean, but one thing I beg of you, never write anything sad home. Ask your camp eldest to please permit you to write to me. Since you aren't writing from home anymore, the mail from home sounds so different. I do hope that you will keep brave and strong, just like you have always managed to do. I hope that you will show your talents, for I bring with mine much happiness to the girls out here. Best regards to your Jew eldest, your loving sister, Ella."

As I read the first card, it brought once again my dear ones close to me, and I cried a lot. I must have read this card a thousand times. One Tuesday I heard my name called out, and I held the precious writing of my dearly beloved mother in my hand. The date was April 21: "My beloved Lydia! We've received your card and had at the same time one from Ella, so we had a Passover surprise. I am writing your address to Ella so that she can write to you, too. They gave me permission to write you, too. My beloved Lydi-baby! I am packing our possessions, for on the twenty-second, we have to be out with our furniture. We are going to a very strict ghetto, Steinstrasse 10. All of our neighbors have different addresses. I am trying to change mine. I will send you a package and also one to Cilly. Cilly has been found; she is in Blechhammer. To Ella I will send a package, too. I will have to get a permit from the committee. I am all broken up about the new flat, I will write to you more on Tuesday. We are not permitted to take our furniture along with us. We can only take our beds and some linen, a few clothing and dishes. Oh, Lydia! Couldn't we come to you? I could be a cook or gardener and Daddy is a good painter. To the Dullag I didn't send you anything, for you were supposed to come back home. I still have to wash, for there where we will be is no water. In one room will have to live two to three families. Maybe I will be able to move together with Uncle Jacob. But it is not too sure yet. The best would be if we could come to you. Mail follows. Dear child! About your braids, keep them clean diligently so you'll have it good. The heartiest regards and a million kisses from your loving parents."

As I finished this card, my hands were shaking. I couldn't believe that here I really held one of my most precious possessions in my hands, my mother's writing, and once again my undying love for them took hold, and it did hurt so very much. What was going on back at home? What did those monsters do to them, that Mother was begging me to help them to come to camp? I was so desperate, I felt as if my hands were tied behind me. What could I do? I was in the jungle of nowhere, with those beasts around us day by night, just waiting for us to do anything to displease them so they could grab their prey, ready to tear it to pieces. One thing at least had brought some comfort, the thought of Cilly. So they found her and she was alive. Although saddened by Mother's plea to come to camp, the thought of Cilly being well gave me new strength to live. And I had been given new hope. Somehow the feeling approached me that this miserable war would soon come to an end and we all would once again be happily reunited.

With my job as room eldest, things weren't so easy. There were those girls that, under no circumstances, would take any order, especially from a younger girl, although I always pleaded with them not to make it harder on me than it was already. Some of the girls would help me, but things got so out of my hands that I went to the Jew eldest and pleaded with her to release me from that job. I told her that I couldn't go on any longer. Her reply was that I would have to inform on those who disobeyed my orders, which, of course, was out of the question. So I just had to suffer the consequences, and a great many times my bread ration, which was meager enough, was withdrawn for the day. Well, I just had to go on for the time being and wait till I could find her in a better mood when I could ask her again to release me of that duty which made life so miserable. With our daily ration of bread we received some *Ersatzcoffe,* as well as some meager soup, and if we were lucky, we would come for the soup when the kettle was almost empty so we could have a few pieces of potatoes in the thin soup left. With those potatoes, we could make, with the spoonful of jam we were given for Sunday, a nice paste and we ate it as a bread spread, which satisfied our hunger a bit. We were surprised the day we arrived at camp when those girls that were there ahead of us had come running and grabbed the soup from our hands because we weren't able to swallow it. We said then that we would rather starve to death than touch that goo. We very soon changed our tune and now when new arrivals came, we waited for them to throw their food away so we could have it. But as far as the food was concerned, it got even worse with each day. And with the food getting less in quantity and worse in quality, our boss, that fat swine, gave a new order to get more work from us, and with this the twelve hour shifts started. With that, all kind of new arrangements were made, which from the rumors we heard, made our hair curl. Rumors went around that our hair would have to be shaved. How disgraceful for us that those men at the factory would see it, or those other men that worked on the outside. But in the meantime we were ordered to wear babushkas like nuns, so anyone could recognize from afar that we were prisoners. Anybody who disobeyed would right away get their hair shaved. Beside this, we had to cut holes in our clothing and sew underneath yellow stars of David with the inscription, *"Jude."* Then our clothing was checked, so that we wouldn't be in any position ever to escape. Across our barracks, which were closed off by fences, were Russian prisoners of war. They worked at times together with us, but to talk to one another was strictly prohibited. Some of them were kind, and there were also some mean ones among them. One old soldier I remember so vividly—he was always so kind to us girls, and when he saw when we were mistreated, I noticed tears running down his face. At times when we worked together and weren't watched closely, he told us about his home in a melancholy way. I soon found out that those tough-looking men, on whose lips one could hardly see a smile, had hearts and feelings, too. When he spoke aobut his Volga River, it was as though he spoke about a tender child. His eyes would get a dreamy look and he would say that he wished, just once more, to see his Volga again and then he would be ready to die.

One day as I came back from the factory this letter was waiting for me: "Lichtewerden, May 1, 1943. My beloved Lydi! All of the girls who have relatives in your camp wanted so badly to write a few words, so our camp eldest gave us permission to write on a sheet of paper, for on a postcard there would have been too little room." After mentioning all the names, Ella wrote, "Tomorrow we will have a little show at our camp. I was busy today preparing everything. We are playing raid and the way I was caught. Of course I am sure that my firm will get me out and that I will be home. Do you remember how long it took me to get ready? And how Mrs. Goodman said that I shouldn't be too sure of myself. At the end of the play we all take a ride under the hill. (Under the hill was a slum-like neighborhood in Bendzin.) Our holidays I spent all right. And because I wouldn't eat any bread, I am sending to you my ration. Please write if you get it. We had some nice days already. Last Saturday we did some exercises out in the fresh air. Although I haven't done any exercises for a great many years, it went just wonderfully. What work did you get? What do you do in your spare time? Is your camp a new one? Write home only gay cards, for since you left, the letters from Mama are awful. And on top of it, we didn't know for over three weeks where they had taken you. And in the committee they didn't know where Cilly was, until I wrote personally to them. And imagine, after four days, I got an answer that Cilly is in Blechammer. I sent the message right away home and now I haven't heard from home for quite some time. They had to leave the flat at home, and have to go to the Kamionkas. (The Kamionkas was one of the very strict ghettos.) There they have to live three families in one room. To Cilly I shall send, through the forms that they sent to me, some regards. How many girls are there with you? And why came there so late news from you? I want to finish my writing, and hope that by now you've gotten used to the camp life. Be always happy, but not so wild, and be very careful at work. The heartiest regards and kisses, your sister, Ella."

Those cards and letters that kept coming from Ella gave me always new strength and vigor. They kept me going. It was just like fuel for a machine. I don't know how I would have taken those first months in bondage without them. They were always so full of hope and life, the way I always remembered Ella. And what an awful death was meant for her! What have those awful monsters done with so great a people?

One day new arrivals came to our camp and among them was very young girl. I think she must have been about thirteen years old. When we heard her story, the way she had parted from her mother, we felt awful. This poor child, what must she have suffered? She told us that after she and her mother were taken to Auschwitz, she was taken from her mother and put, along with many other children, on the truck which went to the gas chambers. With all of those screams still on her mind, she started weeping as she told us all of this gruesomeness: how they had torn the children brutally from their mothers and the awful choir of cries and screams of their beloved ones and the children begging to let them go back to their mothers. Before they undressed for the chambers, a few good-looking girls were taken out, and she was among those. After they waited for an OK to see if they were doomed to die or to pass, she was taken among a group of healthy looking girls, for she was a tall girl and had said that she was fifteen years old. While waiting, she heard that the transport where her mother was had gone to the chambers. Whenever I looked at that girl, I felt that the world had come to an end. And I thought that it might as well. What were we still in for? What would be the end for us all? What were they going to do to my parents? If the war didn't come to an end soon, who knew if any of us would stay alive? And here in all of those hopeless thoughts of mine, a new ray of sunshine came through, for there again came a letter from Ella. I had written to her in my deep sorrow that they cut my braids, and Ella, knowing how much those braids meant to me, how deeply my life was woven into them, here came her reply: "My beloved Lydi! Lichtewerden. Your postcard written April 30, postmarked May 7, arrived today, May 8, 1943. So quickly they have taken your whole pride, your beautiful braids from you? I know what they meant to you and am myself heartbroken over it. Was your hair really so bad? You had always clean hair. Well, now that it is all over, don't think about it anymore. Maybe there was something awful meant for you that has gone with the braids. Your hair will grow again, you're still so young. Haven't we lost in the past the few years much, much more? How did you feel, for instance, when you passed in the train your homestead Gleiwitz? Dear Lydi! By this time you've probably received a little package from me; I will try to send you some more. Ask your camp eldest to permit you to write to me on each writing day. I am not getting mail from home whatsoever. But this is all because of their moving. Don't worry about it, soon you will get mail, I am sure. I will send you a few things that I can do without. Be very economical and take good care of your clothing. Those pieces you have sent to me to camp, I didn't wear them for quite some time. Now I am sending them to you. Everything that I am sending will be written on the inside of the carton. Let everything be to your good heath. That you won't write home about your braids is very wise. Lydilein, don't be sad, take everything in stride. Your ever loving sister, Ella."

Together with me in the room was a girl I had known ever since we came to Bendzin. Her name was Fella Shayer. She had lived not far from Uncle Jacob. I always liked her, for she was such a pretty and quiet little thing, and here in camp, being together in one room, we had become good friends. Fella was all the time so very worried, for her father had been taken away from them when she still was at home. On that awful day at the Punkt, he had appendicitis, and they never saw him again. She was the only child and after that, her mother was her whole life. All of her thinking was about her mother. What would they do with her? She wasn't able to think about anything else. From her mother came almost regular mail under the circumstances, and then all of a sudden, the mail stopped; all of her postcards went unanswered. One day, one of her cards came back marked "address unknown." That meant only one thing, that her mother had been deported. Poor kid, she wouldn't speak one word, but all of the time she brooded to herself. One day she got a high temperature and when I went into the sickroom to see her, a little of her consciousness had gone. She kept asking me if any mail had come from her mother. When I asked the nurse if it really was as bad as it looked, she nodded her head and said that Fella had brain fever. To cheer her up, I told her stories about how I had heard from my sister that her mother was in a camp nearby and that she would see her for sure very soon, but I think that I got never through to her, for she lived in another world already, a world where she was with her mother already. She told me, with a feverish gleam in her eyes, that Mother was with her now, and how very happy she was. She asked me how I liked her, and told me that we should take good care of her mother, not let her work at the factory too hard. She said that now that she had no appetite, her mother could have all of her ration and that I should look to it that she got it. She asked if I had noticed the beautiful flowers that Mother had cut especially for her. With this she pointed to a glass filled with paper flowers. For a few days Fella was delirious, but one day when I came to see her, she looked much better, and it looked as though she was getting back to her own self again. She smiled as she saw me entering, and said, "I must have said a lot of foolish things, I guess." When I left the next day for work, I was so happy at the knowledge that Fella was getting better, it made me want to sing. Although we knew that things weren't all well with her yet, we hoped that her youth would soon bring her to her feet again, and that her recovery was on its way. She couldn't afford to be sick too long, for if the inspection showed up and saw a record of too long a sickness they might deport her to Gross Rosen, which was like Auschwitz, the concentration camp for our district. After we returned from work that day, I couldn't run quickly enough to get my soup and go in to see Fella. While I waited there in line, I heard the camp eldest saying to our secretary, "Get ready the death certificate." My heart started beating rapidly. Who had died? Most of the girls I knew weren't that sick, and then I heard her spelling the name, Fella Shayer. I just couldn't get over it. I just wouldn't believe it. I begged our Jew eldest to please let me see her again, but no one would let me. As I stood outside the barracks so that the air would straighten out my mind, I saw the hearse approaching with the inscription "Gross Rosen" on it. And then I saw them carry out a little bundle in a blanket, my sweet litle friend Fella. *What have they done to you?* I asked myself. Why wouldn't they let me in to see her once more? Was she really dead? One more great mystery which surrounded the Nazi culture, with all its horror. *Good Fella!* I cried to myself.

It seemed to me that, whenever I was really down, there would always come something from Ella to cheer me up. She was the one who gave strength to us all, but there was no one who could give her any hope. Sweet sister of mine, how much pretending she did in her mail. And I grabbed any ray of hope that I could hold onto. Now I realize fully how much was written between her lines. I am so grateful to her that she never let us down. Once again in all my misery came this card, which broke on me like a bombshell. Could such a thing really happen in this darkness of our time? And here are the words:

"My beloved Lydi! Lichtwerden, May 17, 1943.

"I am writing now in a great hurry. Imagine, tomorrow morning at six, I am going to the train station and together with the camp eldest, as well as the Jew eldest, I'll go to Sosnowitz to settle a few things. Only this evening have I known that I am going for sure. They have no idea about it at home. I received through the committee a package from home, with cake and sugar. So much is happening at home that they are in no condition to write. But don't worry about it. The sister of our cousin wrote that everything is at home all right. Dear Lydia! I do hope that by now you will be used to it all. Just don't lose your courage and you will see that everything will be all right. Just keep good watch for your health, and be always happy and gay, just like you used to be. Please write something about your work. What are you working at? How many girls are in your camp? This month is Cilly's birthday. Well, I have to finish, for I am already restless about tomorrow's journey. Many kisses and good wishes, your loving sister, Ella."

Yes, to be careful about my health, those were her words. Always about my health. This was the most important factor in the fight for survival. But how could one stay healthy? Between the danger of those machines in the factory, undernourishment, hunger, and cold constantly with us was bad enough, and then they put certain medicines into the food and you had no way of knowing it, or they gave shots, and you had no way of knowing what they really were. One day a few young girls were taken to the sickroom, and I was among them. We were given shots. I remember everything moving in the room and then I fell into a deep faint. I don't know what those were for; they just kept on saying they were vitamins. Well, you had two choices about it. You could believe it, or you couldn't believe it. But I soon did find out that those were much less than vitamin shots, for whoever heard of getting shots in the back for vitamins? But what was there to do but pray that nothing would happen to us? Anyhow, the place where the shot was given started to swell, and a few days later an awful abcess formed. The agony of it will never be forgotten. Going to work more dead than alive, I was afraid to tell about it, for the picture of Fella always stayed with me. But the place became infected, and I went around half unconscious. The girls told me that I should tell the nurse, but at that time the nurse was sick and there was no one else to go to. The pain became so severe that I didn't care anymore if I died or not. The pain made me faint at times, and then to top my agony, the same sore came on my neck. Still today I have the marks from both of those sores. At work I wasn't able to stand on my feet. Alfred, the Belgian foreman, saw me in my agony and sent me to stay in the restroom, but for fear of being discovered, I bit my teeth deep into my tongue and stayed there as white as a sheet. When I just couldn't go on any longer, I went, half unconscious, into the toilets and there I fell into a deep faint. As I fell and lost my consciousness, it felt like a merciful blessing from heaven as something warm and wet ran down my back. Later when I came to, I discovered that the abcess had opened itself, but until I came to, the girls were afraid to help me, for being caught in the toilets meant severe punishment. And of all the days to come for an inspection, this day our Jew eldest came. The first thing she did, of course, was check the toilet. Seeing me lying there in agony, this evil woman—she had no feeling at all except for herself or her sisters—she grabbed me and kicked me and threw me out. Alfred saw it, and after he had a heated argument with her, I was sent to the barracks. There the Jew eldest's cousin, who was our nurse, poor little her, was to attend me. Can one imagine? The poor little thing, she had had a cold for a few days, and here she actually had to work on me. Anyhow, I guess I have to be thankful to her, for she attended to my sores, and glory, glory, I could stay home from the factory for the rest of the day. As soon as the sores were opened and cleaned, I started to become myself again, but I was weak and sickly for the rest of the war. Those shots had taken the rest of my resistance away from me. When I returned from the factory to the barracks the next day, a letter was waiting for me. After reading this letter, I cried so much, and whenever I take it into my hands so many years after, I still weep. I want to mention that Bendsburg was Bendzin, only the name had been changed by the Nazis.

"My beloved sister Lydia! Bendsburg, May 19, 1943.

"I am finally home. Our first step was the commando and his highness the commandant of the *Sonderabteilung*. Here we settled everything and *Herr Hauptsturmbannfuehrer* Ludwig gave me until five this afternoon off. Dear Lydia! Are you able to imagine all of this? It is all as if I am dreaming. I went to Schrodel (Schrodel was on the edge of the ghetto) in the company I was given. I was taken to a little house with a tiny garden in front of it. As I opened the door to that little room, Daddy kept on looking starry-eyed, so that I got a shock. And in his disbelief he asked, 'What is this?' And we hugged each other. Mama wasn't home, but I was told where she was and went right away to her, to Auntie Mary. Pola stood by the door (one of my cousins). She told Mama a few times that I was coming. Mama just looked at her, what foolish stuff she was talking! But as soon as I entered Mama jumped from the chair on which she was sitting, and as you will imagine, we cried tremendously. From all over, all of our acquaintances came to greet me. Everyone was so happy. It all looks to me like a dream. Together with Mama and Papa resides another family of three and two single girls. Everything is very, very crowded, but let's pray to the Lord that everything stays at least this way. I haven't heard from home for over four weeks. But this was all on account of their moving. Everything is just fine. Mama and Papa are well! Dear Lydi! They haven't received any mail from you, only your first postcard. I read it, and am surprised that you don't want anything. Are all of your things still good? Take good care of everything. Did you get my parcel? Have you got those shoes? I've heard that you knitted some very lovely things for yourself. I hope that you will take good care of all your things, the way I used to, and that you will be able to have them as long. The whole city lives already in the ghetto. They are buidling barracks and a good many were put up already. Everything is in a big uproar. Have you got there some girlfriends? How do you spend your spare time? I am getting ready to leave soon. This night we will have to spend in the Dullag. We have from five in the afternoon to settle the rest of the formalities. Everyone is taken by the Miliz from and to work. Now I shall end, keep your head up high; you see, for me, too, a miracle had happened. The heartiest regards and kisses, Ella."

Who could imagine how much I cried after reading those lines, who will ever imagine what my thoughts were? I was back home with Ella, together with my dearly beloved ones. I saw it all with my vivid imagination. I walked step by step with my sister. I lived every minute through their joy of meeting again. Oh, my love for them was so strong that I hurt. I had never realized how dearly I loved them. Oh, that I could have wings and fly to them. Oh, that I could see them, laugh and cry with them again. Oh, how I yearned for them back home, however humble they should live; for me, home had always meant all the riches on earth. Although Ella had written very often, how she had gotten that special permission I shall never know, but I am srue that she turned heaven to earth to be able to comfort us in those dark hours of our lives. And with all of her writing, it had taken quite some time for the mail to reach me. Her mail came from time to time, but the mail I waited most painfully for, from my loved ones from home, never came. So my mind, wherever I was, whatever I did, was always with them.

We had now two twelve-hour shifts. One was the night shift and one the day shift. The night shift I always shuddered for. It was each day from six to six; they never were satisfied with anything we did, no matter how they demanded a man's work from us on too little food. At times girls fainted from hunger, but the Nazis always demanded more and more. One day they made changes at the factory. We had to produce this and this amount, and if not, our bread ration would be taken from us for the day. Out of fear, we worked so hard that we produced even more than a machine. Long ago we had realized that we had stopped being human and that we had become machinery. I was ordered to a machine which was highly dangerous; one had to be extremely sharp. My machine tied the flax into bundles.

Through the middle went a knife, and if one was a tiny bit careless, one could easy lose a finger, or even the whole hand, and this would mean one's life, for there was no help in any kind of accident. Once it happened, one was doomed to die. In front of me was always the picture of little Fella and the hearse they had taken her away in. But sooner or later we knew that something would happen. My partner by the machine was to remove the bundles. She was one of my roommates, a very temperamental girl, and I was frightened stiff to have her with me. She always did everything sooner than demanded, and one day it happened. She pulled the string while my finger was still in the machine. The next thing I knew, I felt a terrific pain in my finger and I saw blood all over. As I felt near a faint, I just looked at it, trembling. What had happened? I tried to feel my finger, but couldn't feel a thing except pain. As she looked up at me, her face white as a sheet, I just asked her very quietly, with a bit of blame in my voice, "What have you done?" Soon our manager came; him being the devil in person, we all feared the worst, but to our greatest surprise, he ordered me back to the barracks and said I should stay there until my finger was taken care of. He was the biggest devil I had met so far. He had kicked and beaten, mercilessly, many of my friends; he never permitted us to go to the washroom. If one had to go, it was just too bad. And if he caught someone there, he dragged them out and beat them half dead. It was the biggest crime, going to the restroom, or to do anything else except work, work, and again work. So if caught by him, the person could be sure of severe punishment. When he left for a minute, we took care of our most urgent needs. Alfred kept watch and told us when the devil returned. Oh, how feared this man was it is beyond me really to describe. He must have been sent from hell. There were also times that we witnessed him mistreating those Russian prisoners of war. But when they saw him mistreating us, I could see with what hate those men looked at him. The hate in their eyes said, "How much I would like to have you on my side of the fence." No one ever witnessed anything more brutal than this devil with his murderous eyes brutally beating so many of my friends. I had always paid attention to what Ella had written to me and now, somehow, I understood what she meant by telling me to be always industrious and brave. She knew them better than I, so I always tried so very hard never to be caught idle, but I think it had a lot to do with luck, too. Whenever he approached me with his meanness, I, fearful but friendly, answered him in German, and somehow he never mistreated me from then on. This probably saved me when I cut into the finger. After a few days, my finger got well again and with great heart-beating I went back to my old working place. This was only the beginning of it all, for the worst was yet to come, with us yearning and hoping for a better tomorrow, praying to the Lord to please give us our freedom back.

So it was that I started to compose poems. The girls loved them, and for me they were prayers for my home and family. Girls composed songs, all telling of their deep melancholy and their only hope for a better tomorrow. They told stories of Frehlinka, Maidanek, Aushcwitz and all those other dead pits meant for my people. The prayer and hope to end each song was for the sunshine on the outside. And in the dark of the barracks, we sang those songs softly and hopefully, with so much yearning in our voices, the heartbreak of being a prisoner, a prisoner without term, never to end. We kept on searching for a light in the darkness.

SEARCHING FOR A LIGHT IN THE DARKNESS

Yes, the search for a light in the bitter darkness went on. And my only light was the mail from my loved ones. Each piece of mail brought to me a little bit of new hope. Before my brother left home we had made up a few code names, so through all the censoring that the mail went through, we still had left our little secrets and privacy. When life was unbearable after my accident, I begged Ella, of course under code, to arrange for me to come to her camp. Since the Jew eldest had there a cousin, maybe we could exchange one for the other. I was waiting anxiously for her reply, and finally, shortly after Ella returned back to camp from home, this card arrived.

"My beloved Lydi! Lichtewerden, June 5, 1943. I just received your second card, and alos mail from home. And they tell me that they don't get any mail from you at all. Mama is, because of it, very restless. The address home is Bendsburg 0/Steinstrasse 10. Soon new girls are arriving at our camp. Maybe there will be some from Bendsburg; a lot are in Dullag from Rossner's. A brother of one of the girls here, with whom I spoke on my short visit home, wrote to his sister that next week a new registration will start at Rossner's. He had been told that Mama was among the first ones to be accepted and this is on account of the sewing machine that Mama had given there for you and Cilly, remember? For Erika (that meant me), everything has been settled. Now, dear Lydia, you'll have to carry your sacrifice with ease, and you will, I am quite sure. Daddy has received his street identification card and is now headmaster over the rest of the painters at that firm. Your mail sounds now so different than once, as if you have grown about ten years older. Mama talked about you a lot. She is yearning to see you so very much. At home in this tiny room, three families are residing. But you just can't imagine how nice and clean it still is. Mama takes care of the little garden in front of the house and it looks from afar as if there was peace and quiet around. Your little chickens are still with them. If everything just could stay that way. The time I visited home, Mrs. Brenner was there, too. (Mrs. Brenner was a friend of Ella's who had been deported from Punkt; this could only mean one thing, that the deportation continued with its full strength.) How many girls are there in camp with you? The heartiest regards and kisses, your sister, Ella."

My resistance wasn't like it used to be and soon I had a high temperature and a bad throat ache. I felt so very miserable, just like dying. Lying there in the sickroom, I felt so forlorn and remembered the way back at home, when I was sick, Mother would pet me and buy me anything just to make me feel better, for she knew how much I hated being sick, and nothing in the whole world was too good for me. How I cried to myself for what Mother had done when I felt as miserable as I felt right now. I had once bothered Mother a whole night, I felt so bad and just couldn't go to sleep. And poor Mom, working till the late night, she never tired of carrying me around like a little baby and trying to comfort me. Who could have all that patience? Only an angel of a mother like mine. Here, I was a worm with the fear around me of being sent away to the chambers if I was sick too long. This all made me feel so low, so miserable, that the whole world could have come to an end and I wouldn't have cared a bit. After a few days I felt better and I wrote a card to Ella. I guess it must have been discouraging, for the reply came and it was like this: "My beloved Lydi! Lichtewerden, June 18, 1943. Your postcard from May 30 arrived yesterday. Stop already writing all that nonsense, you continuing to write all the time about it. I can't do more than I have done so far. So we just have to wait with a little bit patience for the results. Please do not write about it anymore. So you were sick. You had never to do anything with your throat, how come this time? Have you still all of your knitting which you had made for yourself? Or is it all gone? Dress yourself good and warm. For you must remember one thing, you must stay healthy. Don't be discouraged, life is still ahead of you. After each rain comes sunshine. What fate has in store one just must carry through. Haven't we gone through enough already? And we have always thought not to be able to live it through. But everything goes by, only don't lose your hope and especially your courage. And bite your teeth fast together. How many girls are there in your camp? Is the work there similar to what we do? Write something about it, just leave Erika already alone. My heartiest regards and kisses, your sister, Ella."

After that card, it took quite a while until I received another card, and from home, still nothing. My worries were driving me insane; I didn't know what to think. I couldn't get my mind off home. Ella wrote about the deportations—why weren't they satisfied with all the grief they had done to us already? Why could their evil doings find no end? Polish women were forced to work with us, but they got paid and could go home from time to time, and they were free. They lived in barracks, too, but theirs were much, much nicer and more comfortable, as we found out, and every evening they could be out in the city. They didn't fear for their lives like we did; as long as they didn't get involved politically, there was no crematorium waiting for them, and if they got sick, they could go back home. How much we envied those women, but were they better than we? Why were they so lucky? From those women we found out what was going on back home, and it was very discouraging. On the twenty-sixth of June was Ella's birthday, and this was the last card I got from her, together with the last card from my dearly beloved parents. For the mail had stopped and it was no more permitted for us to contact one another. For the finishing touches had begun, and with its greatest power, and the Nazis were cleaning off the Jewry from Europe. The first thing to do was to break off any relations and keep us blind from everything around. First came Ella's card, and it was so unlike her, for there were only a few words thrown on the card, not like she used to do, always using up each piece of paper. Now the writing was shaky. Here is what she wrote:

"My dear Lydi! Lichtewerden, June 16, 1943.

"I am sitting by a birthday table and in the middle a huge bouquet of jasmine. My thoughts are somewhere else. When did you hear the last time from home? One of the girls here found out that at home everything seems to be OK. I am waiting impatiently for mail. I have read from Ester those few words you addressed to me, and believe me, I am doing fine. I hope very much that our wish will be granted. Just don't lose courage. Many girls came yesterday from Bendsburg. Also, brothers, husbands, and sons, for some of the girls here came through our camp, but they left right away. I just wonder what Max is doing. Best wishes and kisses, Ella."

She mentioned Max, our brother from Argentia, and that meant that she had heard something from him, or some of the boys she mentioned must have been prisoners of war. I was worried; could it be that Max had joined the army in Argentia? And could it be that he was a prisoner of war? As much as I wanted see Max, I just hoped it would not be under those circumstances, for those Nazi-beasts didn't treat Jewish prisoners of war any better than they did the rest of us. As a matter of fact, they didn't treat any prisoners of war as humans. This much we had seen already from the way they treated the Russian prisoners. The next day as I came back from work, the Jew eldest wanted to see me. As I went towards her office with my heart beating loudly, she handed me the card from my mother, the card that Mother wrote to me in the greatest despair of her life. Those dear words were swimming in front of my eyes and the card was covered with my mother's tear drops. Had she known the end was near? The card was so desperate, as if there was something burning under her feet. It was one big cry of agony and for help. Each word was wet from her tears. Were those tears meant to tell me good-bye? How much heartbreak on such tiny piece of paper! My whole life lay in it, everything so dear and unforgotten. And here are those last few words my darling mother spoke to me, for never did I hear from her again; the Nazis had taken my parents from me forever: here are her last few words: "Bendsburg, June 26, 1943. My beloved Lydia, my heart! Why don't you write to us? We're not staying anymore on Steinstrasse, our belongings are in Uncle Jacob's shed. My beloved Lydi, my heart, please answer right away, couldn't you take us to your camp? I could be a gardener, and Daddy is a good painter but right away, for the time is running out, it burns. Cilly has left Blechhammer since May 13, we don't know where to, my beloved sweet Cilly, where is she? Uncle Jacob lives at Robert Kochstrasse 44. My beloved Lydia, my dear heart, my sweet picture always in front of my eyes. We are kissing you a million times and stay as well, from your fearful parents, if we could only be by you." And the card was signed by Mother and Father, for the last time. At the bottom of the card were a few lines written by Uncle Jacob. "Lydia! Until now we have still been spared, but it would just be wonderful if I, my son, and my wife could come to you. Best regards and kisses, your Uncle Jacob."

Well, now I knew that things were at their worst back home. They actually were pleading to come to camp, which was impossible. Such a thing could only happen in a dream. There were no men at our camp and it was like hell already. But, of course, it was better than to have to go on deportation. Everyone got similar mail from home, and the only thing we were able to do was break our fingers in despair. I felt like I was chained. There, the begging of my mother, and here, I was helpless. Our hope was that God would make an end to all of that suffering—the light must come after such a deep darkness. How much darker could it get? One thing must be told to the glory of the Nazis, and that is however much pleasure they took in making us suffer, their own sorrow they weren't able to stand. Those big brave men who had found the greatest satisfaction in killing Jewish children, mutilating people, and gassing them, those monsters were broken when confronted with their own sorrow. But heaven forbid! If they were to suffer, the more they would take it out on us. For instance, the manager at the factory where we worked was the devil in person. One day he was especially wild and Alfred told us to get out of his way as much as possible, for his son was missing in action and now he wanted to take it out on us. His eyes were filled with fury, so he went about kicking and beating, insulting and swearing. And the air raids—hearing them was like music to our ears, but they, those brave and husky man, they ran like the devil was behind them. How much this satisfied us! There was at least something that frightened them.

My dreams somehow always had some meaning, and I remember that the girls came to me and asked what I had dreamed, for most of the time it would come true. "What do you think, Lydia, when will we be free?" But I was sorry to say that, at that time, only the bad dreams came true, for nothing good happened to us. Some of my dreams saved me from from a good many griefs, for they were like a warning. The last mail I received from Ella was a little package and in it was one of her pictures. Did she know what lay ahead? Who knows? But it was like a kind of good-bye to me, for those few words she had written on the back of the picture gave me courage in the future, and it was though I heard her dear voice saying it over and over again. "Without parting there could never be meeting again, never without winter could spring come again. Just think on those May days when the storms blow insane, and when friends have to part, think of the day they'll meet again! If your wish goes broke, never lose your hope, one gate shuts close, but thousands still are open! My dearly beloved Lydi from her sister Ella." And with this our correspondence ended; never have I seen or spoken with Ella again, for she was taken with the rest of her camp to Auschwitz when the Nazis started getting cold feet, when they were beaten on the fronts and had started in a hurry to get rid of all the evidence we had against them.

In my darkest hours of life, I started composing poems. The girls just loved them, and whenever I had an occasion, I recited them. The girls always said that if the war ever ended and we survived I should publish them for the world to hear. Those poems are, of course, in German, and they told of all our misery, all our yearning and sorrow, but they always ended with the hope for a better tomorrow. And so it came close to midsummer, and with melancholy, I looked toward my birthday. My birthday—how nice it had always been at home with all the gifts. Even in the worst times, Mother had always tried to put all she could into this day. And here my only hope was to get some mail. If it was only a sign that my family was OK it would have meant heaven for me. It would have been the nicest birthday gift I could wish for. But as the day came and passed and nothing came, I spent my free time mourning. Topka said, "Don't be sad, you'll see, your parents will set heaven to earth to send you a note, if only a note that they are all right, it will come." But who did we kid? No one got any mail anymore and things were real bad, but I had hoped, like a little girl hopes for good fairy to show up. I still hoped that on my birthday there would come some news. And it came, but a little later, for it must have been around the twentieth of August when I got my birthday present, all right. We saw a few Polish women, all excited, waving to us. Hinda had been in contact almost all of the time with a Pole who used to bring her some food or mail from home. Well, as I saw Hinda coming towards us, this tough girl was hardly walking on her own feet; it looked as if they would give under her at any minute. She was as white as a sheet and soon we were to find out our agony. For on the seventeenth of August, the murderers had cleaned the ghetto of all the Jews and had taken them in cattle wagons to Auschwitz. The way it was told to us, it was too gruesome to believe. It was the blackest day in history. The Nazis gathered those frightened people, and the shooting and screaming was heard all over Bendzin and surroundings. There weren't any Jews left in the ghetto. All of them had been taken to the gas chambers. As I heard this, I couldn't believe it. I was desperate—no, it couldn't be, my parents must be alive, they couldn't have been murdered in such a brutal way. But I knew, the minute I thought about it, that it was true and that I had been made an orphan. And all the time, those awful aonizing thoughts kept going around in my mind. I saw my mother, how they had taken her from Father, and I lived through all the agony. I saw them going towards their destination, but I didn't want to believe that they had gone to their death. I thought that my mother, not being so old, maybe had been taken her for slave labor. And who knows, maybe we would meet. I kept on dreaming. And Daddy, maybe they won't harm him, for after all, they could still have some use from him, too. And everyone used to always like him, for he was such a good worker. But reality stood with me and deep inside I knew that all those thoughts were only dreams of desperation and all of those wishes were only wishes. As we came back this day from work, we closed the shutters and refused to eat a thing. There we lay on our cots and cried in deep agony in memory of our dearly beloved ones. There was no one to comfort us, for each of us had gotten the same taste of deepest agony of mankind. In all of our agony, our Jew eldest burst into the room and shouted that if we didn't stop all that nonsense, we would be severely punished, she personally would see to it. Her own parents had been murdered, but this woman, this witch, just went on as if this all hadn't touched her. What deep loathing all of my friends always felt for her! In our minds, she was the devil's adjutant. But this passed and we tried to stay strong. We saw, somehow, that everything was useless, so we had to go on, to keep fighting for our survival, and perhaps we would somehow, sometime, find some one of our beloved ones. And we vowed to each other that whoever stayed alive would have to tell the world about it all. There were those pessimistswho said that when the Nazis were through with us, no one would be alive to tell, but the optimists said that, no matter what the Nazis did to us, they couldn't destroy all of us, and that someday we would stand there in judgment and demand an answer for all of their crimes. One day American prisoners of war came near our camp and our group eldest had a chance to talk to the sergeant. How fearless those boys looked! I found out later that many of those boys were murdered, too, and especially the Jewish ones were mistreated severely. Those Nazibeasts, they didn't care about the Geneva agreements, they made their own laws and whoever didn't like it just could do anything they wanted about it. They felt that they had the world in their hands and that they could do anything they pleased. After a few days, the Americans were removed, where to I don't know, and no one knew.

One day the *Hauptsturmbannfuehrer* Stoll came to our camp and demanded that we turn in any money or jewelry still in our possession. If by any chance one got the idea of hiding any of it, it would be useless because they would find it and we would be sent to Auschwitz. There it was again, the ticket to death, assured to us with all its glory. So what was there to do but to give everything away, the last thing we had hoped to trade for a piece of bread? But who would play with fire? We went like sheep and turned in our possessions, and the Jew eldest came as the goddess of death, with fire in her eyes, saying, "You'll be destroyed if I catch anything on you." So no one really dared anything. We had to go to the office to turn it in personally and that way the murderers could see all the girls and get an idea for our further use. I stood there in front of him, giving away those last precious memories from my beloved ones, and him smiling in his sadistic way, so big, so strong, and us, so little, so frightened—yes, power was on his side. He could decide over life and death. He was a god in his own right. His lustrous, sadistic eyes kept going over us, undressing us with his dirty smile, looking through each one of us. And then he asked with his brutal voice, "Are you sure that you have turned in everything? You do know that if not, we will find it and it will be very bad for you." Just to hear his voice made us shudder. It gave us a spinetingling feeling. But even this was not the worst, for the worst was yet to come. One day, after we had worked at night and gone to sleep, I was suddenly woken up, for there had come four women doctors to our camp from Auschwitz. At first I was frightened, for my first thoughts were that perhaps someone had come again to harm us. But they right away quieted me down; those women were Jewish and had come to our camp to work, and in order to entertain them a little, I had been called to recite. Among them was a woman dentist, Sabina, and right away she opened her heart for me. She took me out into the yard and listened to my telling her about home, about my dreams and yearning, and how my mother had always told me that once again my life would be sunshine and roses, but that I felt as if the sun would never shine for me again. And then she took me into her arms, hugged me and kissed me, and told me how much she loved me. She said that if she ever was fortunate to have a little girl, it should just like me. And then she told me her sad story. Her being about fifteen years older than me gave me a little security, and soon it was known around the camp that I was Sabina's little girl. Although she shared a small room with the other three doctors, I spent every free minute with her. Since Sabina's room was in the barracks where the showers were, I always stopped at her room afterwards, and she, always with pride in her voice, bragged about her little protégé. "Look," she said to one of the women, "doesn't she look like the Mona Lisa?" And she pointed at my profile, which was wound in a towel and pink from the warm showers. At times she told me that, if the war ended and we were still alive, and if, God forbid, I couldn't find my dear parents, she wanted to adopt me. She wanted me to promise it to her, but to this I wouldn't listen. First of all, my hope kept on glowing in my heart to find my parents alive, and then, too, I had my two beloved brothers, who, thank goodness, were out of Europe. I was always confident that I would meet some of my dearly beloved family again.

Sabina almost didn't survive, but she is alive today and has a nice practice in Paris. Things were really tough for Sabina, as well as for those other three doctors. The Jew eldest was very little educated except from the experience of being a slave-driver, and her jealousy against those highly educated woman was so terrific that after a short time she sent those doctors to the hardest work she could find at the factory. Those woman, being masters at their own profession, just couldn't adjust to this kind of work, but they lived it through somehow. I remember the devil, our manager, when he mistreated my Sabina so badly. She always smiled at it all. A little while later a Russian woman doctor came to our camp; she was also a prisoner of war. She was a nice and kind woman and I got right away to like her. Her name was Lydia, too, and this meant again some luck for me. Soon Sabina had competition, for the Russian doctor called me "dochenka," little daughter. When I got sick, which was lately very often, for the temperature just wouldn't leave me anymore, she sat by my bedside and told me about her life in Russia. The nurse didn't like this at all. She was such a jealous thing, and after I saw that she tried to make trouble for me with her cousin the Jew eldest, I tried to break away from Lydia and went back to Sabina. But although I had a temperature, the Jew eldest made me go back to work. Well, maybe she was right in some way, for once I asked her why she did this to me, and she answered that it wasn't safe for me to be on the sick list all the time. She said that the doctor didn't understand, that she didn't care as long as she could be the good one. Well, the doctor was a very kind woman, which was more than I could say for the Jew eldest and her gang, but in some ways it made sense—it wasn't good to be to on the sick list. From then on, however sick I felt, never again did I go back to the sickroom, out of fear that her prediciton might come true, for in front of me was always the picture of little Fella.

Back at the factory, I was given easier work as the group eldest had arranged. She was so wonderful, and how fortunate we were to have her, for in the other departments were some like witches. Those days that I felt ill she gave me assignments near to nothing. One of those times, our boss, the murderer, caught me. With murder in his eyes he came after me. I ran and hid and then my group eldest got hold of me and hid me someplace, for if the boss found me, the worst and most horrible punishment was in store for me. I was shaking like a leaf. Later when the boss left, the girls described how he was looking for me and had described me to them. They said that he had been ready to kill. From then on, I lived a life of constant fear that he would come to the barracks and get hold of me, for if they made roll call, it would be the end for me. I lived quite some time in terror. Every time I saw him come to the factory, I tried to hide my face in fear of being recognized. But as some time passed, I could once again breathe easily, for I was confident that by now he must have forgotten about me. Some time later he caught a girl named Frieda, who is dead now. She was very young and beautiful, always very quiet. Her group eldest hit her once and she rebelled against it right when this murderer came along. He took her to a place of detention, her clothing ws stripped from her, and she was beaten bloody. When she was given permission to go back to the barracks, the girl was so swollen that we weren't able to find her face. But this was not the end yet. One day *Hauptsturmbannfuehrer* Knoll arrived, the pig that had taken all the jewelry from us, and this girl again was taken to a detention room. It looked like a slaughter room, for this room was used for all kinds of gruesome detention and therefore the blood had never been cleaned off so it could be a warning for us. She was taken in there, her clothing torn off her, and this heavy and strong man hit her naked little body fifty counts with a strap. All through the night we could hear the gruesome screams from this poor girl. The next day when she was released, she couldn't stand on her feet. She became gravely ill, and after her recovery, the hearse from Gross Rosen came again and they took her away from us. This was one of the most gruesome warnings for us so far. We knew that the Nazis were capable of any horrorifying deeds, but for us to see such was just too much. The Nazis came quite often from Gross Rosen to pick up some live burn material. Any girl that was sick for long was taken away. This was also the reason that the sickroom stayed empty. The winter was the most unbearable of all, for the cold was out to kill us. We stood in the awful frost and worked. The huge doors were constantly open and the icy winds nearly blew our heads off. The cold ate at our hands and feet, but not once would I cry to myself out of desperation. We bound paper bags around our feet, for the frost was biting them. But this they forbid us. There we had to stand in the freezing cold, hardly clad, and the frost made us so very miserable. We were taken out on those cold winter nights to pile the bundles of flax, and there we had to stand, helpless, freezing, the time past midnight, and working with the last bit of strength. How a human being could live through such was then beyond us to imagine. But soon we were to go through much worse. And even this torture was nothing to compare to all of the horror to come.

I remember at times I was sent to the boiler room to refill some tools with grease, and the German man there had such a sneaky look on his dirty face that it gave me the creeps. Once we got to know a new foreman who was a German named Karl, but I soon found out that he, too, had no great a sympathy for the Nazis. He was an invalid who had lost an arm at the fight for Stalingrad and was sent home. Nothing gave him more pleasure than to tell us, when we were under his care, about the beating his fellow Germans had gotten.

His eyes were aglow when telling us about the fight for Stalingrad, and for me, it was music, it gave me new hope; I couldn't hear enough of their suffering. It comforted me so much and gave me a great deal of pleasure. I knew how to hate already. The Nazis had been our best tutors for it. I rebelled against the thoughts that Mother used to teach us. She always said that we should love our enemies and find the goodness in people. *A lot of good it has done,* I said to myself, *when they'll be down on their knees and when I will be able to walk over them the way they have walked over us. And the more I see them suffer,* I thought, *the more I shall love them.* Karl was so different from all of them. How kind and considerate he was! He always called me his little sister, and at times he tried to get me away from the hard work and gave to me the easiest that he could find. But this luck was not too often, for he wasn't on my shift too often. Those few times he was with us, he showed all that kindness to us. This made me change my opinion that all Germans were rotten; there were a few nice ones left. How sorrowful he looked when we got punished for nothing at all. Once it was a Sunday, very cold, and we were sent to a bin to clear out all of the merchandise there. Not too many were guarding us and, luckily for us, Karl was our foreman. At that time we had a discussion with him. He just couldn't understand that our faith in God was still so great, and he said, "You fools, if there really was a god, do you really think for one moment that he would let you suffer the way you do? All the agony over you, what did you young children do to deserve this?" And he would go on like that and talk to himself in a rage. From that day on I really liked him. For here I knew was one of them against them. How nice—if only more of them were like him, what a wonderful world this could be. But there weren't many like him. As a matter of fact, there were so few like him that one could call that figure miniscule. And in all this, I was in so many ways lucky. A guardian angel must have kept watch over me, for whenever I was sent to the boiler room, there out of the machinery room Karl would appear, for he really was a machinist. And so he would always be first at the boiler room whenever I went. Come to think of it, I don't remember once having been there alone with the scary German in the boiler room. Then one day, our shift changed and we went on to the day shift, and something horrible happened. The girl who took my place on the night shift went to the boiler room and was raped by this awful man. How awful! This girl was the daughter of a rabbi, and she was driven nearly insane by the attack. It dawned on me little by little that Karl had known this devil and had kept watch over me. But such was life, for we were in a jungle and those beasts could do with us whatever they wanted, for we were weaponless and on their side was all the power.

One day things started to liven up back at the barracks, for we were told that a new transport would arrive from Auschwitz. For us, people coming back from Auschwitz was like a return from another world, for most those sent to Auschwitz were doomed to die. I remember trembling and waiting. Maybe one of my beloved ones would be among them. Each of the girl had about the same thoughts. When they arrived and stood outside to be counted, they were welcomed by our beloved Jew eldest. We looked through the windows to get a glimpse at them and then I heard a scream that went through my bones, for I saw a girl that had come before from Auschwitz. She had been told that her mother had gone to the gas chambers, but here she was running, pulling her hair and screaming, *"Mamale, Mamale."* Whoever didn't live this scene could never, even in his wildest dreams, be able to imagine it. For outside, among all those hairless, shaven girls from Auschwitz, was her mother. Her mother hadn't seen her yet, for she knew that her little girl had been sent to the chambers with hundreds of other children. And then, when the women were brought into the barracks and the girl fell over her mother, her mother stared at her. When she came back to reality, she broke down and wept, "My Sarale, my Sarale!"

At times such things would happen, when children met again with their beloved ones whom they believed to be dead, but I had never witnessed one so happy as when a mother and child met. With all my joy for Sarah, I felt somehow a little jealous. Why couldn't I have been this fortunate? I would ask myself, *Why couldn't my mother have been among them, or Cilly? How wonderful this would have been.* And in the middle of my selfish thoughts, I heard a screaming voice and like a ghost, a girl came running towards me with the words, "Cilly, Cilly are you alive?" As I mentioned in the beginning, Cilly and I were very much alike and at times, people thought we were twins, so I felt right away that this was the door to a mystery. As the girl approached me, I stood still, only to see what she was about to say, for most of the time girls would stop in the middle when they felt they made a mistake by telling the whole and gruesome truth. I wanted to know what she was so frightened about, what had happened to my sweet and beloved sister Cilly. As the girl came towards me, she stopped all of a sudden and asked, "How did you get out alive?" So I asked her what she meant, and she asked me if I didn't remember that I was taken among the sick ones from Blechhammer to Auschwitz. As I started to cry, she saw that she had made a mistake. She said, "You aren't Cilly, isn't it so? Who are you?" And then I broke into tears and told her that I was Cilly's kid sister. She said it was amazing that we two looked so much alike, and then she told me the whole story. She had been together with Cilly in Blechhmamer. Cilly was waiting for a transport to take her home, for she was among the sick girls who had been given special permission to return home. She was so excited she just couldn't wait for the transport to pick her up, for she was so disgusted that she had even lost contact from home. She was only living for that moment. When the transport came, Cilly was in such a hurry that the girl was unable to warn her, for she, having been in Blechhammer for a longer time, had some kind of experience. She noticed on the black truck the tiny inscription "Auschwitz" and she knew right away what Cilly's destination was. "Oh, Lydia, if I only could have gotten near her to warn her. But she was the first one to run into the truck with so much happiness and hope on her face." Those girls had no chance at Auschwitz. The Nazis didn't even bother to put them through the selection if they came with a transport of sick, although Cilly had been hardly sick at all. "If I had warned her, she could have hidden, and when the transport left, she could have said that she was in the washroom. Knowing there was no way home anymore, she could have gone among the healthy girls and they would have removed her from the list and she would have been able to go for slave labor, perhaps."

Oh, Cilly, oh, Ella, I wept to myself, *what have you done? Why didn't you leave well enough alone and stay together? Where are you and what have they done to you?* But my hope wouldn't fade. I said to myself maybe, if a miracle like that that happened to little Sarah, maybe I would be fortunate, too. Somehow deep inside me, I felt that Cilly must still be alive. They couldn't have taken her to the chambers, not my Cilly, so full of life, part of my own life, it just couldn't be. *Somewhere, somehow I will meet her,* I said to myself. But I kept on brooding and my friends scolded me to stop it already, for I would make myself sick and it wouldn't help me find Cilly anyhow. After that I tried to avoid this girl, for I was afraid of what else she might be able to tell me. With the new transport of girls, we were so crowded that our room was taken away and given to about thirty new girls. From then on, we were given cots to share with other girls. Those that were working on day shift were made to share the cot of one of the girls from the night shift, and on those days that they worked together, they just had to sleep together on those tiny hard cots. And things were getting worse and worse with each day. Our camp eldest had been changed quite some time ago because it was said that she was too kind and we must have someone tough. She really hadn't been too bad; as a matter of fact at times, she gave us more to eat, and at times she fought with our Jew eldest, who woke us in the middle of night, barely dressed, to make us stand outside in the cold for hours, just to show us that she was the boss. We did not know whose interference it was that caused the change for our camp eldest, but we had an idea. And so the camp eldest was exchanged and our new camp eldest was a prostitute who was very tough. Just to see her from afar was enough to make our blood freeze in the veins. Since I had heard the bad news about Cilly, my only thoughts were with her. One day while I stood at work at my dangerous machine, tortured with thoughts about Cilly, Alfred came along. He was like a guardian angel; he told me to go get some coffee. And here I will explain what he meant.

There in the same factory was a canteen for the Germans and for those other Aryans working for them. Fresh coffee was always brewed at lunch time—of course it was coffee in name only, for it was cheap Ersatz. Anyhow, the workers there would eat at the canteen, and at times we were sent there to bring some of this gooey coffee to our bosses. For us, of course, it meant a great deal to get a little bit of this warm drink. But this luxury was not for us to consume. At times,

Alfred sent me to bring some coffee in his name, and then I got it to drink. And so it was this time. As he watched me, so broken-down from my sorrow, he came toward me, and this is why I went to get some coffee. To get to this canteen, I had to pass a long corridor and go over the stairway which led through our part of the factory. As I started to climb the stairs, I heard a scream and as I looked down, I saw the girls around my machine. As I slowly started to climb down the stairway, my feet were ready to give under me. I saw a gruesome picture in front of me. Alfred's finger had been cut off completely. And here is how it happened. Jadzka, the girl that I worked with, was so careless. I had been so frightened of working with her since my accident. When Alfred sent me to the canteen, he worked in my place, and right away it happened. She pulled the string too early. I was used to her way of work and would be so very cautious, but Alfred didn't know her system and the big misfortune had caught him. Right away we were questioned—where was I when it happened? Alfred, in his agony, winked his eyes at me and said that he had oiled the machine and carelessly pulled the string. If things had come out the way it really was, nothing would have saved us two. Our gratefulness towards Alfred found no end. He actually saved our lives in his unselfish way. The girls asked me if I realized what Alfred had done for me—he gave me my life back. Now I know that Cilly watched over me, for just the thought of her had made me so sad, and that had made Alfred send me for coffee. If not for that, who knows, I might have followed my little friend Fella to Gross Rosen. There was no need and no help for such in camp. I'll always remember Alfred, how wonderful he was to all of us and all the good he did for me. He was away from the factory after the accident for quite some time, and we feared that we would never see him again. We heard from his friend, the other Belgian, that he was taken back home. In a way we were happy for him, for he hated working for the Nazis, but in another way it made us sad, for he was a ray of sunshine for us. And then as if our prayer was answered, he came back, the same wonderful self again.

One night I had a funny dream. I dreamt that I was warned to hide my valuables, which consisted mostly of postcards from Ella and those two postcards from Mother, as well as some pictures from home. I had also saved a few pieces of jewelry, nothing of value, only they had sentimental value for me. It wasn't worth much, but for me, it was more than all the riches on earth. In my dream, my mother told me to pick up the roof of the barracks. I never knew that there were planks to pick up, but Mother advised me, in my dream, that I should put there everything I wanted to save. After I told my bed-mate about the dream, we told a few of our friends to put all of their valuables together and we would try to hide it there. At night when everybody was asleep, we tried to raise the planks and they really gave under our hands. As I lay there thinking about it, I wondered how I came to have such a dream. But the next day I found out that my dream saved me. As we stood there at work, the group of girls that came to release us came in looking like ghosts. What had happened back at the barracks?

As we left for work early in the morning, trucks with SS men were arriving, and they started searching among our possessions. Everything was taken away from us, everything a girl possessed, from her mail from home to her last piece of clothing. At first the girls thought that we would be given striped prison uniforms, for they had to undress and later they were given some clothing. We were so very frightened by hearing part of what awaited us. And so as I stood there, my dream came into my mind. How fortunate I had been and how lucky! For I had told a good many girls about my dream and a good many of them had tried to hide their valuables. How happy and relieved I was, to have been able to save part of my possessions at the nick of time. If I had waited, it would have been too late. All those thoughts went through my mind. I knew that someone must be watching over me. After that dream, I started again to be confident in life. As we were walking towards our barracks, part of my confidence started to dwindle. With each step I took, I felt a heavy burden take hold over me. My feet became all of a sudden so heavy, and fear came over me. As we came towards the gate, there was such a quietness, like a cemetery. We saw the cars of the SS and quite a few of these Nazis were around to bid us welcome with their filthy smirks on their faces. We were taken in right away, and right away we were ordered to take off all of our clothes and to dance around a group of filthy SS men. The earth could well have opened right under me and buried me underneath, for I felt like drifting. I, who never even like to get undressed in front of my own mother, was here naked in front of those fat swine. If the performance of one of the girls wasn't to their satisfcation, she would get whipped. *Oh, agony of life, oh, dear Lord,* I cried to myself, *why, oh why, do we have to go through such, haven't we suffered enough already?* And when the line came to me and I had to dance around in front of those pigs, I closed my eyes and pretended to myself that I was in my blue ballerina gown with no evil around me to look at my innocence. And this, too, went by and at last I could hear the voice of the Jew eldest—for the first time, music to my ear. "Lydia, it is all right, you can go out now and get dressed." I could have kissed her for it. And when I came back out, oh, glory, I got back the clothing I had worn before, but only one piece of each item. Then we had to go to another room where again we were told to remove our clothing, for here we were told that a doctor would check us thoroughly—and did they ever check us thoroughly!

Those that were in ill health would be going on vacation. We knew the vacation place, all right—the gas chambers and the crematorium. We were tormented by fear. After I was told that I had passed, my number was given to me, and I had no name anymore. I became a number, but at least I passed the selection and wasn't doomed to die. From that day on, things got so tough in camp that horror was the only word for it. A few of the girls were taken away, those unfortunate ones who weren't lucky enough to get the dog tags. From that day on, the SS took over all the camps. From now on our guards were SS and two of them, rotten prostitutes, SS women, were assigned to us as camp eldest. They were taught to be real tough with us. Everywhere was SS. Our eyes couldn't find any rest from the blackness of them. Even at the factory we were watched by SS women guards, and they were so horrible, with their filthy way of talking, like they were at home in their brothels. If one of the girls had to take care of a very urgent need, she had to salute the prostitute and ask for her permission—which, of course, most of the time would be denied. At work our foremen had nothing to say anymore, except for the murderous manager, and to him all the power on earth had been given to do with us whatever he desired. And did he ever use that power. For if he had been before the devil before, now he was even worse. We asked ourselves if we would be able to live through it, and what more would we have to live through? When would the end come?

After the Nazis' defeat at Stalingrad, we were given new hope, for we saw that the more those beasts tortured us, the more they were tortured by the thought of their own defeat. After all of our possessions had been taken from us on that awful black day when the SS took over, Alfred told me that if I had any valuables, I should bring them to him at the factory and that he would hide them for me. I knew that it was just a question of time before all of our hidden possessions were found, and then Alfred made that nice offer to me. I had hidden a good pair of shoes, for my mother had ordered them for me and we had turned our shoes in a long time ago, for they were pure leather and the Nazis wanted them for their own children. Together with the pictures, my mail, and a few other items, I gave the shoes over to Alfred. I could finally relax, for if all that stuff had been caught with me, I would have been in great trouble, and always when they came to search, I was stiff with fear. Dear Alfred, how very concerned he was, and how much he despised them, for he felt each bit of pain with us. I noticed him spitting after them. One day, out of the bule sky, Alfred came to us to say good-bye. The Germans had ordered him some place near the borders and with his heartbreaking kind of fun, he said to us jokingly good-bye. Dear Alfred, how heartbroken we felt to see our ray of sunshine going from us. How much we admired him, although he made himself look so stupid. If one was to portray his life, no one could fit into this role but Jerry Lewis. He was such little a man with such a big heart. Then he came toward me and whispered into my ears that those things he had taken to hide for me were in the good care of his buddy. Whenever I wanted them back, I could tell him. Alfred wanted a favor of me, that I should let him have one of my pictures. I agreed to it, for I had six pictures of me and my parents, copies of that picture we had taken one week before they took me from them. I asked Alfred to look for my parents wherevere he went, and if he found them, to tell them about me.

With Alfred gone, everything looked hopeless. Now we realized how much comfort he had been to us. Alfred came from time to time for a brief visit, but we didn't see too much of him. His buddy, who now took care over my things, was a little different than Alfred. He didn't joke much with us, but he was also a nice man. If at first I was frightened that he wouldn't want to bother with my stuff, my fear was soon taken from me, for one day he whispered to me that he was taking good care of it. How kind of those men, for if it ever had come out, they would have been punished for it. One day he, too, wanted a picture from me and I gave him the same one I had given to Alfred, under the same condition that if he ever found my parents, he should tell them about me. And he, too, in his kindness, promised it to me. He said that whenever I wanted some of my belongings he would be happy to bring them to me, and if I had something else to hide, he would be glad to do it. If I had thought that there was no other good person around than Alfred, I found out now that his buddy, too, was as great as he was.

Then that wonderful day came when we heard that the Russian army was near the Polish border. It was only a small question of time before our liberation was here. But defeat was something the Nazis just couldn't take, and with each day that brought them nearer to their own destruciton, they made our lives more unbearable. Like mad dogs, they took everything in stride, for we knew that their end was near, but we still had to go through hell. We didn't realize that most of us would die. Then, the sounds of the air raid were for us like a promise from heaven, and the bombardments sounded like the most beautiful symphony. When the air raid sirens sounded, how precious life was again! How utterly delightful it was to see them run for a change. How heavenly to see their frightened faces! What cowards they really were—here they could kill young and old with the greatest satisfaction, but when they felt death hot on their own shoes, how their faces grimaced with fear for their own dirty lives. One night we were awakened to find that our group eldest, Mrs. Potash, had been taken away. This was already the year 1944. When we saw Mrs. Potash ready to leave, how beautiful she looked as we saw her for the last time. Like a goddess, she was just breathtaking. She told us that she was going home. Home? Where to? For there was no home anymore. We later found out that she and her husband had been among the richest people of Sosnowitz, and her husband, who had been in hiding, was bringing her to join him—for a very large amount of money, of course. As fantastic as it may sound, we believed that she was taken away because she had once been caught speaking to an American prisoner of war. When she told us, "Good-bye, children," with tears in her throat, we had a feeling that something evil was going to happen.

    She told us that if any of us girls had relatives out of the country, we could write a few words and she would try writing the addresses in code into her little autograph booklet. I wrote to brother Max in Argentina, "Max, have you, Sigfried, and Uncle Heinz completely forgotten us?" In those few words I wrote my outcry of fear in my most desperate time of life, for I didn't know if I would ever see any of my beloved ones again and I wanted Max to know how very desperate I was. When I met my brother in 1960 after twenty-three years apart, he reminded me about this note. When he received it one day in 1944, he felt relaxed, for he thought it was meant to show him that all of us were well and alive. How did Mrs. Potash do it? How did this woman get this note through? As she left into the dark night with a few of her belongings, we cried, for we felt that we would never see her again. With each day to come, we saw by the way the Nazis tortured us that it was really going downwards for them. For the more they would torture us, the more we knew that freedom was near. Now we could hear the bombardments very clearly, and the Russians working with us told us the good news that their people had liberated Poland. My heart bled as I cried, "Oh, Mama, if you and Papa had only been in hiding, you might be free now!" I hoped that Mother and Father had gone into hiding, and I dreamed how I would live every minute of freedom with them. Whoever was able to hide and pull through up to now would be free. For as we had heard, the Russians were now near the Oder River, and from there, it wouldn't be long before they were by us. How I enjoyed every minute, just thinking of it. How sweet I thought revenge would be. But things didn't turn out that way for us.

    At the factory there was hardly anything to do. One could see that there was something in the air. Inspectors showed up as often as they used to, and then the rumor went around that who knows if we would be able to stay here and wait for our liberation. Where could they possibly take us? Auschwitz, we had heard from the Poles outside, had been sabotaged and the whole death factory destroyed. Some said that the Nazis wanted to destroy the evidence, and still some said that the partisans had done it. And then it was said that because Auschwitz was in Poland, the Russians must have it by now. So, we thought, the Nazibeasts couldn't do a thing, and would have to leave us right here. But one day as we returned from work, we saw some people—or were they still people? For they really didn't look like people any more. They dragged themselves along, their prison clothes half torn away, with their shaven heads and bare feet here in the cold winter. Some fell and were beaten to death by their guards. They looked like a parade of ghosts, only skin and bones. We soon learned who they were because one girl had gone with our guards to bring our bread ration to camp, and while waiting outside, she saw another transport go by. Someone from that group told her that they were evacuating, for the Russians were near. They had already been without food and drink for three days. Where they were going, only heaven knew. As the girl told us the story at camp, we were frightened to death, for some rumors went around that the shooting nearby came from a forest where the Nazis brought the prisoners. They were shooting them all in order not to leave any evidence of their horrorible deeds. As a matter of fact, one of the guards told us that we shouldn't be too happy, that not one damn Jew would be around when all of it was over—they would first kill all of us.

When I couldn't look at those nice dreams of the future to come, one day I asked the Belgian to please bring me my things that he had hidden for me. In my coat I sewed a hidden pocket in which to put my mail and pictures. The next day he brought all of my things. With tears in his eyes, he asked me what I thought the Nazis were going to do to us. Some of the girls said that we should hide behind the loads of sacks at the factory if the time came that we were to evacuate. With only four of us that had thought about it, we thought that they wouldn't possibly search for us. Then we thought to perhaps raise the roof where we had once hidden our valuables, hiding there in those holes where no one would possibly look for us. But the only thing that kept us from it was the thought of food and drink. How long could we stand it? And to be caught would mean disaster for sure. So we went around worrying for the future to come. Behind us was freedom and in front of us death lurked in each corner. After a night of awful dreams, I saw myself in rags and around me little children were crying, begging me to help them. And I saw a caravan going in the desert. The caravan was us girls and we were the horses, pulling big black hearses. We were famished and huge camels were our guards, and as I looked closer, I saw that the camels were whipping us to make us go quicker and quicker. As I looked closer yet, I saw the camels turning into SS guards and each of their faces looked like Hitler himself. When I woke up, I decided to take all of my things from the Belgian, for I had a premonition and I felt that something bad lay ahead of us. Ever since I was a little girl, whenever I dreamt about little children, always aggravation lay ahead of me. As I stood so thoughtfully, my mind wandered far away. I saw freedom behind me, with all its glory, and I wanted to stay alive so badly. What had I had from life so far? Although I had been persecuted since I could remember, it hadn't mattered, for we had been all together and had hoped together to be free. How quickly my dream had ended. So soon I had to leave the Land of Play, so soon to leave my childhood. And then, all that time later, we lived in constant fear. And so, I thought why shouldn't I be granted a place in the sun once more? That there were millions of others who once had dreamt the same dream didn't enter my mind. At that time, there weren't millions left to dream that precious dream of freedom. The death factories of the superior race had seen to that. But thousands were still left to step out of the ruins and to be the witnesses to all that horror and disaster. *Oh, Lord, please let me be one of them,* I prayed. *Please, merciful God, don't let me fall to those brutal Nazibeasts, and I vow to you to be a witness on this earth. I shall be a witness for my people who were destroyed by the devil and his adjutants. I shall help you when the day of judgement will come.* Did the Lord to listen to my plea? I am confident he did. For to have lived through the next episode of my life in hell, there must have been someone above who kept watch, for how, how could I have lived through an episode like this? How could a person, after being in hell, actually come back to life again? But about this, I shall tell later.

As I stood there, so deep in my thoughts, some of the girls passed me and asked what the quietness was so all of a sudden. How could I explain to them what went through my mind? As we came back to the barracks that day, we heard so much bombing and the air raid sirens wouldn't stop. Now, many of our guards had disappeared all of a sudden and such a quietness settled around us. We started to sing that maybe tomorrow we would be free. There was no question about it anymore, for even our Jew eldest was like sugar to us all of a sudden, and even our two camp eldests were like honey. Who wouldn't have been hopeful that time? And as we walked slowly—hardly any roll call anymore, hardly any counting of us numbers anymore—towards the factory the next day, we asked ourselves where was all the German efficiency they used to have? Were they afraid to show their faces already? We vowed to each other that we would find them, just let us see freedom first. All of a sudden as I stood sorting the flax, the group eldest from the hothouse came running and as I saw her frightened face as she went towards our group eldest, right away it went like a thousand needles through my body that my dream had come true. Then our group eldest approached us and told us that we should assemble and as I stood there trembling, one of the girls asked me why I was so frightened. Maybe we were to come back to the barracks because the Russians were not far and the Nazis wanted to show themselves in the best light. But my forfeeling was one of the worst ever, and my teeth knocked on one another. "No, Rivka," I said. "I think that for all of us, misfortune has come right now." Rivka was one of the girls I had known from Bendzin; she had been a neighbor of little Fella. She was a very strong girl, although not the Mona Lisa in person—we had always made fun of her nose. The nose really was a scream and her face was because of it very funny-looking. Although the girls made fun of her, she was a wonderful sport and would most of the time join in the laughter. But one name she was furious about, and if anybody was so bold as to call her that name, she saw red. "Turnip" was the name, and when it was said in Polish, it had a little insulting flavor in it. Hinda just couldn't call her another name but Turnip, and the results were heavy fights.

Anyway, that fateful day, we were assembled and as we were just about to leave, we saw a sunny face, and there stood Alfred. We didn't speak to Alfred that day and I have never seen him since, but I think that he is alive in Belgium today. Then our watch started to come, one by one. Quick, quick, hurry, hurry, in two hours we are leaving Graeben. Oh, merciful heaven, why so quickly, why couldn't we wait a little while longer? Why couldn't we be given those few precious minutes more? Maybe freedom was here, not far away. But as the SS man had said to us before, the Nazis weren't going to leave any evidence. In an emergency they would destroy all of us, just to have to fun from it. As we came toward the other part of the factory, everyone was already waiting for us. Our group eldest explained that any minute that we wasted would be our own time. We were allowed to take a few things along with us, but if we lost all that precious time, we just would have to leave the way we were. Now it was already nearing the end of 1944, and in the coming hour we were to leave. I had my thin and measly coat, which was better than nothing, and in the secret pocket I felt my most precious possessions, my mail and pictures from my so-dearly beloved ones. I just knew that this would be my guardian angel. I put on my nice knitted clothes from home. I had hidden them with Alfred, but now no one would pay any attention to them so I was safe to wear them. How secure I felt in them, for I knew how proud Mother had been of them, me having knitted them myself. I remembered when Mother bought the wool for me, very cheap yarn, but for such a high price. Somehow with those few pieces of clothing I always felt safe. And then I put on my good shoes, for who would pay attention to them now? Those shoes, from lying in all those hiding places, were by now dried out, but they were still much better than any of the shoes given to us by the Nazis. Who knew what stood ahead of us? It was a good and secure feeling to have sturdy shoes on my feet. The magazine where all of our clothing had been taken when the SS took over our camp was open, but only those real bad pieces were left. When a girl tore her own clothing, by special permission, she would be given some pieces from there. Now this magazine was opened and we could take anything we wanted. Why their great concern over us all of a sudden? It smelled fishy. And again the speculation started. Some of the girls said it was because the Russians would be there soon and the Nazis were trying to get into their good graces. And some of the girls, among whom I was, asked what difference it made, for after they had killed us, they would have everything back anyhow. I wouldn't touch any of that clothing, for I felt that taking anything would mean writing my own death certificte. Anyhow, I had my two precious dresses from home and who could carry so much? Who knew where we were going? Remembering those men who had walked passed our camp, the way they looked, how famished, with their clothing in shreds, I just wanted to have water and bread with me. And clothing? Only what I was able to put on. For the last three weeks, our bread ration had been very meager for we had to share a loaf bread with about ten girls. Now we were to find out why. Now we were given two loaves each. There was hardly time to speculate what was to happen to us anymore, for all of a sudden, the whistle sounded and the march into nowhere began. The march into heartbreak and death. I wish to honor all of my friends that fell on that fateful march in this chapter, all those young and wonderful lives, all those who fought until freedom was knocking at our door, only to be torn away from it without seeing its glory.

After marching about fifteen miles, we were given permission to rest for a few seconds, for those devils adjutant wanted to rest themselves. Although many were in cars, still a good many of them had to walk with us so no one got the idea to escape. Some of us fell out of tiredness, and there were a good many sick ones among us. I wasn't feeling too good myself, but I had been given some secret strength to go it all through. While we rested for that tiny little while, the shooting behind us, near the Oder River, continued. What were we doing? We were actually running away from our freedom. But there was no way to escape. Still we speculated that if the Nazis took us to the woods, we knew that they meant to kill us and we would try to escape. By this we, I mean Topka, Frieda, another Topka, and me. Frieda and I, knowing German, would take care of everything when we came to a farm, but in the meantime, there was no means or way to escape. And so we continued to wander. It didn't take long before we were wrecks, too. Many fell on the way, unable to march another step, and those were shot by the SS. They would never leave behind any witnesses. After a long and weary march, we were permitted to rest for five precious minutes. We took out some of the water that we had taken along, and sipped at it carefully, always the fear for thirst with us. We tried to be as careful as possible with our bread ration, cutting very thin slices, for we didn't know when we would get again a piece of bread. But somehow when one is so hungry for a piece of bread, never having had in those past few years enough to eat, the sight of those loaves just wouldn't let one resist the temptation. How long can two loaves last? The fear of hunger took over again. Any little piece we ate would make us choke. After resting this little while, we were ordered to get up quickly and get going, for, as were told, we were still to make thirty miles today. With a lot of cars going past us, and watched with eagle eyes, we still had a rest period. The cold was biting on us barely dressed girls and sometimes the wind or fear would bring tears into my eyes. But at least we still had something to eat and to drink. This was the most that counted right now. Oh, if the marching would only stop already! And the fear that the feet would give under one! But we still had so much hope, for the shooting from afar continued. When we heard bombing, the guards ducked under the trees, for, as we understood, enemy planes were going by. Their enemies were our friends. Oh, we didn't care if we fell that way—only to see them drifting with us and to be able to see the fear of death in their gruesome eyes was satisfying enough. Then they started to chase us, just as if they were going mad. On this chase, so many of my friends gave up, and there I saw them lying in a bloodbath. Then something took hold of me, as if I heard Ella's voice from far away. "Be brave, Lydia, don't ever give up! You are still so young, your whole life is still ahead of you. Haven't we gone through enough already, and we had always thought we would not to be able to live it through? After each rain the sun shines again!" Sweet Ella, I could hear those words of courage as though angels were above me. I tried to give courage to others—me, among the youngest in the group. As my friend Topka walked next to me, hardly able to go another step, I kept on whispering, "Chin up, Topka, you will see that their end is near and soon the sun will shine for us again."

Topka, with her kind and sorrowful smile, asked me what made me believe in all that nonsense still. "Don't you see, Lydia, they are taking us to a secluded spot where they will kill us." And the chase went on until the deep night. We walked like ghosts. Our ears were ringing from exhaustion, and then we asked one another what the end would be. Would we have to march through that awful, cold night? What had they got in their evil minds, those minds that always worked overtime for the devil? A few of us had a plan. We whispered it to one another. We should strike, for we saw that there was nothing good waiting for us, and to kill us all right there was against their plans. So let them do to us what they wanted, we were not going to go another step. Of course, someone had to have the courage to start it and give word to the Jew eldest. She was to give it further to the command. And it did do some good, for we were told to sit and wait near a farm. The SS guards went in to those farmers and we were given a shack for the night. I think by marching we would have been better off than by taking rest in that awful place. As they opened for us that empty, filthy shack, I could not believe my ears. There, in that tiny place, five hundred girls were to stay overnight. The outside would naturally be guarded by the SS. In this misery, all through the night, the cries and prayers went to heaven. It was all so merciless. I remember still that I hadn't even enough room to stand on both of my feet. So I first stood on one, and then I changed to the other. This was one of the longest nights I thought ever to stand through. If they had given to us enough room to sit at least—but this was another way to torment us, and, of course, in such a situation, almost everyone turns into a beast. The kicking, fighting, and swearing arose. No wonder, though, for most the time we stood on each other, and with no support, how could we help it? I looked so helplessly at those bare, cold, and dirty walls. Oh, Lord, let this gruesome night go by already! And then, as if, a thousand years had passed, outside, the dawn came. We heard the voice of our commander ordering us to get ready for our march. At least we would be able to breathe again. Anything was better than the awful night. I said to Topka, "Nothing could be more gruesome than that night. This must have been the worst that we have to go through." How mistaken I was, for those Nazibeasts just had so much gruesomeness still in store for us that it seemed our suffering would never end. And so the march for the next fourteen hours began. And now it was much worse than the previous day.

Lydia prior to being taken to camp age 9

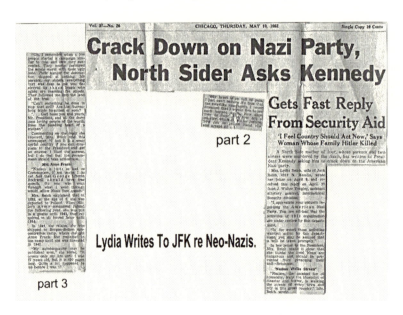

Article in the Albany Park News in Chicago

Mass grave of tens-of-thousands at Bergen-Belsen

Sign the camp Bergen-Belsen

Childhood, a poem by Lydia Rychner-Reich

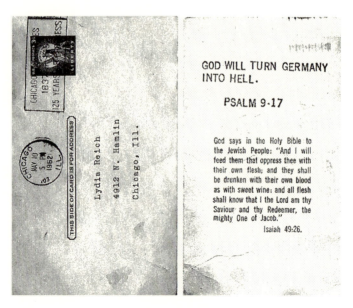

Christian group supports Holocaust Survivors

Sister Cilly, their mother and Lydia—Gleiwitz—1936

Card Lydia received from her mother while in camp

Front of card from Lydia's mother.

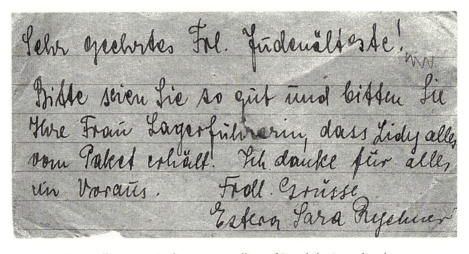

Sister Ella writing Lydia in camp telling of Bread she is sending her.

Card from older sister Ella received in camp.

Jack and Lydia's wedding photo.

Part of Lydia's family (Lydia in center.)

Lydia's nuclear family (Lydia smallest, far left.)

World I Accuse You, a poem by Lydia.

Lydia's father's business card in Germany prior to Jews being taken.

Jack and Lydia at their wedding (photo #2)

MY MOTHER

My Mothers porcelain face illuminates every wonderous place
Rosey her cheeks as she laughs and she weeps
Giving and caring to all she adores
Never it seeming to be any chore
Her heart is so tender she just doesn't remember
A childhood forsaken dear loved ones were taken
Mama and Papa had perished a whole family she cherished
The ghetto is finished not all has diminished
My Mother not so lucky as I
To have a Mother with a beautiful porcelain face

Lydia's oldest daughter Jeanie's poem about her mother.

Letter from Lydia's granddaughter (Carly) after she spoke about her experiences at Carly's social studies class.

Photo showing Lydia at the FRONT of crowd of survivors (holding flag) only four days after Liberation April 1945.

Brother Max's poem to sister Lydia. Page 1.

Brother Max's poem to sister Lydia. Page 2.

Tear stained card to Lydia from her mother just prior to her mother's death in another camp. (Front of card)

News letter 1

MY VOYAGE THROUGH HELL by UPF Member, Mrs. Lydia Reich

Let me introduce myself. My name is Lydia Reich. My husband and I reside in Illinois. My husband has had Parkinson's disease for almost nineteen years. We are both Holocaust survivors. Surviving is nothing new to us.

Let me draw you a picture of what hope and faith can do. I was born in Germany right into the Hitler regime. My family and I were deported to Poland right before Hitler's army invaded Poland. I had been torn from my parents arms when I was fifteen years old. After slave labor, I was taken to the death camp of Bergen Belsen and thrown into the barracks, where typhoid was rampant, to die an agonizing death. But I swore that I would survive. With no food and no water, we were each given a little place to sit on the floor. My pillows and blankets were decaying corpses. From a barracks of five hundred girls, only a handful survived. On the 15th of April 1945, I was liberated from this nightmare. All this and much more I have documented in an autobiography, for generations to remember.

Jack, my husband, who is distantly related to me (my uncle married his cousin), had found me after the war. We had known each other since early childhood. Shortly after Jack found me, we got married. We now have four children and six beautiful grandchildren. What a wonderful, caring husband and father Jack always was and is. Even with his disability of Parkinson's, he will always be there with a helping hand. Let me tell you, after all of our pain and struggle, Parkinson's is not going to stop us from living. Sure, we have our ups and downs, but we are so grateful for every day that we are together. We just celebrated our Golden Anniversary, and somehow I got Jack on the floor to dance a polka and a tango. It was not easy, but we did it! This shows you that where there is a will, there is a way. Jack has been on Mirapex* now for five months and, with his other medication, has had much improvement. In the coming months, his dosage will probably be increased and we are optimistic for continued improvement.

I must stress again that we are so grateful for every day that we are together. We are free and alive. There is so much hope out there. Oh, the tomorrows are going to be so beautiful. Just remember, Parkinson's is not fatal. We are living in such exciting times. Did you ever think how blessed we are with all the choices we have now? But none of us should rely on the medicines alone; compassion and love go a long way. Jack and I appreciate each other. We laugh and perhaps sometimes will cry together, we are only human. However, Parkinson's will never hurt us, and you know why? Because our love is so strong that we can overcome all of the hurdles. We both have seen Hell and right now is our Paradise. Before we go to sleep at night, we reminisce about funny episodes in our lives. Then my sweetie has a good night of sleep. I know that being supportive of your loved ones, showing that you are there for them and giving them hope, is so important. Please remember to give them hope. I know that hope is a healer.

In my eyes, Jack is still the dashing young man that he was fifty years ago, and I know that he believes vice versa. Parkinson's is really only another inconvenience in our lives. A better tomorrow is near. Tell your loved ones, assure them of it; the better tomorrow is near. With hope and faith we will all jump over this hurdle. No, Parkinson's will not interfere with our zest for life. We have been to Hell and back, and we will be darned if our survival will have been in vain. Remember to drink happy thoughts in your lives. Give love and hope, maybe they will not heal but maybe, just maybe, they will slow the progression of the disease. For me, all of those come easy because I adore my man.

Now, also remember, we have to be active and let our voices be heard. We have been pushed to the background long enough. The number of Parkinson's patients totals well over half a million and some even say a million. Do you realize that including caregivers for family members this number is in the millions? But, no matter how many we are, we all must give a little time, if only a little, and let our voices be heard. We will not go away. We are the voices of our loved ones and we want to be heard. Our loved ones are hurting and we are here to love and protect them. My love and admiration to all of you. We shall survive!

News letter 2

Wi is gewein iber der End die gantz Menschheit?
Wenn fun die kworim hot sich gelejt heren der Echo "Barmherzigkeit,"
Und wu seit Ihr Alle gewein, wenn das Feter hot gebrennt
Unter die Kerper fun mein Volk, zeidenen bei telefonische hendt?
Wenn men hot uns gefirt wie die Shug fun die Herd?
Ihr hot Alle geschwigen, kejner fun zij gestert!

Fu Wu seit Ihr nur geweist Die Kreiselt fun jeden
Wenn mein Unschuldig Volk, fun Tiger zertreten?

Hakenkreiz, Symbol fun Vasklavung, Mord und fun Schand,
Is 4 soch Plotzer bejubelt in land!
Fundament fun Zerstirung, Groji und Sorgen,
Mit zein Finsterkeit vertet, zu zerstiren den kumenden Morgen!
Nazism, mit sein Schmutz und Schande,
Arbeitet weiter mit zejier blutigen Propaganda!
Afilu Interpol, Miter fun Gerechtigkeit iber der globe,
Mer zu helfen mein Volk, Sei schockeln den Kopp!

Allmechtiger in Himmel, giv es klingt wie Nokum,
Ich bet um Barcelerung gerichten Rachmunes
Nemm Dir up far mein Volk, as der Telvel soll schwelgen,
Und mir nit mehr fun Verzweiflung sollen muzen leiden;
Ihr starke Nationen, Ihr hobt's am Gewissen,
As mein Friedvolles Volk, in Flammen zerissen;
Und wenn mein Herz wet nit mehr schlagen,
Well ich stendig Dir noch klugen,
Und mein Neshume wet schreien, "Welt gib mir bescheid,
Wu, oh wu, is die Menschliche Gerechtigkeit;"

Lydia's poem "World I accuse You" in YIDDISH, page 1.

Lydia's poem "World I accuse You" in YIDDISH, page 2.

"World Without Jews", a poem by Lydia and friend (deceased.)

Poem from Sister Ella, page 1.

Poem from sister Ella, page 2.

Tear stained card to Lydia from her mother just prior to her mother's death in another camp. (Back of card)

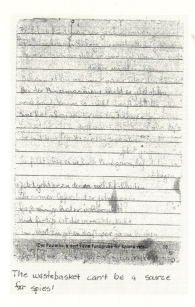

Propaganda warnings on Nazi stationary.

Food ration card. (front)

Food ration card. (back)

Red Cross letter. (back)

Red Cross letter. (front)

Lydia's sibs Max and Ella.

Sister Ella's last card sent to camp in which
she reminded Lydia to stay out of harm's way. (front)

Sister Ellas last card to Lydia. (back)

Steven Spielberg's Shoah letter.

THEY CAME FIRST for the Communists,
  and I didn't speak up because I wasn't a Communist.

THEN THEY CAME for the Jews,
  and I didn't speak up because I wasn't a Jew.

THEN THEY CAME for the trade unionists,
  and I didn't speak up because I wasn't a trade unionist.

THEN THEY CAME for the Catholics,
  and I didn't speak up because I was a Protestant.

THEN THEY CAME for me,
  and by that time no one was left to speak up.

Stand Up poster

Wonderful Mother, a poem by Lydia's daughter Belle, written at age 16.

DEPARTURE FROM GREABEN

For now there was no marching anymore, only chasing, and so we were running, a helpless people, with freedom and death side by side. As the night approached again, we passed a small town. Or was it a big one? I really can't recall it that vividly, for my feet hurt so much and everything ached so agonizingly that I hardly realized what was going on around me. Everything was hopeless. As we passed those houses, one of my friends asked, "How about going into one on our way? We can tell the people that we are lost from a group of German refugees." We knew that it was senseless, for who would believe us? And then there was the fear of being caught—what would we have to go through then? Maybe it was worth the chance, for as the Lord says, "If you help yourselves, I will help you, too!" but fear was hurling all around, and we just had no strength for any risk. So we were brought to the train station called Jannowitz. From then on, things that happened are just too gruesome to recall. Now we had become cattle, or even worse. Who ever heard of beating an animal bloody to ship it in a freight wagon? For there were prepared freight wagons for us, with two tiny windows. The wagons were to be sealed, but then the Nazis changed their evil minds and took us to cattle wagons, each wagon to seat one hundred of us, and here hundreds of girls were chased and whipped about. Some of my friends were unable to walk into the wagons and they were beaten to death with clubs and other weapons. Their bodies were thrown on separate wagons and locked up, some still alive and in agony, some dead already; they just threw them in with such satisfaction, and their growling laughter sounded in my ears for many a year to come. The Lord is my witness, with a few of those that survived, that everything I say is the whole truth.

As I was about to go into the wagon, I saw Hella, one of our cooks from camp, in such agony that she couldn't walk into the wagon. I felt so sorry for her, I was afraid that the beasts were going to throw her on the wagon of death. I took her around the waist so that she would be able to support herself on me. I realized the grave situation, for if they wanted, those Nazibeasts could throw me together with her into that awful wagon. As I supported her, I remembered Ella's boldness at Punkt, when she said in a fearless voice, "Five Jews, all are employed," and how this had saved us on that fateful day. So I went forward with Hella, she half alive, and I told the murderer on the platform that she was my aunt and that she was a little bit tired from the journey. He looked with his murderous eyes, and asked me if I was sure that I would take care of her. I promised that I would and so we came on the wagon. Then she fell into hysteria and some of the girls asked me why I had done it, because this woman had never done anything good for me to deserve it. I ignored them. Then, having hardly room to sit down in the wagon, I let her rest on me and tried to nurse her with the little water I had left. I also gave her the little bit of bread I had left. I just didn't understand better than to help, me being still so naïve, not knowing that people will many times repay goodness with advantage. But I still am glad that I did it and I would do it again. Soon, my precious water supply was gone. Most of the girls had no water anymore, and with Hella lying on my bag where the bread was, there were only crumbs left. But what did it matter? I was so happy to have been able to help her. Later when all of us were famished, she herself had plenty of water left and plenty to eat, too. Later in Bergen-Belsen she had a good position, under the circumstances, and she acted as if she didn't even know me anymore. But it doesn't matter, for one shouldn't expect to be rewarded for a good deed. There stands someone high over us who rewards us for everything, and I was always grateful for every good deed I was able to perfrom.

We were squeezed into this filthy cattle wagon under much, much worse conditions than cattle taken for slaugther, and in such a predicament, fights and mistrust always begin. Like everywhere, those who were stronger won over the weaker ones. With Hella lying all over me, and her having quite some weight, my hands and feet fell asleep. In this misery, the wagons were going faster, faster, but to what destination? It looked to us as though there was no end to it, as though we were stranded on a desert and no one knew or cared what was going to happen to us. Like a ghost ship, the open wagons chased through rain and storm.

Some of the girls jumped out, making an end to all their suffering. Although we were soaked to the skin, we still prayed for snow to fall, for we had no water and we were so thirsty that most of us were in high fever. The fever burned so badly on our lips that we cried for a littler water, so when it snowed or rained, we thanked the Lord for it. With it, we wet our dry and blistered lips. Although I was all wet and frozen, the thing I remember the most is that whenever it rained or snowed, our spirits were highest. But at times, there was no rain or snow and even though we could to dry out in the wind, the thirst came back again, and then the hunger came. But the hunger didn't bother us as badly as the thirst. By now we had been out for a few days in the open wagons and the Nazis brought to us guards, Ukrainians who had joined the SS. And heaven forgive me, those were the worst yet. Why, those people really were the devil in flesh and blood. Did they ever enjoy seeing us in our agony! They tortured us so badly, just unbelievable, and the guard sitting in front of us enjoying his food and slurping his drink. With a sadistic smile he called me and asked if I wanted a little bit to drink. Me being famished, what did I care that his filthy mouth had touched the bottle, at least I would be able to get a few drops of liquid on my dried-out tongue. I went towards him with thankfulness in my eyes and reached out my hand for the bottle, half full of precious liquid—and he spilled it over my shoes. The girls leaped toward my shoes and tried to get hold with their hands of some of that precious liquid. It looked as if they were about to tear my shoes from my feet. The guard stood there, screaming for laughter, as if he was about to go into pieces. Our thirst was so awful that we didn't look at him as such a sadist and we pleaded and begged, "Please, please have a heart, bring us some water." We noticed that, on another wagon, they had brought the girls some water, but we found out later that those guards had done the same fun things with the other girls. They spilled the water right in front of the eyes of those parched girls. At last it looked as if we had softened his heart, for he said that we should leave him alone, he would get some water for us.

He brought a tiny bit in and the girls jumped over him to grab the precious liquid out of his hands. Some of the stronger girls refreshed themselves a little bit, but the weak ones, among which I was, were unable to get near. The guard enjoyed it so tremendously that from then on, he would bring in few drops of water. Most of the time it would be spilled anyhow, for one wanted to grab it from the other's hand.

To go out for some urgent need was out of the question, so it was lucky that some of the girls had brought along a dish which would be our toilet. If we were fortunate, we got water to drink in it. Our prayer for snow continued. Although we got soaked through, how good and blissful it felt. Me, not being able to stand on my feet any more (and who was?), I reproached myself, *Why, oh, why, didn't I try to escape on our way to the station?* Looking Aryan and knowing the German language perfectly well, I was so stupid not to have tried to save myself from all that torment. For some of the girls did escape. Even at the station, so heavily guarded, some of the girls said it was no use. Our destination was death, so any try would be worthwhile. A few were caught, and a few got killed, but a few that escaped from that inferno are alive today. And my brain worked and worked for a way to get out of this, a way to escape, for anything was better than to have to stand this kind of torture. A person always thinks, when things look very bad, that there just can't come anything worse, but there is no end to the suffering one can endure. Things can always get worse, as we were soon to find out.

We endured this awful misery in those open wagons for one week, and then we heard up in front in those other wagons crying and weeping. What had happened? The news traveled soon to our wagon. Those torturers of ours had prepared closed wagons for us. Having heard while we were still children that many of our people had been taken to the crematoriums in closed wagons, we felt that here lay the end station to our dreams. All of our suffering and hoping had been in vain. After so much suffering, we were doomed to die. Good-bye, beautiful world, good-bye freedom. I had always thought of freedom as a pretty maiden with flowers in her hair. She was chasing after us, but she would come too late, she couldn't outrun the devil. She was just too slow. No, the world is not cruel, who had ever said such? The world was our paradise—only the people in it are so cruel. I would spend my sweet sixteenth birthday in the gas chambers. And here again, it was as though I could hear my mother whisper in my ears. "Don't despair, Lydilein! They haven't killed you yet; you will see, once again your life will be sunshine and roses!" And then my tears ceased falling.

They unloaded us in a hurry, rushing us to the closed wagons, for there was no time to lose if we wanted to stay alive to greet the pretty maiden with the flowers in her hair. Water and food was next to heaven for us right now. The Nazis started to count us again, to make sure, heaven forbid, that none of their cattle had escaped. For if one dared to, bulletins with a description went out and the watch over us was reinforced. Again, one hundred girls were to go in one wagon. The gruesomeness of this picture was never to be forgotten. And then fortune did smile on us a little, for how utterly awful did we imagine our future, and all of a sudden it looked a little bit brighter. How come they changed their minds about gassing us, we asked each other, for in the wagons were two little fenced-in windows and, glory, they left the doors a tiny bit open. They could afford it, for we were heavily guarded, and in an emergency, if an air attack occurred, they wanted to be able to escape themselves. After making the best of our new home, we found, oh, glory, that there was place for each of us to sit. Me being all the time together with Topka, we changed places so that one could put her head on the other to rest. With our two places combined, we were able to rest a little one at the time. Since the guards had been changed, they didn't know us yet so well, so our Jew eldest, always the boss, had taken all the ones that were our personnel at camp and they received a special wagon. Now Hella, back with her crowd, didn't know me anymore. As each of us found our seats, we were ordered to be quiet. If we behaved, we would get something to eat. Since we hadn't had any food since we left Graeben, most of the girls had hungered for a few days already. They brought around soup—well, it looked more like dishwater, but for us it tasted heavenly. Then a wagon eldest was chosen to provide discipline, always with their sadistic efficiency. And then we were given the most precious of it all, water.

A few kettles with water were brought and each of us was given a ration of water. And then what heaven, what fortune! Our wagon eldest was given a bread ration for us, and to top it all, a salty little cheese. It felt as if the angels sang to us of happiness to come. It turned out that this little cheese was just part of their torture, for the thirst that we suffered from it later one can never, but never, imagine. While we consumed our long yearned for feast, who thought about later? Why would they want to torture us still? Fortune had come to us and would stay with us from now on. The Nazis saw that it was hopeless and that doom was near—or so we thought. But some of the girls were so cautious already. They said it looked more like the last meal to them. As soon as the first hunger was appeased, and the thrist quenched, one just couldn't help but feel hopeful again. I said, "Who would have thought of that, to once again get a piece of bread and again drink water to satisfaciton?"

But all good things come to an end, and soon the bitter night approached. Again we spent it fighting, pushing, and pleading to the Lord. Now the thirst came in such a murderous manner, for the very salty cheese started to act up. We tore out our hair for thirst. As I lay there in agony of thirst, a hand reached towards me in the dark of the night with something cool and wet. Not far away from where I sat was a lady who had known my sister in Bendzin. She had seen me crying of thirst, and she had a little can with her which she had filled with her water ration. She reached it over to me so I could take a few sips. Just like an angel out of the dark, she came. For the next three days, Lady Luck stayed with us, for we received our water and bread daily. After those three days, then the worst came to us. For from then on, hunger and thirst really began, and for the next six days, we weren't given anything. Nothing to eat, nothing to drink. Six such awful days, in which many of us were ready to go insane. Six days, we cried and even laughed out of despair. Or were we halfway insane already? Who knows what went through our minds, for we weren't human anymore. When the wagons made station, we went towards the fenced windows and begged little children for a little water. Some of them, if alone, felt sorry and tried to help us, for even those little ones saw how famished we were. But if they were with their parents or any grown-ups, those people pulled the children away, asking them if they didn't know that here were those awful Jews. Those horrible Jews—how few were left, how tormented, how degraded we were! But the people still ran as if the plague was on their tail, and all of those grown-ups on the outside, seeing us in despair, laughed and spat at us. How could people be so heartless? At times, when the train passed a little creek, we were permitted to leave for a few minutes and the first thing we did was drink from that precious liquid called water. However dirty it was, it still meant heaven for us. At times, we undressed in the cold and washed up, but it didn't help us much, for the insects came in swarms over us. So it went on for the next six days in the wagon cell, and each day we were promised that today we would come to our destination. Everything around us was so very quiet, such a quiet that it made us shudder. We knew that this was our destination, all right, for all around we saw prison clothing with the yellow star of Jude and the prison numbers. The one thing we didn't know was that those who wore this clothing were part of a group who had escaped previously. We thought the Nazis would now take us into the woods to kill us. As we were sitting there quietly, one of my girlfriends told me that now was the time, now or never. "Let us make a break, for death is lurking somewhere around in the quiet of this peaceful woods. If we let the chance for survival escape right now, our doom is near." So slowly, we started removing our stars and numbers, and as we were getting ready, all of a sudden our wagons were closed. New orders had come and we were to leave this place in closed wagons. We tried to relax, for the fear of those woods and things to come had worn us out, not to mention the hunger and thirst. As the wagon wheels started rolling again, we passed stations with passenger trains coming from the opposite direction. If the doors of the wagons weren't shut, girls jumped into those passenger trains. Some of those girls survived, but many of them got killed. Suddenly one night, way past midnight, our wagon doors were pulled wide open. Spotlights blinded our eyes and we were surrounded by countless SS who were there to bit us a welcome. With guns, with rifles, and with clubs they chased us from the wagons. We were afraid to even breathe. As the spotlights moved around, I could see that we were at a little train station. That station probably was a peaceful little place, but right now it was more like the foreshadowing of hell. After they counted us and made sure that none of us were lost, we were ordered to march. There still were some very smart and courageous girls among us, and two of them, even in this lighted foreplace of hell, escaped. How much did I envy their courage later. But as we were marching towards the woods again, my thoughts went around one and one thing only. I asked Frieda, "Can you imagine something more heavenly than to have reached finally our destination? Can you imagine what paradise, after such a long time, it will be to be able to have a cot to put our heads onto? Isn't it too good to be true?" The only wish I had was once again to have a place to rest, even if it was only a a measly cot like we used to have in Graeben, with mattresses filled with straw. Frieda nodded her head and tears ran down her cheeks. Impossible to imagine that, after having been crammed in those wagons like cattle, now we would be able to have again a place to rest, some water to drink, and some food. That those closed wagons, in comparison with what was to come, were paradise, we wouldn't have imagined in our worst nightmares. Who would have thought it? So long was the march towards our destination, so filled with the hatred in the voices of the Nazis' henchmen, so endless, so hopeless. Exhausted to our last draw of breath after two and a half hours of endless marching, we were finally told to stop, and there we saw that we were about to enter hell. The huge gates were wide open, the fences were loaded with electricity, and all around us were the camp commandos and huge spotlights which made us dizzy. Through such peace we had marched until we reached this camp, and no one would have thought that here in these beautiful surroundings lay one of the most murderous of all camps ever to be created. We had reached Bergen-Belsen.

BERGEN-BELSEN

As those huge gates closed behind me, my first thought was, *Why, oh why, didn't I have guts enough to escape before?* For as I saw it, this was the end. I did not realize yet how bitter an end it would be, and how much suffering there still lay ahead of us. Dead tired, we kept marching into the huge camp, obeying the orders of the Nazibeasts as if we were machinery. Everything inside me was numb. If only the orders from those murderous lips would cease, those nightmarish orders! If only those reflectors would stop shining into my eyes! And then we waited in the awful cold, trembling from fear and desperation. What were we waiting for in this graveyard? The decison made our blood freeze in our veins, for we were marched towards a place which looked very much like a crematorium with its large and fearful chimneys stretching out like ghosts into the black night, so very frightful to our tormented souls. And one big prayer went from each of us up to the dark sky: "Oh, merciful God, please have mercy with us, please help us in our deep despair!" As we waited outside for our turn to enter this gruesome place, the chimney began to smoke, and we asked ourselves, have they started already? Those girls that had food left shared with one another so that we wouldn't leave the Nazis the satisfaciotn of having food left over. In twenties we entered that place of horror. As we entered, we saw no women inside, only SS men. We were ordered to undress and any who possessed more then one piece of clothing had to put it on a certain pile. The rest of the clothes hung on a stand, which as they said with their gloomy voices, would go for disinfection.

As we started to undress, all the time under commands which seemed to include only a few words—and the most heard was "schneller, schneller."

"Quicker, quicker." What happened from then on, I am unable to describe, for there had never, in history of men, been anything so inhuman since the beginning of the world. These Nazis would not believe that we had been robbed already and that we had no jewelry left. Their feverish greed and search went on; they just went on searching everywhere. Those filthy, brutal beasts, this superior race, to remember this day even today makes my blood boil. How can you forget such? How can anyone forget such, ever? Then they tried to beat and whip it out of us, us, standing there in the nude, with our young and famished bodies. How much I prayed for the floor to give under me and that it would swallow me right there and then so that I would not have to go through that awful disgrace in my innocent shame. But the floor wouldn't give under me, and I had to go through it all, with all of its horror. Then we were ordered towards the showers, which as we understood, meant only one thing—here comes our end. Afraid to speak another word, I thought, *If the end has to come, please, merciful God, let it come quickly,* for we had heard that gas is not a hard death and that one dies quickly; one doesn't suffer so badly, so let the end come already. As we entered the washroom each of us was given some gooey and messy soap; it felt as if the victims from whose fat the soap had been made were still fighting with death. This awful soap, how it made me shudder, as if one still could hear the groaning of those victims. All of a sudden, as if my mother was nearby, I heard a voice whispering into my ears, "Lydilein, it isn't the end yet, stay brave and you will see, your life will once again be sunshine and roses." At home in the worst times when we went around hungry, Mother had always planted roses and flowers in our tiny garden; I enjoyed them because they meant fulfilment of my dreams. The world could be bitter and dark, but for me it was paradise as long as I had my sunshine and roses. But then all of it went away; the sunshine and roses were gone. And now here I was, so far away from sunshine and roses that it hurt to think about it. It was as if she was singing me a lullaby; with her sweet voice whispering into my ear, I suddenly stood up straight and thought to myself, *Let them do to me what they want to to, I shall bite my lips tightly together and will pretend to myself that it all is only a nightmare.* As we turned on the showers, which until the end we had thought were filled with gas, to our greatest surprise, water came out. At the end of our strength, we started crying. As we were ordered by the SS, who were always arounds us, to soap ourselves good with this gooey mess, all of a sudden the water stopped. Up to now it had been as cold as ice. But no water came anymore, and we realized that that was all the water given to us. Then their fearsome voices shouted for us to get out, and we went into another room. This room was freezing cold, and here we waited for another few hours. Standing and waiting, waiting, in this painful cold, with us undressed—for what were we waiting? At last we got our clothing back, but most of it was gone. If a girl could find half of it, she was very fortunate indeed. The first thing I looked for was my coat, for in it I had my precious possessions, mail and pictures from dearly beloved ones. To my great luck, I found my coat, and as I was squeezing it tightly to my heart, I felt that all of it was still inside.

I must have been the only person so fortunate, for it really sounds fantastic, but it is the whole truth. Having hold of my coat, I looked around for the rest of my clothing, but except for my knitted dress and some of my underwear, I didn't find a thing. Then as I looked up on the stand, there were my shoes! Although they were all dried out from the oven, it still was a miracle to have them. From then on, each of us was halfway dressed in that bitter cold. We were ordered to stay again outside in the freezing cold; hardly dressed, we were again to wait, wait, wait. The night was so cold and gruesome, but we were alive, and that was the thing that really mattered, although some girls were so disgusted that they said they should have killed us. But the light of hope kept on glowing in me, the hope for survival, the hope that all of it must end soon, the hope that all of our suffering would not have been in vain. I was only waiting for the minute to come when we would be given our barracks and we could have a warm place to rest, a little cot, a tiny one, only to have somewhere to put our heads again. How very disappointed we were to be, and how much I regretted later that I had not escaped. From how much agony and disaster I could have saved myself. And I kept on asking myself, *Why, oh why, didn't I do it?* For we were taken to barracks, all right, barracks with the windows broken and the floors so awful and filthy that the stench made us nauseous. The barracks were empty, for hundreds and hundreds of girls were to lay there on the dirty, cold floor. There was nothing inside except the filth and the stench. What were we to do in the awful cold, hardly dressed? We lay on the cold floor taking a little rest. The worst treatment was not enough for their horrible minds. As the day finally started to dawn, we heard around us voices; names were called as some girls from other barracks sneaked in. The place was so well guarded, but still the curiosity wouldn't let some of them rest, and there took place a heartbreaking film in front of our eyes. Sisters and aunts, mothers and daughters and other kin found each other. Auschwitz, they said, was no more, and many had come to Bergen-Belsen from there. How desperately I looked into those faces, how desperately I waited to hear my name called. *Why can't I be that lucky?* I asked myself. Although a very small number of the girls found relatives, it seemed to me that everyone except me had found someone. Then, a shock ran through me, for one of the girls from my camp who had a sister in camp together with Ella had found her sister. I jumped toward her, choking on my words. "Where is Ella?"

"Ella is dead," she replied. I couldn't move. I just stood there like I was coming out of a faint.

What, Ella, my sister, so full of hope and life, was dead? "It can't be," I screamed out in hysteria, "tell me that you are lying. Where is Ella? She is here somewhere among you, I know," I screamed in my agony. "You all are only jealous of her because she is so pretty, everybody was always jealous, I know that is it, that is why you are lying to me, just to hurt me, because I am her sister, to hurt the both of us."

Topka came near me and kept on stroking my hair, trying to bring me back to reality. "Do you think Ella would want you to behave that way, do you think it would make her happy to know it? You can't help her anymore, but you can help yourself by being strong. Maybe Cilly is still alive—no one had seen her going into the chambers—there is always the possibility that she is still alive, maybe they did go into hiding, or maybe your mother will be among those girls here. Don't you see how awfully big this camp is? There will be more occasions to find things out. Meanwhile, keep strong, Lydia, for my sake, for your sake, let's keep on fighting for our survival. I haven't found anyone, either." Dear Topka, her heart breaking, how much she wanted me to stay strong, for as she kept saying, my courage gave her always new hope, but if my courage was gone, she thought that all of our hope would go with it. When I quieted down, I found out everything about Ella. From the camp where Ella had been, they had taken hundreds of girls quite some time ago to Auschwitz, and from all of those hundreds of girls, only seven were alive. The girl told me she remembered Ella's name had been called out when they came to Auschwitz because they wanted to take her to work at the office in charge of the extermination.

As they called out her name, how very pretty she had looked still and how proudly she had answered their questions. The girl even recalled that Ella had worn one of her nice sweaters. But Ella had to do some filthy work for the commandant who was in charge of her, and she wasn't able to take it. From that moment on, she lost all of her zest for life. Before she was taken to the gas chambers, she told to one of the girls, "Lola, the war will end soon, and not many of us will stay alive, but I have somehow a feeling that my little sister Lydia will make it through. You must promise to me, please promise, and then I will die peacefully, that if you live through this war—you will, I am sure—search for my little sister. Help her to find my two brothers, for as things look, she will no one have left in this world except them." And then Ella was gone. Gone to eternal peace, my life-loving sister Ella was murdered by those brutal Nazihands in the prime of her life. That day I didn't have much time to think about it, for every few minutes there was another roll call, or we got new numbers, or there this, here that, there some kind of punishment, for what I still don't know. We had to kneel in the cold and wet for a couple hours. They kept on counting us as if we were their most precious possessions in the world. Our Jew eldest from camp had again found a position here. She was to become our block eldest. Again Lady Fortune smiled at her, even in this camp of dead, for she was to choose her own helpers. Who would it be but those who had been her personnel back at Graeben. Group eldest, room eldest, watch guard, and so it went on and on. I was among a group that was marching along the camp for some food, when suddenly from far away I heard my name being called. The quiet was so awful in this well-guarded camp. Everyone turned their heads toward me, some with a little envy, some with anxiety. Whoever had found me, it must be someone with power around here, for who else would have dared call my name? I was frightened and very anxious to see the caller. Who could it be? And then the person came running towards me, out of breath, repeatedly calling my name; here came my friend Sarah from Bendzin, who had been with us among those deportees from Germany. During the war, she had disappeared from Bendzin and we had heard that she was taken to camp. Here she stood in front of me, telling me she was block eldest, to my great joy, at the next block to where I was right now. She told me that I must come over to her block later on. As we continued our walk, I just couldn't believe that I had, here in the camp of dead, found a chance for survival, for to have found my girlfriend Sarah meant much help. Many of the girls told me how very lucky I was, and Topka was so happy. She said that she had told me I would find someone sooner or later, and I told Topka that as soon as I could get some help from Sarah, I would get her into her block, too. The same day I went to Sarah, and now I met my biggest disappointment. As I tried to sneak myself into her barracks, I saw that the block was under more awful conditions than the one I was in. If in my place the filth made us nauseated, it was here much worse. The whole block was occupied by Hungarian Jewish girls. As I looked around in this jungle, for there must have been more than a thousand girls, I knew you had to really be tough to work in that place, and I kept on thinking I was sure that none of my sisters would have been able to hold such job as Sarah.

But she was from now on my greatest hope for survival. Here Sarah had her own tiny place, with one of the most wonderful possessions, one I hadn't seen for quite some time—her own cot. Oh, to be able to put one's head on such again, what paradise it would be for me! For hunger, thirst, and filth was the trademark of this camp. That there still could be anything worse, we didn't think of. I stood in front of Sarah again, pleading with my eyes. Please help! For she was able to help. And I felt how lucky I was, and how happy Mother would be to know that Sarah had found me, Sarah, such good a friend of mine. As I stood there in front of her, she didn't seem the same as before. She talked to me very little, and I had thought that we would have much to talk about. She told me she had seen Cilly in Auschwitz one day for a second from afar. As if in a haze, she had seen her going towards the chambers, but she could, of course, be wrong. Anyhow, I was there standing in front of her in my deep desperation, wanting to hear more, wanting to talk about old times, and the most, wanting Sarah to help me. She put a bowl of warm soup in front of me. Soup! I had eaten hardly a thing for a few days, and I had already forgotten the taste of soup. It tasted so heavenly divine. It was cooked with plenty of potato peelings, and I later found out that potato peelings were only given to some, for to find such later in the soup was the greatest luck. Those potato peels tasted so wonderful, but in the middle of my feast, I couldn't swallow a bite, for I remembered that across the block was Topka waiting for me, so hungry, so anxious. How could I eat up everything, knowing that? Sarah looked at me with surprise, so I ate up quickly. As I finished, I saw that Sarah wouldn't speak a word and I was to go back quickly, for if another roll call came and I was missing, who knows what might happen to me. After I saw that Sarah wouldn't ask me if I wanted to stay with her, which I thought was natural, I just brought it over my lips and told her how much I wanted to stay with her. Her reply was the most shocking for me. "No, Lydia, you misunderstood me when I told you to come and see me. I wanted to give you some soup, for I knew how very hungry you must be. Yes, of course, we were once very good friends, but this was back almost a lifetime ago. I can't help you in any way." How could she speak to me this way?

I replied, "And how about our friendship, have you forgotten it? For old times sake, please? Sarah, help me, take me to your place! Anything you want me to do for you, I shall do!" Her cold reply was, "No, Lydia, I made other friends at Auschwitz. Those bind me much more than the friendship I had with you ever will, so if you want, I can give you once more some soup, and this will be about all that I can do for you." With those words she turned away from me and it meant good-bye, or good riddance. As I returned to my own block, Topka, seeing my face, didn't ask much, for she knew without asking that all of our hopes had burst just like soap bubbles.

When she heard that Sarah had told me I could come back once again for some soup, Topka's hopes were still high, but I told her that I would rather die than go beg for another bowl of soup. Topka tried to persuade me that here was no matter of pride, that we were about to drown and we just had to grab hold of any blade of straw in order to find a way to survive. The door was still open and I kept on thinking that maybe her conscience would bother her, and probably the next time that I went over, she would help me. Yes, that was it. How foolish of me to try being proud; she must have time to think things over. Maybe she wanted to ask for permission, and she didn't want to tell me until she was permitted to take me over there. But all my hopes vanished when I went to her the second time; she hadn't changed. So I vowed that never would I go see Sarah again.

Life at this place was so awful that I wondered at still being alive as each day dawned. Sometimes the Nazis gave us a small piece of bread. On a lucky day, we got a little watery turnip soup. If one had no dish, one could trade half of the soup to borrow a dish from someone else. A few days later, women from the Ukraine came to our block and it became one big nightmare. Now there was no place left even to sit. One was kicked and stepped on constantly. Although those women were themselves prisoners, they hated the Jews in such a fanatic way, it was unbelievable. When we got our small pieces of bread and tried to save a few bites for later, they grabbed it from us. If we tried to hide it, they found it. We just weren't able to fight those strong and big women. The washroom situation was so horrible that the thought of it still now makes me nauseated. The camp was like the land of the livng dead. Corpses were a common sight in Bergen-Belsen and some of our girls were assigned to work details. They had to take the corpses over to the crematorium, and those corpses gave out an awful stench, for they were already decaying. During the day we saw pushcarts, filled with hundreds of skeleton-like bodies, being pulled by some of the girls.

This horrible camp, who could have thought of such a monstrous place? In which sick mind was so much evil designed? This camp was so huge, it looked like a town. With hundreds of barracks, it looked like a forlorn world. Or was it still part of this world? So many people were suffering and so many were dying every day. But if I thought that I had seen all the misery that this camp had to offer us, I was very mistaken. For I was to see much more later.

We were told that we were to go to work, and if we stayed on at work, we would get each day on our return a bread ration. It wasn't much, but to know that one would get the piece of bread was a comforting feeling, and to be able to get out of this horror even to work made the day pass quickly. But in those awful nights, one nearly died of thirst in this sticky place with hundreds and hundreds of girls around. We were stepped on, walked over, and without a place to lay down our heads. The hunger hurt so badly, it just wouldn't let you find any sleep. With working, we imagined that things would get better, but then we saw what we had to do. I was sixteen years old and so weak and hungry, I could hardly drag my feet, but we were taken to the forest commander.

There we were told to carry, two girls together or one alone, huge trees, which were so heavy they pulled us to the ground. Five miles we had to go with each load, and we weren't permitted to go slowly, either. For the next few days, we had to do that kind of work for about ten hours at a shift. Hardly dressed, the bitter cold bit at us, but when we came back to the camp, at least a slice of bread waited for us. The work was hard and we had hardly anything to eat, so we just knew we couldn't keep on like this. But some girls warned me to try stay at work as long as I could, for the Nazis would make a selection, and whoever was unable to work, they would take over to the typhoid section of the camp. The typhoid section— this was the greatest fear of it all—we had heard was even worse than the gas chambers. For whoever was taken over there was doomed to die one of the most gruesome deaths. But this all I was to find out a little later. With hardly any food to eat, many of my friends knew that we wouldn't be able to go on much longer. We looked already like the living dead.

One day, sure enough, the day of judgment came. This fateful day was like a nightmare, never to be forgotten. We were called outside so they could see our physical condition, and the selection began. One group was to go on this side, the other on the other side. We wondered what they meant by it. We were soon to find out. Topka and I and many of my friends from camp were marched toward the typhoid section. Among us were little Sarah and her mother, along with Rivka, the girl we always teased.

Well, Lydia, your time has finally come, I said to myself as we walked towards our goal, crying, weeping, and pleading. We were put into Block No. 217, the typhoid section. This was one of the worse blocks in the section. This time we had a welcoming committee, too, but they weren't live people, only dead bodies. The stench that welcomed us was frightful. This little block had over five hundred inhabitants and there was no place to move. Topka and I were given a tiny piece of floor next to each other near the end of the block, but those who were near the walls were the fortunate ones, for they had at least a place to lean. At night they stretched their feet on us, so what could we do? They had been there before us and they were stronger, bigger, and older. Our new group eldest was a fat slob, an ugly creature, who, when she was given food for us, would steal most of it. The first impression of this place was worse than hell. Here there were no washrooms, no water, nothing at all. If one had an urgent need, one just had to do it. If you were lucky enough to have a can, you used it. If we were very lucky, we were permitted to go outside once a day to perform certain needs in a corner. If you just weren't fortunate, you just had to do it where you were sitting, right inside the barracks. At times, we loaned each other a tiny can and passed it toward the door. As it went over a good many heads, everyone got something of it on the head. No, anybody who hasn't lived through such can imagine this picture of torment. The next day when we were permitted to go outside for a few minutes, I ran towards the barbed wire which cut our camp off from the other part of the camp. From afar, I saw Sarah coming. I called her name out loudly in my agony. As she was nearby and had seen me, I pleaded and begged her to help me and take me out of this camp. "Sarah, don't you see, I am doomed to die, this is the end!" Her cold reply has haunted me ever since.

"So many are dying, so what difference does it make if one more will die?" And with those words she walked past me. And so my life in one of the worse hells had begun. No food, hardly at all, no water—how long would we be able to live? I knew that from now on, it was only a question of days. No, never had there been anything like it.

And the great dying began. Next to me a lady went insane and at times she tried to choke me and tear my hair out. I was frightened to death at looking into her insane eyes. Lice were crawling all over us. They invaded us by the millions—the biggest nightmare forever, the lice and the Swastika. It seemed there wasn't anything around but lice. They swarmed all over us, and we spent our whole time trying to get rid of them but it was just like dimming a fire with gasoline. The more we tried to get rid of them, the more they came in swarms all over us. I wore my knitted dress from home, and here it was a fortress for millions of lice. Typhoid was all around us, too, and all around were people in an agony of thirst and pain. The screams from their unconscious minds were enough to make us slowly go insane.

Five Hungarian sisters were not far from where I sat. Those girls must have come from a very wealthy home, but those poor souls didn't last long. They were the ones that went first. However much misery there was around one, there were those girls to make one's life even more miserable. However down we were already, those girls, not master of their minds anymore, laughed at the most tragic situation. I despised it so much, but I was frightened to show it, for those were the tough ones. Those five sisters somehow had a feeling that they had found a friend in me.

Each day until her choking voice could speak no more, one of the sisters announced to me that another sister had passed away. Looking around me I saw how animal-like those girls had become. With more than half of us insane, I couldn't help but feel that here was the end of all humanity. How far away was my home—did I ever have a childhood? Or was I born into this awful bondage? It was impossible to think back. Everything just sounded so insane, so unbelievable. Weak from hunger and thirst, most of the girls were unable to walk.

Each and every day we had to go out on roll call. At times when the wind blew and the storm was strong, we were made to kneel down in the horrible weather for hours and hours. Those who were unable were beaten with clubs until they couldn't move anymore forever. Once or twice we were allowed to take out the dead, and then we had to burn them in front of our barracks, and the stench was so awful that soon the barracks were full of sick and nauseated people. Wherever one stepped, wherever the stench blew, there lay mutilated, dried-out bodies. Once those were girls in the prime of life, but now it was impossible to look at them. The typhoid took over so quickly in our barracks, I was frightened and I told Topka, who was frightened just like me, that I was sure we would get it and our end would be like the others. Here I pointed to the burning bodies outside. In my great despair, every time we were able to go outside for a little while, I looked around to find someone who had known my parents, or maybe to find one of relatives, and maybe they would help me. But there was no such luck; except for Sarah, I found no one, and Sarah I had to forget. Sarah's words came into my mind: "So many die, so there will be one more." But I didn't want to die, I wanted to live. Each time I felt that I was near death, for the hunger and thirst was unbearable, in my greatest despair when I felt that I just couldn't go on any longer, I heard Mother's sweet voice whispering into my ears, "... and your life will once again be sunshine and roses." Then I would go on fighting for my life, but the odds were so very much against me. The screams of agony around me were so frightful.

One day I heard a tiny voice: "Please, Mamale, don't leave me! Mamale, stay with me." I looked toward the voice, for it was familiar to me, and there stood little Sarah, the little girl from our previous camp who had found her mother under such fantastic circumstances, both saved from the gas chamber. Little Sarah had been all the time together with her mother, and here her mother lay on the floor, with little Sarah kneeling beside her holding her head. Her mother begged her for a drop of water and little Sarah sat there helplessly as her mother died in her arms. How can one ever imagine all those sadistc deeds the Nazis performed in the name of the Fuehrer?

In my coat I had, together with my other most precious possessions, my diary and a pencil. And here I would write in poem form about our life, but I had to be very cautious, for if I were caught, it would have been the end. The end was near, this I felt. It seems funny that I held out so long. Some of the girls read my writing, and they were touched to tears by it. I went out looking all the time in case I might find someone and maybe a miracle would happen. Once I came across a girl my age, and this is how I met Anna Frank. Of course, how I was I to know she would become famous, how was I to know that I would really stay alive? She told me a few things about herself and I showed her some of my poems and told her that if we stayed alive, the poems would tell a lot of our horror. She spoke the same language as me, and she became interested in everything. She said that, one day, if the war ended and if she stayed alive, she, too, would have a lot tell. I told her that if I survived, I would write everything down and try to get the whole world to read about it. Somehow to talk with her was so soothing; such peace came from her. She was so different from most of the girls in my barracks. I liked her from the first moment that I saw her, for she reminded me a lot of my sister Cilly. I met her a few times and later, when I couldn't find her anymore, a lady told me that she thought she had died. Later when I heard about her diary, I knew she was the girl I had a short friendship with at Bergen-Belsen.

Back at the barracks, things got worse and worse. Oh, they gave us from time to time a little water soup, and at times a few pieces of turnips were swimming in it, but a worm probably couldn't have kept alive on it. When we got those few pieces of turnip in the soup, Topka and I slowly drank down the soup and saved those few pieces of turnip in a little can. We mashed it, and whenever we felt a faint coming on from hunger, we took a little lick from it. Those lucky occasions were few, and there were many days we were without anything to eat. At times I was so hungry I felt like eating pieces of my coat. Once Topka said, "Oh, Lydia, to be able once again to sit at the table and to have bread to eat to satisfaction."

"Oh, Topka," I replied, "don't talk about it, for I feel a faint coming on, for there can't be such any more, to have once again enough bread to eat." If I had known that I would marry a baker later on and never be hungry for a piece of bread again! For bread was the one thing that we never saw in the typhoid section. One night Topka dreamed that she sat with her parents by the Seder table, which we Jews set on the evening beginning Passover. Her parents could see her, but they still asked where she was. One of the family answered that Topka, too, had died. After the dream she told me with tears in her kind eyes, "Lydia, I have a feeling that my parents are dead, for they said by the table that Topka is dead, too." This time I wanted to talk her out of that nonsense because she had always been so brave, and even in my autograph book, she had written so nice a dedication. From that dream on, though, she started losing any interest in anything that went on around her. Her love for life somehow dwindled. When she told me that, with her parents gone, there was no use for her to stay alive, I scolded her badly, for how could she be sure of it? It was only a dream, but she was as heartbroken as if someone really had told her that her beloved parents were dead.

She still was the stronger one of the two of us. I can say now that I don't know what I would have done without her, for when the typhoid had me in its claws, she was the one who tried to comfort me as much as possible in this disastrous hell. Although she was infected with this gruesome disease, too, she didn't suffer as much as I did. The agony of this high fever, with nothing to drink, was just like smoldering in hell. My only thought and only pleading was for a drop of water, but instead I was kicked, beaten, and stepped on, for so many died around me. Those cold bodies, they were all over me, under me, they were all around, like a big, ugly snake trying to get hold of me, for wherever I turned, there was another corpse staring at me. Those cold, lifeless, famished bodies—it seemed all like a nightmare. You try to escape, but they just hold you in their iron grip. Those days when we were allowed to take out the bodies, we thought we would be able to find some peace, but they died at such a pace that it seemed the more we took out the bodies, the more died. With each day, new victims of typhoid were brought in, and they died quicker than they could get acquainted with this awful place.

One day I heard such agonizing screams that I looked to see where they came from. I looked into the tormented eyes of Rivka, funny face Rivka, the girl we used to have so much fun with, she who had always been full of life. Here she was lying down and screaming in agony. Rivka, too, had been among those girls who had received those shots at Graeben when I received mine, that time I was in so much pain from those awful abcesses. And now her whole body had broken out with them. Then, those two abcesses were enough to drive me out of my mind, and here she lay without water and no help, for everyone was afraid to go near her. She was rotting away, insane from pain. Her whole body was such a mess. I held my ears, for I couldn't stand any longer hearing her screams of agony with no one able to help. As I approached her, hardly able to walk, she recognized me, and pleaded "Lydia, please give me a drop of water."

But I was helpless, for I had no water. Then it came to me that it was just a question of time and I, too, would probably lie in the same agony. Each cry of anguish would hurt me, too, for I suffered along with that poor girl who was unconscious and half insane from pain. As they beat on her with their clubs, they didn't know that they eased her pain, for she never regained conciousness. They helped her by beating her in her agony into the other world. With her gone, we somehow felt a little relaxed. I was happy for her because she would not to have to suffer this awful pain anymore. But with me, things got worse and worse, for the typhoid had taken hold of me. I felt that the end was here. The awful thirst was such that, when they let us out, I drank water from the dirty, filthy creek where most of the girls did some washing and some perfomed their most urgent needs. The stench that came from that water was less than pleasant, but I closed my nostrils and drank down that cool, soothing liquid, typhoid itself. But what could I do? The fever burned me down and I was happy and grateful to at least have this to drink. To our despair, we weren't able to go out often to get even that filthy water to drink. Then came days when we heard shooting from afar and girls brought in leaflets which it was punishable by death to possess. Some of the girls had smuggled them from work into camp; some of them were in English and some were even in German. Those leaflets said, "Hold on, we are near and coming to liberate you!" What hope, what joy! Could such really happen? Here in our hopelessness, waiting for death to come, something beamed inside me, and I tried so hard to stay alive. But one just couldn't help it, for death came each night to take its toll.

One night, while we were lying there one on the other with the screams of dying around us, we heard continued shooting, but this time it sounded nearby. Hope arose in us. Then the whole barracks, which was like a huge casket with all those dying girls around, sang the song of the partisans. The spirit got hold of us; let's not give up, let's try to fight for our lives, for liberation is near. Soon I felt that I was in no condition to fight any more. I wasn't even able to go out on roll call. I could only crawl; I felt so weak and near death that the only thing that kept coming to my mind was that the liberators better come soon, or I would be dead. Food, hunger? I didn't care for any food anymore. Only water—this was the only thing I cared for. The next day there was no roll call, and how lucky for me, for I wouldn't have been able to get out. Before the monsters came to chase us out on roll call, I told Topka that I wouldn't be able to move. But Topka wouldn't hear about it. "Lydia, I will help you, you must go out, please try once more!" I wanted so badly to try, but how could I? My feet felt like lead and I was hardly even able to speak anymore. But they didn't come that day, not the next day, and not even the third. Not far from me were some girls form Lithuania. How much I always admired those girls, for they kept on going. They weren't only beautiful, but so full of life. Nothing, but nothing, was able to break them down. When almost half of us lay dead, they were still up and around. In their beautiful Yiddish they kept saying that it would soon be good, that we would see.

How much did I wish to be able to believe those words so full of glory! That night the shooting grew louder, and those girls, so full of hope, said that our liberators were near. "Kids," they shouted, "don't despair and don't give up." Not far from us was another girl with whom I had made friends quite some time ago. This girl had been made an orphan by the Nazis at the beginning of war. She was so quiet and nice all the time. Even to make friends with others, she was too shy. I liked her from the beginning. Never would she have any arguments; always she let someone else be in it right. She had an aunt who was most of the time around the place. One day her aunt brought her a little red beet. We had been without any food for the last few days and I felt my heart stop beating. She gave me a bite from her beet, which made my heart beat again. I had promised that if I stayed alive, I would never forget her. She, too, was very weak, but at that time not so very bad as many of us. She tried so much to help me when I couldn't move in delirium. This day, she told me that she wished the most to see freedom and then it wouldn't matter if she died. To live for freedom, those were the only few words on our lips, and it seemed, that despite all of our prayers and with all our hope, it still only was a dream.

This was April 15, 1945. As the day started to dawn I said to Topka that I thought this was the end. "I don't think I will be able to go any farther." I just begged her, if she should be fortunate enough to stay alive, to look up my brothers and try to find some of my beloved ones. Maybe the big inferno had not swept all of them away from this earth. Topka was weeping, "Please, Lydia don't speak such. You know that it is not so, you must keep fighting. You always did."

But as I gasped for air with my dried-out throat, I whispered to her, "I just can't go on anymore." I lay there, knowing and feeling that the end was now on me, but we in the back hadn't realized that in front some commotion was going on. Those girls from Lithuania had disappeared all of a sudden, but we hadn't paid much attention to it. And then we felt such sudden quiet from the outside. Early in the morning, plenty of shooting had gone on outside, for the Hungarian guards on the tower had shot down any girls they saw coming out from their barracks. But now, we hadn't even noticed that the barracks had been opened and no one was watching us. This camp, always watched and guarded with such a dreadful efficiency, lay all of a sudden deserted.

A few bold girls sneaked out to see what was going on, but as I mentioned, many of them were shot down by those Hungarian facists. And then the shooting ceased and peace like never before entered the camp. We were so used to almost anything that we didn't pay too much attention to it. Then, I don't recall exactly, it might have been at noon or later—who knows, for our lives had been timeless for so long it seemed to me, looking back, like a thousand years. As I felt that I was falling deep into another world, a world of no return, I could hear so clearly now my beloved mother's voice. It seemed that with it I could hear angels singing and I could see in my agony of dying my two sisters in their festive white dresses and Daddy the way he always had looked on Yom Kippur, with Mother having lit the candles and going to the temple to pray for the day of judgment. All the woman were white-clad to show their innocence before God, white, the way my people were always put in the grave. Had I joined them already? Was I meeting them on my way to heaven? *For heaven must come now,* I thought, *for I have gone through hell on earth.* And then I saw my mamale waving to me, whispering with her golden voice, "No matter what, Lydilein, don't give up, you'll see, your life will once again be sunshine and roses!" Here it was again, my mother's voice like a guardian angel, pleading with me not to give up. And it seemed as though Ella was waving to me and saying, "Be courageous like you always used to." All of a sudden it dawned on me that, now that I was giving up my better fight for life, I must stay alive to fulfill the promise I had given to my mother that I would tell the world everything that had happened. My two brothers came into my mind, and I knew I must stay alive. But I knew, with my strength leaving me, that all of it was too late. I just couldn't go on any longer. And as from far away, I heard a hustle outside, soldiers voices, but somehow different from those German's sadistic orders. These voices were soft and kind. And then the barracks shook; it was like tanks were rolling over the place. And as I was falling and falling, I still heard my own voice saying, "This is the end," but from far away I heard the voices of the Lithuanian girls: "Children, they screamed, "get up, we are free!"

The British had come to liberate us. As if a magic word had brought me back to life again, with the last bit of strength and the last bit of breath left in me, I fought the man armed with the scythe and tried to sit up. With my agonized, watery eyes I looked wildly around and saw all the girls with happiness in their eyes.

Was it really true? Yes, it was true. For all of a sudden the strength seemed to come back to me. How was I given all of a sudden inhuman strength? On all fours, I crawled out after the girls to welcome the maiden with the flowers in her hair. Yes, it was true! Freedom had opened her arms to us. As I witnessed this moment I had yearned for almost all my life, I saw a girl falling at the feet of the soldiers and kissing their boots. I stood motionless, tears running down my cheeks. How can I ever put in words what this minute meant for me? How can I describe this most joyful moment? No, there are no words for it, for all the words, poems, and songs that have been told about freedom are really too poor for it!

FREEDOM

And here is what happened. As the British tanks approached this island of the dead, Kraemer, our *Lagerfuehrer,* the devil's adjutant, warned the soldiers not to enter, for typhoid was raging in the camp. But as the soldiers explained later, they didn't pay any attention to Kraemer. He was taken prisoner and they entered the camp. The gruesome sights they witnessed were enough to make one sick deep down to one's stomach, for the hunger had been so bad that some of the inhabitants of the camp, in their rage and half insane from hunger, were nibbling on the corpses. The British took over command right away and those Nazis that didn't have enough time to get away were put to work cleaning up the corpses that lay around in the hundreds and hundreds. The British took out those dying in the barracks and put them into hospitals right away. Most of them died anyhow. We were told that anyone who was sick should come out, for the person would be put into hospital. Who wasn't sick? I was so sick and unable to stand on my feet that I had once again to learn to walk. I wouldn't trust the Germans anymore, for into their hospitals we would have to go. Although they were under British supervision from then on, I had a feeling that if I were to go there, I would die in the end. When the British went around to look for the sick, I hid behind Topka. Although I was so very ill, I tried with all of my strength to get out of it. When one of the girls came over to our block to see who from our camp had survived— she had always adored my complexion and my lips especially—her words were, "You know, Lydia, all of your loveliness has gone, but your beautiful lips still are left." Yes, my red lips—cut like a heart, they shone out from my ghost-like face. I thought that, having lived through typhoid and so much horror, I would be able to do without a hospital, but it took a long time until I got back on my feet again. Many of my friends did die thereafter. Many of the girls, not being used to rich food, died of dysentery. My little friend who had once saved my life with the piece of beet, she had lived to see freedom. She lived to the day when those torturers of ours, those assasins, met their destruction. She lived to the day to see how they were treated, the stones and mud that were thrown at them when one of the girls leaped toward one of those beasts who once had called themselves the superior race. She beat, kicked, and spit at him. Now I could understand my mother when she had told me there was no revenge for such. How miserably little they were now that their power was broken. How they crawled to our feet and how frightened they were at a bit of mud thrown after them. How they ducked when passing us. No, there must be something higher, more holy than this. We weren't able to put judgment upon them by throwing stones or mud after them. Even when humans have passed judgment upon those beastly murderers, there will always be a higher court. My little friend had yearned for the day of freedom like Moses had begged to see the holy land, and she, too, died thereafter. As they came to take out her small, famished corpse, I kept watch over her and I made them put gloves on their bloody hands so as not to touch her innocence.

With the glory of freedom, we still were left to stay for quite some time in those filthy barracks. Hearing at night the bombing around us made us shiver. Why wouldn't they let us get out of here? What if the Germans came back? A new fear—I asked myself, *Is this freedom? Is this what we waited for?* Yes, those first soldiers who had come to liberate us were the most wonderful guys in the world, but now that the relief forces were here, they were so different. Although they didn't treat us with kid gloves, I was still grateful to them and looked up to them as our liberators. Although I suffered a lot later on from the hands of the British, I shall always remember that they were the ones who liberated me, and in this respect, I guess, I shall always be grateful to them.

To my great surprise, one of the healthy girls died. I was unable to eat at the time of our liberation; only drinking kept me alive. At times we got milk, sometimes juice, and good, disinfected water. From my illness, I was unable to eat a bite, and this was my luck, for most of the girls that had fallen over the food died at such a pace that it was almost as if the Nazis still had us in their claws. Rumors went around that the Nazis had poisoned the flour so that the bread now was poisoned. Many said that some had died because of it. I don't know for sure. I am sure that the Nazis were capable of doing any of those things. I wouldn't touch any bread for quite some time, and Topka and I hid it under our clothing for fear the time would come again when we were hungry and needed the bread. The bread, meanwhile, got moldy, but we didn't dare throw it away. We were suspicious of everything.

As I was able to get up on my feet a little, I went out. I saw a rabbi who was in the British Army. He said he would send mail to Israel for us mail. Since my brother was there, my first thought was that he must hear that I was alive. The rabbi gave me a postcard and on it I wrote my first few words about my liberation. Then the Red Cross came around with forms we had to fill out so any relatives that were alive would get the good news about us. The postcard came many, many months thereafter to the hands of my brother. It took months until he found out that one of our great family was alive. I read a letter much later that my brother from Argentina had written to Sigfried in Israel with the sad words, "Well, we have to accept the fact that no one of our beloved ones is alive anymore. For so many months have passed since the war ended and there is nothing, not a word from them." As I found out later from my sister-in-law in Israel, one day my brother came home, put his head on the table, and cried bitterly. At last she found out why. One of his friends from back in Gleiwitz had emigrated to Israel, too. This friend had liked me as a little girl and always joked with me, and he told Sigfried that he found a list of the survivors of Bergen-Belsen. On the list, he found my name.

It took a long time to get in touch with my brothers. I was very sick, but I did recover. For a few weeks after our liberation, I broke out on my body just like Rivka had before she rotted away in Belsen. This time I had help; I was not doomed to die like her in agony. I was treated right away, although it took a long time for me to recover, but I fought it through. When I held the first mail from my beloved brothers in my hand, it was heartbreaking, but I felt that it had been worth fighting for.

After a few weeks passed since our liberation, Topka felt not too well. She told me that she would go to the hospital to recover a little. I had great disdain for the hospitals, especially with the German staff around, but as I saw, Topka had made up her mind that she would go, for she said she wanted to get out of that filth. Who could blame her desire to lay once again in a bed? She promised to stay for a short time and then we would be together again. I thought it would be for the best, for lately she had become so careless. Even when I was sick, I had always tried to get to a washroom, if only by the filthy creek, so that I could undress and wash myself, but Topka would just lay around and wouldn't even go out to wash herself. Maybe it was for the best, I thought. But Topka never returned. When I went to see her at the hospital, she complained to me about how awful the Germans were treating her, the fun they made of the sick, and that she was sorry to ever have come to this place, where instead of getting better, she got worse with each day. "Lydia, I only wanted to rest—what have they done to me? I can hardly move," she said. When I went again to see her, there she lay, so helpless. She told me that she was unable to leave the bed, so she cried out for help when she had an urgent need, but the nurses wouldn't even show up. She was doomed to lay there, helpless, in all of it. "And it hurts and burns me so much," she told me. I was furious. How could they dare still do such now that they were defeated? They still wouldn't give up their evil ways.

One day I was riding on a train when I heard a German woman talking to another while she herself held her nose closed. "Pfui, how it stinks here now that the Jews are let out." No, they still wouldn't give up. After I found one of my cousins, I saw how badly he had been beaten up by a gang of Germans after the war, and I knew I didn't want to stay in this part of the earth any longer. I felt I had to leave this part of earth that had caused me nothing but heartbreak and tears, the earth on which I still could see blood everywhere. No, I just couldn't stay any longer. I begged my two brothers to get me out as quickly as possible, but the doors wouldn't open to us handful that were left. The British wouldn't let us come to Palestine. I don't want to mix here into politics, for I was too young to be able to understand it, but I know that politics had a lot to do with what happened. Argentina, where brother Max was wasn't eager to open its gates to us either. I was so desperate to leave this gruesome part of the earth that I would have gone to any part of the earth, only to be able to leave here. At times I felt that I must go on searching for my beloved ones. Maybe some of them were still slaves. Well, about Ella and Cilly, there wasn't any doubt any longer; they had been killed. But what had become of my parents? Were they really dead? Soon I was to find the gruesome answer. One of the girls I met later on was very distantly related to me. She had been together with my beloved parents almost until the end. They had been taken from Bendzin the day of my birthday, the day I had waited so very anxiously for mail at camp. With the rest of the Jews left in Bendzin, they were taken to Auschwitz. Those brutal murderers had torn Mother from the hands of my father and taken them, after robbing them of everything, to the gas chambers. The same was true with Uncle Jacob, his wife, and his son, little Pinjush. Aunt Mary, the widow of Uncle Samuel—she had seen all of it coming and she ran away towards Grodziec and was shot on the way. Here I stood in the ruins of my youth, an orphan, homeless and alone. But the letters that kept on coming from my brothers, they kept me alive. They always gave me new faith for a better tomorrow. As I saw it, here I was, the youngest, the only survivor of our once-so-precious home. I gave again the vow that, no matter what or when or how, I would write someday about it. My English is poor, I can't express myself the way I should, I know. But in its poorness, it is written with my whole heart and soul. I pray the Lord that all I have written will not have been in vain. Maybe it wll promote better understanding among mankind.

After a long wait to get out of this part of the world, I lost my patience and I found out there were Alijahs, illegal emigrants, going to Israel. I was among the first ones to register, but because of my tender age, and being sick and weak, they wouldn't accept me. They said we would have to go through a lot before we reached the port of our destination. Then again, we were told that those who were caught by the British would have to go to jail. Things there would be real tough, but for us it would be too hard to go through such again. The first to be permitted to go were the healthy and bigger ones. I told my age as two years older, and then finally the day came when I was told, together with a lot of other girls and boys, that we were to get ready for the Alijah B, which was the illegal entry to Israel. The trip was as memorable to me as everything else always will be, for after weeks of wandering the borders, we were brought on a small decommissioned freighter, the *Katriel Jaffa*. But the *Haganah*, the Jewish defense group who had arranged our trip, was happy to get ahold of anything that could bring us over. For four weeks we were in the hot sun with hardly anything to drink, and again I suffered such thirst that I took to drinking the salty water from the ocean. On this voyage I got sick again. Here I asked myself, *Is this freedom? Is this what we prayed for? Was it really worth having fought for?* Like a *fata morgana,* or mirage, I saw another world and another life, a much better one than I had known so far.

Again I joined the fight for our freedom. A British warship caught up with us soon, but although we were deadly exhausted by now, we still wouldn't give up. After four weeks of exhaustion, we were near the harbor of Haifa when the warship came toward us helpless children who had waited and wanted so badly a better tomorrow, to build out of the ruins a new future. But the British started throwing salvos of warning into the air. We still wouldn't give up. As the warships anchored near our little crate, we started to resist. We shouted over to them to kill us, to get over with what Hitler had left. As they saw it was hopeless, that we weren't going to give up, they started with firehoses, seven of them. They tried to frighten us into drowning. Well, if this was what the rest of the world stood for, let it be. Many kids were caught in the stream and their screams of agony put us into reality. Here was another enemy. Blood squirted from those cut pieces of flesh where the waterhoses reached. Here lay again destruction in front of us. No, they wouldn't let us reach the gates of the land the Lord had promised to us.

Right there in front of me a fight went on. They wouldn't let us enter those gates of freedom. Here, we knew, lay the groundstone for the survival of our people, and we woudn't give up. After the ship had been filled almost halfway with water, we saw that they would really drown us, for it was about to reach the drowning point, and they saw that we wouldn't give up, for once my people had given up and look what it had done to them. So the British threw gas bombs at us. As the gas approached us, the last thing that came into my mind was that this was really the end. The Nazis couldn't destroy me, but here on the shores of Israel, those so-called liberators were killing me. *Good-bye, Sigfried, good-bye Max, I will never see you again.* All my fighting had been in vain. As I fell down to the floor of the vessel, I felt water beneath me, and people were stepping over me. As I came to, I almost drowned, for I had fallen down in my unconsciousness to the bottom where the water was already very deep. As the gas let up, I regained consciousness. Then ladders were put up and we finally gave up the fight. There were many casualties among us, and we were were taken over to the British warship where we were kept prisoner. How history repeats itself. This time, again, to go to the toilets we had to ask for permission. This time it wasn't the Nazi guards, only our liberators. After being kept prisoner on that ship for a few days, they finally brought us to our destination. As the ship left the harbor of Haifa, our hearts bled. Where were they taking us? Where and what was going to be our destination? We came toward the island of Cyprus, but for each mile that we came nearer to our new prison camp, a piece of our hearts was left behind. We had been so near freedom, but it was still not meant to be. Here again we were brought to a camp with barbed wire and watchtowers high above. Another concentration camp, again in bondage.

    The day we arrived, the sun burned on us mercilessly and we had to wait again for hours to be given some water to drink. The food they had prepared for us was so ridiculous. Six crackers we were given on that fortunate day. Then with all of the formalities taken care off, we were again given cots and tents, and not to forget, our water ration cards. Freedom, the maiden with the flowers in her hair, the way I had always imagined in all of my dreams, was far away now from reality. As I looked into the faces of those British soldiers, I thought of that day when we had kissed their boots and called them our saviors. *How funny life is,* I thought to myself.

    Here I had many new friends and quite a few had been together with me at camp in Graeben. Life on Cyprus was not very enjoyable. We made plans to get out of there, for the British had a certain quota, which was so fantasticly low that it would have to take years before we saw the shores of Israel again. I and my group were among the youth and the children. Negotiations were made with the British to let at least the sick and underaged out, but it was senseless. Soon we knew that matters would have to be taken into our own hands and we were prepared for all kinds of emergency. No, I wasn't on the Exodus, but I met many forced migrations in my time on Cyprus, saw many beaten and broken-down people and children, robbed of their last belief in humanity. Had the whole world once again forgotten us? I don't want to accuse the British for this part of my life, for deep in my mind I shall always remember they were my liberators. To write all about Cyprus, I guess, I would have to write another book. But this I don't want to really mix with my life of desperation, for as bad as things were on Cyprus, with hunger and the heat, it really was nothing to compare with my other life in bondage.

Here, next door to us was Israel, with my people fighting for us. My people, how proud I was of them! After all my suffering at having been born a Jew, I finally realized that it had not been in vain. Here I came to think of it, here on this little island I finally was proud for having been born a Jew. No, my people are not vengeful, my people are forgiving. They will cry in their agony like every normal person, but they are not hateful. How very proud they made me. There goes a saying that time heals all wounds, that we will forget. We will never forget, for this was a deep wound cut into our souls. With any wound, even after many, many years pass, one still can feel a hurt. Like tiny needles, this hurt will quickly pass until another time.

I left Cyprus, and after two more confinements—jails, so to say—I was allowed to step on the holy ground of Israel. Israel, like a goddess reaching out her arms to welcome the sick and the homeless, with its beautiful valleys and most beautiful sights of modern and ancient times. Looking into the blue sky of Israel, I saw how clean and how peacefully it looked down on me. I sent a prayer to heaven that the Lord might keep it and watch over it. With all those enemies surrounding this little land, built out of the ruins of destruction, Israel gave new life and new hope for the homeless, the unwanted Jews, in their greatest cry of agony and despair. May the Lord always bless this holy place so that the unwanted shall feel wanted again.

For the last seven and a half years I have been in America and I have become a citizen. To hold the citizenship papers in my hand was one of my happiest occasions in life. Now I belong, and with all the gratfulness in my heart, I want to pay tribute to those who were not as fortunate as I was, to those who fell to those brutal Nazibeasts, to all those so dear to us who we have lost but not forgotten. Yes, they have vanished from this earth with the words, *"Sehmah Israel!"*—"Hear me,

God of Israel,"—on their lips. Out of the ashes comes still their prayer for forgiveness for the souls of their torturers. They fought on this big battlefield of humanity and died a hero's death.

What about my sunshine and roses? Yes, I found them, for my husband is my sunshine and my sweet children are my roses. Jack, my husband, went through experiences most similar to my own, and he understands me so well. All of our wishes and prayers are the same. My happiness is his goal. It seems to me as if fate wanted to make up for all the sorrow it had brought to me in my early youth. No one could wish for more happiness than I have found. May the Lord always keep watch over him, for I love him so dearly. My roses, my children, have all the loveliness I could have wished for. The names of the beloved ones that Jack and I lost are combined among them. Genia, the oldest, has the name of my dearly beloved mother. Joachim David, whom we call Joey for short, his first name is that of my father-in-law and the middle name is that of my father. Little Angel Belle Edith carries the proud name of Jack's mother and my sister Ella. I hope so very much that my children will grow up to be worthy of the names they carry and I wish for them to be as great and as wonderful as were those to whom those names belonged once. I do hope that my children will grow up with healthy minds and that no prejudice will ever spoil them. They are now too small to realize how ugly the world can be. My biggest prayer and hope is that men will come to realize that there is no such thing as a superior race, that all of us are created equally before God and our fellow men. Maybe I will be successful, in that my writing here might contribute a bit to the understanding of mankind. Now that I have told of my desperation, I can relax, and I will be able to finally find peace, for I have told the world of the shame that was brought upon my people by a sick mind and an evil people.

Now that I am leaving my world of desperation, I bid good-bye to you, my dearly beloved ones. To my oh-so-dearly beloved mother and father, sisters Ella and Cilly, I pray the Lord that wherever the ashes might have blown, the earth that covers them shall always be blessed. Oh, how very much I loved you, you know, and how very much I miss you, only the good Lord knows. I want to thank you for all the love you gave me, and for all the goodness and love that you taught me. I know that everything I am and have today, I thank you for, for you were the inspiration of humanity!

Now that I carry my fourth child under my heart, which I shall call the name I always wished for, the name of my so-dearly beloved sister Cilly. The baby should come by July fourth. Isn't this significant? So, with it let freedom ring all over the world. I hope that I will never have to wander again and I pray the good Lord for peace on earth and good will toward men.

On the seventh of July, I had a little girl, and named her, of course, Gacilia, for my sister Cilly. Holding this precious little bundle in my arms meant the fullfillment of all my dreams. She is such a joy and looks even a bit like my beloved sister Cilly. Every time I look at her, there go prayers to heaven that all the sorrow should be spared and that the world will finally realize that no weapon on earth can be as powerful as love and understanding.

EPILOGUE

After liberation, Jack Reich (my husband today) heard that I was still alive. He searched all over for me. In 1947, Jack found me living in Haifa, Israel. Jack and I got married in Haifa in 1948. That same year, Israel declared its independence and all of the surrounding Arab countries attacked Israel. Jack went into the Israeli Army. I did not know where Jack was stationed as there was no mail or telephone service. I then discovered that I was pregnant, and so I hitchhiked all over Israel, from Army camp to Army camp, to try to find Jack. Eventually, I found him. A Yemenite family took me in and I stayed with them for several weeks. Their home was near where Jack was stationed so I was able to visit him every day.

Our first child, Genia (later changed to Jeanie when we came to the United States), was born in Haifa in October of 1948. After the war was over, Jack worked as a baker and I cleaned houses to support us. By 1952, there was such poverty in Israel that we decided to leave. We went to France and stayed with some family for a few months. We wanted to emigrate to Canada, but we were rejected by the Canadian government. I found out in France that I was pregnant again. Then, we heard that there was still one Jewish refugee camp left in Germany. We went to Germany to Wolfratshausen, a suburb of Munich to that refugee camp. In December of 1952, our second child, Joachim (Joey) David was born. We stayed in Germany for about one year.

Soon thereafter, President Eisenhower of the United States enacted a new law allowing all German-born Jews to emigrate to the United States with their entire families. In 1953, a Jewish agency called HIAS helped us get to the U.S. We took a plane to New York, but we wanted to be with Jack's family in Chicago. At that time, his brother Mark, his brother Robert, and his sister Lucy and their families were in the Chicago area. So we moved to Chicago and Jack got a job at Imperial Bakery with his two brothers.

Once we had been in the United States for a few years, we wanted to have an American-born child. In January of 1959, we were blessed with our third child, Beila (Belle) Edith.

In 1960, Jack and I bought our first apartment building as a business. Jack, however, continued to work at the bakery. I started going to night school to learn how to type and to write and speak English better. Jack drove me there every night. I started writing my memoir at that time and then became pregnant with my fourth child. I finished my book shortly before Cacilia (Cindy) Francis was born in July of 1961.

Over the years, Jack and I bought four more apartment buildings. Eventually, Jack left the bakery to work full-time at the buildings.

Then, in 1978, when he was only fifty-three years old, Jack was diagnosed with Parkinson's disease. Jack continued to work at the buildings every single day, helping the tenants, fixing everything imaginable, taking down the garbage … you name it. In 1992, Jack finally retired from working at the buildings as the Parkinson's was taking its toll on him.

Jack and I have been very involved in Parkinson's organizations. We received an award from the United Parkinson's Foundation (now the Parkinson'sDisease Foundation), and met Muhammad Ali. I have searched the world tirelessly to try to find newer and better medicines, and for a cure for my beloved Jack to help him in his terrible fight against this disease. I have talked to doctors all over the world, as well as to drug companies in my quest to help Jack. Fighting this dreadful disease together, particularly the last five years, has been our second Holocaust. Watching Jack suffer so has torn me apart. I thought that after losing almost everyone I loved to the Holocaust that I would never feel such suffering again. However, watching Jack and what this horrendous disease does to a person have brought back much of the pain of my past experiences. I pray that someday in the near future there will be a cure for Parkinson's. Fortunately, however, Jack and I are still together after sixty years. Jack is eighty-two and I am eighty.

We are blessed to have such wonderful children and their spouses and children. Jeanie married Don Blum. Joey married and had three children, Adam Michael (twenty-eight years old), Benjamin Aaron (twenty-five) and Nicole Yvette (twenty-one). Joey remarried Kimberly Baldwin. Belle married Ron Kolman and has two children, Carly Laene (sixteen) and Zachary Alexander (thirteen). Cindy married Lee Masover and has two children, Samantha Elizabeth (ten) and Alexandra Monique (eight). Our lives are filled with joy when we see our beautiful grandchildren.

My desire today, first and foremost, is that the Holocaust not be forgotten and that my family members and Jack's did not die in vain. However, my next deepest desire is that a cure be found for Parkinson's disease. I also wish that every person would have access to proper health care. I have seen firsthand how awful it is to have a disease, but to be denied access to full healthcare and medicines is a tragedy. In particular, I see how hard it is to be elderly and in need. I only wish that I had more time and energy to help that fight as well.

978-0-595-44553-0
0-595-44553-5